TEACHING
BASIC, ADVANCED, AND ACADEMIC
VOCABULARY

A Comprehensive Framework for Elementary Instruction

Robert J. Marzano

MARZANO
Resources

555 North Morton Street
Bloomington, IN 47404
888.849.0851
FAX: 866.801.1447

email: info@MarzanoResources.com
MarzanoResources.com

Visit **MarzanoResources.com/reproducibles** to download the free reproducibles in this book.

Printed in the United States of America

Library of Congress Control Number: 2019032471

ISBN: 978-1-943360-33-8

Production Team

President and Publisher: Douglas M. Rife
Associate Publisher: Sarah Payne-Mills
Art Director: Rian Anderson
Managing Production Editor: Kendra Slayton
Content Development Specialist: Amy Rubenstein
Copy Editor and Proofreader: Evie Madsen
Text and Cover Designer: Rian Anderson
Compositor: Kelsey Hergül
Editorial Assistant: Sarah Ludwig

TABLE OF CONTENTS

Visit **MarzanoResources.com/reproducibles**
to download the free reproducibles in this book.

CHAPTER 2

Tier One and Tier Two Terms for Individual Students

CHAPTER 3

Teaching Tier Three Terms

ABOUT THE AUTHOR

Robert J. Marzano, PhD, is cofounder and chief academic officer of Marzano Resources in Denver, Colorado. During his fifty years in the field of education, he has worked with educators as a speaker and trainer and has authored more than fifty books and two hundred articles on topics such as instruction, assessment, writing and implementing standards, cognition, effective leadership, and school intervention. His books include *The New Art and Science of Teaching*, *Leaders of Learning*, *Making Classroom Assessments Reliable and Valid*, *The Classroom Strategies Series*, *Managing the Inner World of Teaching*, *A Handbook for High Reliability Schools*, *A Handbook for Personalized Competency-Based Education*, and *The Highly Engaged Classroom*. His practical translations of the most current research and theory into classroom strategies are known internationally and are widely practiced by both teachers and administrators.

He received a bachelor's degree from Iona College in New York, a master's degree from Seattle University, and a doctorate from the University of Washington.

INTRODUCTION

The Importance of Vocabulary Knowledge

The importance of vocabulary development is almost self-evident. It has been referred to as the heart of oral language and the basis for domain-specific knowledge (Marulis & Neuman, 2010). Some researchers have noted that teaching vocabulary is tantamount to teaching about the world around us (Stahl & Stahl, 2012). Others have noted that vocabulary plays a major role in one's general success in life (Beck & McKeown, 2007; Neuman & Dwyer, 2011). At a more academic level, vocabulary knowledge has been linked with learning to read (Stanovich, 1986) as well as reading comprehension (Anderson & Freebody, 1979, 1985; Beck & McKeown, 2007; Beck, Perfetti, & McKeown, 1982; Cain, Oakhill, Barnes, & Bryant, 2001; Cunningham & Stanovich, 1997; Davis, 1942, 1944, 1968; Farkas & Beron, 2004; Just & Carpenter, 1987; McKeown, Beck, Omanson, & Perfetti, 1983; McKeown, Beck, Omanson, & Pople, 1985; Mezynski, 1983; National Reading Panel, 2000; Scarborough, 2001; Singer, 1965; Stahl, 1983; Stahl & Nagy, 2006; Stanovich, Cunningham, & Feeman, 1984; Storch & Whitehurst, 2002; Thurstone, 1946; Whipple, 1925).

With these impressive endorsements, it seems quite logical that teaching vocabulary should be a focal point of K–12 instruction. Interestingly, this seemingly obvious endeavor met with disfavor in the 1980s after a Seattle Pacific University Professor William E. Nagy and University of Illinois Professor Emeritus Richard C. Anderson (1984) study estimated that students encounter 88,500 words in grades 3–9 alone. This would probably put the K–12 number of words students encounter upward of 100,000. Of course, it would be an impossible task to teach all of these terms in isolation. Teachers would literally have to address over forty words per day! This simple arithmetic led some to reject the notion that K–12 educators should even try to teach vocabulary directly. For example, authors Steven A. Stahl and Marilyn M. Fairbanks (1986) explained:

> Since vocabulary-teaching programs typically teach 10 to 12 words a week or about 400 words per year, of which perhaps 75% or 300 are learned, vocabulary instruction is not adequate to cope with the volume of new words that children need to learn and do learn without instruction. (p. 100)

Indeed, some suggested that *wide reading* was the only viable way to help students gain a knowledge of this massive array of vocabulary. For example, vocabulary instruction experts William E. Nagy and Patricia A. Herman (1987) explained that if students spend twenty-five minutes per day reading at a rate of two hundred words per minute for two hundred days, they will encounter about a million words, and if they learn one in twenty of these words, yearly they will add 750 to 1,500 words to their vocabulary. Why, then, should teachers spend any time directly teaching vocabulary when wide reading can produce such impressive results?

While wide reading is always a good idea, the logic of relying on wide reading in lieu of direct vocabulary instruction does not hold up under close scrutiny. Authors Isabel L. Beck and Margaret G. McKeown (1991) argued that "research spanning several decades has failed to uncover strong evidence that word meanings are routinely acquired from context" (p. 799). Similarly, as a result of a study about elementary school students, researchers Joseph R. Jenkins, Marcy L. Stein, and Katherine Wysocki (1984) asserted that it takes multiple exposures to learn a new word:

> Although, the present findings show that fifth graders can learn word meanings incidentally during reading, this learning apparently does not come easily or in large quantities for educators interested in building vocabulary, prescribing large doses of reading many not be the most efficient means of reaching this goal; heavy exposure to words in contexts may be required, and in many cases specific contexts may not be sufficiently rich enough to allow readers even to derive word meaning, not to mention learn them. (p. 782)

Finally, M. S. L. Swanborn and Kees de Glopper (1999) found that learning words in context is a viable strategy only if students are already familiar with the content, the text does not have a great many unfamiliar words, and students are at the secondary level. Otherwise, learning words in context is a relatively inefficient way to acquire new vocabulary.

In effect, wide reading is not going to adequately address students' need to develop extensive vocabularies, especially at the lower grade levels. This conclusion received official recognition in 1997, when the U.S. Congress commissioned the National Institute of Child Health and Human Development (NICHHD) to convene a national panel to conduct a comprehensive review of the research on reading. The panel, known as the National Reading Panel, completed its review in April 2000 and published *Teaching Children to Read: An Evidenced-Based Assessment of the Scientific Research Literature on Reading and Its Implications for Reading Instruction—Reports of the Subgroups*. In that report, the following components were identified as focus areas for reading instruction: phonemic awareness, phonics, fluency, vocabulary, and comprehension (National Reading Panel, 2000). Of these, vocabulary was singled out for special consideration. Authors and editors Michael L. Kamil and Elfrieda H. Hiebert (2005) reported, "Vocabulary holds a special place among these components. Vocabulary is not a developmental skill or one that can be seen as fully mastered. The expansion and elaboration of vocabularies is something that extends across a lifetime" (p. 2).

Finally, studies on direct vocabulary instruction have consistently shown positive effects. In 2015, researchers Robert J. Marzano, Katie Rogers, and Julia A. Simms reviewed a number of meta-analytic studies on the effects of direct vocabulary instruction, as table I.1 shows.

As Marzano et al. (2015) described, these are rather strong and consistent findings. They note that each of the studies listed in table I.1 actually represents multiple studies. Indeed, summarizing the findings from multiple studies is one of the defining features of a meta-analysis. More specifically, it summaries the effects of multiple studies in the form of a quantitative index referred to as an *effect size*, which can be translated into an expected percentile increase or decrease in student achievement depending on the sign (that is, plus or minus) of the effect size. To illustrate, Marzano et al. (2015) explained that University of Michigan doctoral student Loren M. Marulis and educational studies Professor Susan B. Neuman's (2010) meta-analysis examined sixty-seven studies involving 216 effect sizes. They computed an overall effect size of 0.88 for the influence of vocabulary instruction on students' language development, which translates into an expected increase in language development of 31 percentile points (Marulis & Neuman, 2010). This means a student who is at the 50th percentile in terms of language development would be expected to rise to the 81st percentile after direct vocabulary instruction. Even a cursory analysis of the projected percentile gains in table I.1 attest to the potentially positive effects of direct vocabulary instruction.

Table I.1: Meta-Analyses on the Effects of Vocabulary Instruction

Meta-Analysis	Focus	Effect Size	Percentile Gain
Elleman, Lindo, Morphy, & Compton, 2009[a]	Effects of vocabulary instruction on comprehension	0.50 for words taught directly 0.10 for all words	19 4
Haystead & Marzano, 2009	Effects of building vocabulary on academic achievement	0.51	19
Klesius & Searls, 1990[b]	Vocabulary interventions	0.50	19
Marmolejo, 1990[b]	Vocabulary interventions	0.69	25
Marulis & Neuman, 2010	Effect of vocabulary training on word learning	0.88 overall 0.85 for preK 0.94 for kindergarten	31 30 33
Mol, Bus, & de Jong, 2009[a]	Effects of interactive book reading on oral language	0.28	11
	Effects of interactive book reading on print knowledge	0.25	10
Mol, Bus, de Jong, & Smeets, 2008[a]	Dialogic reading on oral language	0.50 for preK 0.14 for kindergarten	19 6
National Early Literacy Panel, 2008[a]	Interactive book reading	0.75 for preK 0.66 for kindergarten	27 25
Nye, Foster, & Seaman, 1987[b]	Language intervention	1.04	35
Poirier, 1989[b]	Language intervention	0.50	19
Stahl & Fairbanks, 1986[a]	Effects of vocabulary instruction on comprehension	0.97 for words taught directly 0.30 for all words	33 12

[a] As reported by Marulis & Neuman, 2010
[b] As reported in Hattie, 2009

Source: Marzano et al., 2015, p. 10.

There is little if any argument anymore regarding the importance of directly teaching vocabulary. Unfortunately, there is still a major problem associated with vocabulary instruction—it is virtually impossible to directly teach all the new terms students will encounter. Even teaching the 88,500 terms Nagy and Anderson (1984) estimated across grades 3–9 would take up a major part of teachers' available instruction time. While on the surface this problem appears insolvable, there is a relatively simple and straightforward solution.

Three Tiers of Terms

Beck and McKeown (1985) offered the simple solution that not all vocabulary terms should be considered equal. Rather, they posited three groups of vocabulary terms that form the basis for a comprehensive approach to vocabulary development based on not only frequency but also the role the words play in the language. Authors Isabel L. Beck, Margaret G. McKeown, and Linda Kucan (2002) further exemplified these tiers.

Tier one terms are very frequent in the English language. Examples from tier one are terms like *big, clock, walk,* and *baby.* "Words in this tier rarely require instructional attention to their meaning in school" (Beck et al., 2002, p. 8). *Tier two* terms, which may occur in text but rarely orally, are words that may not be frequent enough for teachers to assume students know their meanings. Tier two terms include *nimble, scrawny,* and *dexterity.* While students might have come across these terms, they probably won't encounter them enough in texts to have learned their meaning from context. *Tier three* terms are highly infrequent, like the word *germination.* Beck and colleagues (2002) noted that tier three terms should probably not be the subject of vocabulary instruction simply because they are so rarely used. However, although terms critical to subject-matter knowledge might be infrequently used in general language, they are necessary to understanding academic content. Words like *meiosis* and *mitosis* in science fall into this category. This means instruction for tier three (subject matter) terms should be a critical aspect of K–12 vocabulary instruction.

The concept of three tiers of vocabulary provides a framework teachers can use to design a comprehensive and viable approach to vocabulary instruction. The instructional approach to each tier should be different. While the work of Beck and colleagues (2002) provided the foundation for this vision, it did not actually articulate the terms to use to manifest this vision. This book adds that part to the vision.

Here in these pages, I present lists of tier one, tier two, and tier three terms, along with instructional approaches that ensure students have a working knowledge of those terms by the time they enter middle school. The list of tier one terms is comprehensive, so educators do not need to address any tier one terms other than those in this book. By the end of fifth grade (and ideally before), all students should have mastered these terms. The tier two terms in this book are sufficient but incomplete. Students should have a working knowledge of a significant portion (if not all) of these terms by the end of the fifth grade. At the secondary level, teachers might wish to identify other tier two terms as students encounter them in reading. The tier three terms in this book address mathematics, English language arts (ELA), science, and social studies through the fifth grade. At the secondary level, teachers should identify tier three terms specific to their subject areas and ensure students understand them.

This book represents a comprehensive framework for vocabulary instruction at the elementary level. I firmly believe if K–5 teachers address the tiers one, two, and three terms in this book in the manner recommended, students will enter the secondary grades with a strong foundation for literacy development and academic achievement.

Identifying Tier One and Tier Two Terms

Arguably the most important part of manifesting a comprehensive vision of vocabulary instruction is to identify tier one, tier two, and tier three terms. I generated the lists in this book systematically. Let's consider the process for identifying the tier one and tier two terms first.

I identified the tier one and tier two terms in a series of related efforts that spanned three decades. The specifics of those efforts are described in a number of works (Marzano, 2004; Marzano, 2010b; Marzano & Marzano, 1988; Marzano, Paynter, Kendall, Pickering, & Marzano, 1991). Briefly, though, I based the tier one and tier two terms in this book on extensive analysis of high-frequency words that classroom teachers then vetted. This effort began in 1988 in the book *A Cluster Approach to Elementary Vocabulary Instruction* (Marzano & Marzano, 1988) and progressed through a number of iterations over the next thirty years. The result of these efforts is a list of 2,845 tier one terms and 5,160 tier two terms (see appendix A, page 61). It is important to note that these terms are organized into 444 semantic clusters. The first 420 clusters contain both tier one and two terms. Clusters 421–444 contain only tier two terms. To illustrate, consider cluster 102, titled Bodies of Water.

- **Tier one terms:** *lake, ocean, puddle, river, sea, stream, bay, creek, pond*
- **Tier two terms:** *brook, cove, current, delta, gulf, inlet, marsh, outlet, rapids, strait, surf, swamp, tide, tributary, waterfall, waterline, bog, eddy, estuary, fjord, geyser, headwaters, lagoon, marshland, reef*

Semantic clusters provide a rich semantic context for students to obtain an initial understanding of unknown words. To illustrate, assume a particular student already knows the meaning of all the tier one terms in cluster 102 except *bay, creek,* and *pond.* The simple fact that these terms are in the same cluster with *lake, river,* and *ocean* provides the student with some concrete characteristics relative to their meaning. The same holds true for the tier two terms in each cluster. Students who know the meaning of some or most of the tier one terms will have a rich semantic basis with which to understand terms like *inlet, eddy,* and *estuary.* Simply stated, teaching vocabulary in semantic clusters aids student learning of those terms (Graves, 2006; Marzano, 2004; Marzano & Marzano 1988).

I organized the semantic clusters themselves by their level of basicness, as articulated in the book *Teaching Basic and Advanced Vocabulary* (Marzano, 2010b). In brief, though, I analyzed tier one and tier two terms relative to their frequency in English. I then assigned each word a weight ranging from 1 to 5, with 1 indicating the highest level of frequency and 5 indicating the lowest level of frequency. To illustrate, in cluster 102, Bodies of Water, the term *lake* has a weight of 2; *pond* has a weigh of 3; *cove* has a weight of 4; and *estuary* has a weight of 5. As described in Marzano (2010b), I classified all words with weights of 1, 2, or 3 as tier one terms, and all words with weights of 4 or 5 as tier two terms. Using these weights, I assigned an average weight to each cluster and then ranked the clusters based on these average weights. Appendix A (page 61) contains the 444 clusters in rank order in terms of how basic the words are on the whole.

The clusters themselves are organized into larger groups referred to as *superclusters*. The superclusters can be thought of as clusters of clusters. A list of sixty superclusters with their constituent clusters follows.

1. **Auxiliary and Helping Verbs:** 1, 3, 4, 342, 411

2. **Pronouns:** 6, 7, 8, 11, 12, 34

3. **Cause and Effect:** 10, 273

4. **Physical Location and Orientation:** 9, 17, 20, 21, 22, 23, 25, 26, 37, 49, 390, 430

5. **Measurement, Size, and Quantity:** 13, 15, 18, 19, 28, 33, 73, 130, 327, 373, 374

6. **Time:** 2, 16, 24, 29, 52, 59, 79, 83, 126, 144, 233

7. **Comparison and Contrast:** 5, 27, 252, 299

8. **Color:** 57, 415

9. **Verbal Interactions:** 14, 61, 100, 105, 177, 198, 207, 255, 345, 346, 383

10. **Animals:** 32, 35, 64, 65, 70, 82, 95, 117, 155, 188, 189, 194, 309, 310, 341

11. **Importance and Goodness** 58, 72, 243, 368

12. **The Human Body:** 75, 76, 80, 115, 140, 157, 160, 191, 213, 336, 437

13. **Trees and Plants:** 36, 108, 192, 269, 421

14. **Acquisition and Ownership:** 41, 89, 148, 171, 184, 426

15. **Parts of Dwellings:** 91, 113, 123, 134, 217, 284

16. **Vehicles and Transportation:** 93, 97, 120, 128, 159, 234, 318, 331

17. **Money and Goods:** 104, 109, 116, 122, 201, 214

18. **Actions Involving Walking and Running:** 63, 308, 339, 408, 409

19. **Attitudinals:** 30, 31, 285, 369, 431, 439, 440

20. **Water:** 87, 101, 102, 127, 296, 352, 353, 391, 424

21. **Sounds and Noises:** 84, 103, 156, 165, 175

22. **Food and Eating:** 48, 51, 74, 86, 124, 136, 153, 162, 174, 176, 208, 222, 232, 246

23. **Literature, Composition, and Writing:** 53, 71, 112, 138, 248, 256, 279, 319, 320

24. **Arts and Entertainment:** 54, 77, 239, 244

25. **Seeing and Perceiving:** 135, 195

26. **Clothing:** 47, 62, 125, 129, 145, 178, 212, 224, 263, 354, 435

27. **Texture, Durability, and Consistency:** 202, 323, 441

28. **Movement and Action:** 38, 39, 40, 44, 66, 141, 147, 169, 170, 182, 199, 215, 216, 247, 280, 281, 282, 283, 300, 301, 302, 322, 338, 403

29. **Structures and Buildings:** 60, 106, 121, 190, 210, 321, 324, 335, 364, 365, 366, 399, 400

30. **Shapes:** 69, 99, 142, 193, 218, 270, 303, 326

31. **Contractions:** 42, 81, 85, 150, 235, 274

Some superclusters are quite large, such as supercluster 28, Movement and Action, which is comprised of twenty-four separate clusters. Others, like supercluster 3, Cause and Effect, are quite small. It is comprised of only two clusters. The cluster and supercluster structures provide a great deal of instructional flexibility, which is discussed in depth in chapters 2 (page 29) and 3 (page 37).

Understanding the Resources Necessary for Effective Instruction of Tier One and Tier Two Terms

To teach tier one and tier two terms effectively as this book discusses, teachers should have access to the following resources.

This Book

While it is not essential that every teacher in a school read this book, it certainly is helpful. This is because the approach outlined here involves some components not part of traditional ways to teach vocabulary at the elementary level. Some of these nontraditional approaches include teaching words in semantic clusters, relying on incidental learning for tier one and some tier two terms, and having students self-evaluate their knowledge of terms. If every teacher engages in a schoolwide cooperative study of this book, it will provide a common understanding of the research and theory behind this comprehensive approach to elementary vocabulary instruction.

The *Building Basic Vocabulary* Student Notebook

Each student should have the student notebook *Building Basic Vocabulary: Tracking My Progress* (Marzano, 2018a) to keep track of his or her progress on the tier one and tier two terms. Individual students use this resource to keep track of their progress relative to acquiring a working knowledge of the tier one and some of the tier two terms. As described in the introduction (page 1), the tier one and tier two terms are organized into semantic clusters, which are ordered in terms of the constituent terms' general frequency levels, with those *most basic* clusters (that is, those clusters with the largest concentration of high-frequency words) listed first. Figure I.1 presents a sample page from *Building Basic Vocabulary*.

The pages of the student notebook contain the tier one and some tier two terms in each cluster. As figure I.1 depicts, the tier one terms for cluster 122 are *buy, sale, spend, earn, purchase, pay, sell, bet,* and *owe* and the tier two terms for cluster 122 are *afford, budget,* and *bargain,* which are referred to as *challenge words.*

It is important to note that while the student notebook contains all the tier one terms, it doesn't contain all the tier two terms. To illustrate, consider the tier two terms in cluster 122 (see appendix A, page 120).

- **Tier two terms for cluster 122:** *afford, bargain, budget, deal, discount, donate, invest, lease, market, repay, scrimp, subscribe, auction, insure, peddle, ransom, redeem, render, retail, splurge, wholesale*

The student notebook does not contain all the tier two terms in appendix A (page 61), but it does contain some. The terms included are those that students might have enough background experience with to develop their meanings from incidental learning, as is the case with tier one terms. For example, the tier two terms for cluster 122 in the student notebook include *afford, budget,* and *bargain.* As students interact with these terms in the context of the tier one terms in this same cluster, they will most likely glean a sufficient amount of information about the words to attach meaning to them when they encounter them in the future.

buy	4 3 2 1		pay	4 3 2 1	
sale	4 3 2 1		sell	4 3 2 1	
spend	4 3 2 1		bet	4 3 2 1	
earn	4 3 2 1		owe	4 3 2 1	
purchase	4 3 2 1				
CHALLENGE WORDS					
afford	4 3 2 1		bargain	4 3 2 1	
budget	4 3 2 1				

Source: Marzano, 2018a, p. 76.

Figure I.1: Cluster 122, Actions Related to Money and Goods.

Another reason all tier two words are *not* listed in the student notebook is because there are simply too many of them. There are 2,845 tier one terms and 5,160 tier two terms in appendix A (page 61). If all the tier two terms in each cluster are listed in the student notebook, they might overwhelm students and detract from the teachers' focus on ensuring students have a working knowledge of the tier one terms. As it is, the student notebook contains 2,889 tier two terms, leaving 2,271 tier two terms in appendix A *not* in the student notebook. This is not to say that teachers should not supplement the list of tier two terms in the student notebook using tier two terms from appendix A. We'll discuss this in chapter 3 (page 37).

The *Building Basic Vocabulary* Online Tool

The online tool, available at www.marzanoresources.com/resources/building-basic-vocabulary for tier one and tier two terms in the student notebook, is extensive. Teachers, students, parents, and guardians can access this resource. The tool has a search feature that allows the user to access any cluster quickly and efficiently. Figure I.2 (page 10) offers an example of how the clusters are organized in the online tool.

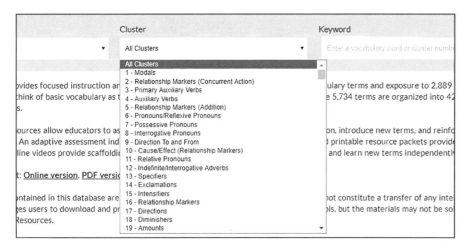

Figure I.2: List of clusters in online tool.

Once the user identifies the cluster for the focus of instruction, he or she activates the Search function and two resources are immediately displayed, as figure I.3 depicts.

Cluster	Supercluster	Vocabulary Words	Video	Download
1. Modals	Auxiliary and Helping Verbs	can, cannot, could, may, might, must, shall, should, will, would	▶	📄PDF

Figure I.3: Search function activated resources.

One of these two resources is a downloadable PDF, which I refer to as a *folio*. In this case, figure I.4 depicts the first page of the folio the user selected—cluster 79, Parts of a Day.

Figure I.4 has a list of the tier one words in the cluster. For each term, the folio provides a visual representation along with a simple description of what the term means. Each folio also includes activities to help students determine how these tier one terms are used, along with two brief activities that allow students to obtain a sense of how well they understand the terms.

A video accompanies each cluster, and the user can activate it by clicking on the play icon. Each video provides a visual representation of each term along with an audio explanation of the term. This is particularly helpful to English learners (ELs) who might have difficulty reading the PDF information. We'll discuss using these videos in more depth on pages 21–22.

79 PARTS OF A DAY

Check the words you already know:

- [ ] day
- [ ] evening
- [ ] hour
- [ ] minute
- [ ] morning
- [ ] night
- [ ] noon
- [ ] second
- [ ] tonight
- [ ] afternoon
- [ ] midnight
- [ ] overnight
- [ ] sundown
- [ ] sunrise
- [ ] sunset

Many people eat dinner in the **evening**.

Day
Noun
A **day** is one period of twenty-four hours. There are seven **days** in a week.

Evening
Noun
The **evening** is the part of each day between the end of the afternoon and the time you go to bed.

Hour
Noun
An **hour** is a period of sixty minutes.

Minute
Noun
A **minute** is a period of sixty seconds.

Morning
Noun
The **morning** is the part of each day between the time people usually wake up and noon.

Night
Noun
The **night** is the part of each period of twenty-four hours when the sun has set and it is dark outside.

Source: Marzano, 2018a.

Figure I.4: First page of the folio for cluster 79, Parts of a Day.

The Tier Three Terms

The tier three terms are more difficult to determine than the tiers one and two terms simply because the tiers one and two terms are primarily a function of frequency of use. As previously described, tier three terms encompass the vast majority of unique terms students encounter, but they encounter these words quite infrequently. This is depicted in table I.2.

Table I.2: Tiers One, Two, and Three Terms Found in School-Based Texts

Number of Words	Frequency of Encounter	Tier
6,700 (7.57 percent)	One time or more in one year of reading	One and two
8,650 (9.77 percent)	Up to three times in ten years of reading	Two and three
6,350 (7.18 percent)	Up to three times in one hundred years of reading	Three
24,600 (27.80 percent)	One time in one hundred years of reading	Three
42,200 (47.68 percent)	Up to three times in ten thousand or more years of reading	Three

Source: Adapted from Nagy & Anderson, 1984.

The findings in table I.2 are based on the Nagy and Anderson (1984) study, which estimated that students will encounter about 88,500 words in the reading material taught in grades 3–9. Nagy and Anderson (1984) referred to these terms as *written school English*. Table I.2 indicates that of these terms, students will encounter 6,700 one time or more in one year of reading; 8,650 will be encountered up to three times in ten years of reading and so on. Perhaps the most striking aspect of these findings is that the vast majority of the 88,500 terms in written school English are words students will rarely encounter. For example, 24,600 (27.80 percent) of these terms, students would encounter one time in one hundred years of reading, and 42,200 words (47.68 percent) students would encounter three times in ten thousand or more years. Stated differently, 75 percent of the terms students will encounter rarely, if ever, in their reading.

Clearly, tier three terms are a vast galaxy of words, most of which are so far removed from the literary experiences students will have in life as to be inconsequential in terms of teachers' direct instruction. For example, taking time to directly teach the tier three term *germination* would not be worth the return in terms of enhancing students' knowledge base. There is, however, a relatively small set of terms within the tier three galaxy that do warrant teachers' direct instruction. These are the terms specific to academic subject areas students encounter within the academic topics. Hence, if the term *germination* is considered important to a specific academic course, it should be taught directly. Teachers' direct instruction on such terms can pay great dividends to students.

For this book, Marzano Resources identified the terms for ELA, mathematics, science, and social studies for grades K–5 (Dodson, 2019; Simms, 2017). The researchers identified the tier three terms using a different underlying perspective than the tiers one and two terms. Tiers one and two terms are based on frequency of use in English. One might say the 2,845 tier one terms and 5,160 tier two terms represent the 8,005 most frequently used terms in English.

The tier three terms in this book have little, if anything, to do with word frequency. Rather, using various sources of standards and national assessments, the researchers first identified the most important topics (referred to as *measurement topics*) in ELA, mathematics, science, and social studies in grades K–5. These topics comprise a number of standard statements. The researchers then analyzed the statements and then identified the vocabulary necessary to accomplish the knowledge or skill in the statements. For example, table I.3 contains topics and associated vocabulary terms for grade 4 ELA, mathematics, science, and social studies.

Table I.3: Tier Three Topics

Subject	Topic (Critical Concept)	Related Vocabulary
ELA	Analyzing Text Organization and Structure	*introduce, section, link, transition, main idea*
Mathematics	Measurement Conversion	*kiloliter, kilometer, mile, millimeter, pint, quart, ton, yard, liquid volume, mass*
Science	Waves	*amplitude, frequency, mass, midline, period, wave, wave cycle, wavelength, crest, energy, longitudinal wave, matter, medium, oscillate, transverse wave, trough*
Social Studies	Participating in Government	*campaign, candidate, demonstration, elected official, monitor, petition, political party, public official, vote*

Chapter 3 (page 37) describes how educators must teach these tier three terms in the context of specific units of instruction. For example, the term *campaign* should be addressed in a unit that deals with the topic Participating in Government.

In all, there are 2,141 tier three vocabulary terms for these four subject areas (see table I.4, page 14).

Table I.4 shows the number of words and topics at each grade level for ELA, mathematics, science, and social studies. The number of unique words at each grade level are in parentheses and the number of topics immediately follow the number of words. Science involves a few topics that span the grade bands. One topic spans grades K–5, and two topics span grades K–2 and 3–5. It is important to note that words at one grade level might also appear at another grade level, but the expectations relative to students' levels of understanding increase from grade level to grade level. For example, the mathematics term *denominator* is listed in grade 3 and grade 4. However, at grade 3, *denominator* is associated with the topic Fractions, and at grade 4 it is associated with the topic Fraction Addition and Multiplication.

The terms in this book represent a comprehensive treatment of the tiers one, two, and three terms at the elementary level. If students master these terms by the end of elementary school, then teachers need only be concerned with the tier three subject matter–specific terms from grade 6 and up, and selected tier two terms specific to certain tests. Quite obviously, this would relieve middle school and high school teachers from the great burden of addressing terms foundational to the more complex concepts students will encounter in the higher grade levels.

Before getting to the comprehensive list of tiered vocabulary terms in appendix A (page 61), in chapters 1–3, the text digs a little deeper into teaching tiers one and two terms as a schoolwide effort, teaching tiers one and two terms to individual students, and teaching tier three terms.

Table I.4: Distribution of Tier Three Terms and Topics

	K	1	2	3	4	5	Total
ELA	(66) 17	(68) 20	(63) 19	(57) 19	(62) 18	(66) 15	(382) 108
Mathematics	(85) 10	(40) 9	(60) 14	(63) 14	(85) 15	(59) 14	(392) 76
Science	(76) 6	(63) 8	(89) 8	(75) 10	(97) 12	(65) 7	(465) 51
Science Grade-band topics	(11) 2	-	-	(15) 2	-	-	(26) 4
	(7) 1	-	-	-	-	-	(7) 1
Social Studies	(67) 5	(127) 14	(145) 12	(205) 21	(172) 17	(153) 19	(869) 88

Note: Quantities in parenthesis are the number of terms. Quantities immediately following and not in parenthesis are the number of topics.

Summary

This introduction briefly laid out the research and theory behind the need to design programs and practices that ensure all students leave elementary school with a working knowledge of all tier one terms, selected tier two terms, and selected subject-matter tier three terms. This was once thought impossible in part because some educators believed that it was best to develop vocabulary through wide reading, but mostly because educators had not identified the appropriate tiers one, two, and three terms. Research has demonstrated that wide reading in isolation is not sufficient to ensure students understand these critical terms. Also, Marzano

Resources conducted a series of studies to identify the tiers one, two, and three terms which form the basis for the approach in this book. For instructional purposes, the tier one and tier two terms are organized into semantic clusters. The tier three terms are organized into topics that educators will teach students in the context of specific standards for ELA, mathematics, science, and social studies.

CHAPTER 1

Teaching and Reinforcing Tier One and Tier Two Terms as a Schoolwide Effort

Vocabulary instruction is not a unidimensional construct. Rather, there are different types of vocabulary, each requiring its own instruction strategies. When educators use the term *vocabulary*, they can be talking about one of four different types. Figure 1.1 depicts these types.

	Receptive Vocabulary	**Productive Vocabulary**
Oral Vocabulary	Words understood when heard	Words used in speech
Written Vocabulary	Words understood when read	Words used in writing

Figure 1.1: Relationship between receptive, productive, oral, and written vocabularies.

Relative to the four types of vocabulary are the distinction between receptive and productive vocabulary and the distinction between oral and written vocabulary. *Receptive vocabulary* refers to the terms a person understands when he or she hears or sees them. Students cannot necessarily use terms in their receptive vocabularies. *Productive vocabulary* refers to the terms a person understands *and* uses. In this book, we'll focus on enhancing students' receptive vocabularies. The purpose of vocabulary instruction as this book describes is for students to recognize and understand the meaning of the elementary school tiers one, two, and three terms when they encounter them in print or orally. The type of instruction that this book describes is not designed to ensure students can use the tiers one, two, and three terms effectively in writing or orally, although it certainly will help.

Considering Tier One and Tier Two Instruction

Ensuring students have a working knowledge of tier one and tier two terms should be a focal point for vocabulary development at the elementary level. This implies that some of the current vocabulary instruction practices at the elementary level might change. I have two critical recommendations for this change.

Recommendation Number One: Don't Have a Separate List of Sight Words

Many schools use reading programs with their own list of sight words. However, it is completely redundant to teach and reinforce the tier one and tier two terms in this book and also teach the sight words in a specific reading program. To illustrate, consider the following sight words teachers commonly introduce at the kindergarten level.

- *a, all, am, an, are, as, at, away, back, ball, bell, big, bird, blue, book, box, brown, but, by*

These are obviously high-frequency words; a reasonable expectation is for students to recognize them immediately—hence, the term *sight words*. However, when teachers present them to students as a simple list, there is no context to provide semantic clues as to their meaning if students don't happen to already have these words in their receptive vocabularies.

Virtually every sight word teachers present to students in the elementary grades is in this book as a tier one term because sight words are derived from the same high-frequency word lists as the clusters. The difference is the tier one terms in this book are organized into semantic clusters. For example, the kindergarten sight words *as* and *at* are in cluster 2, Relationship Markers (Concurrent Action)—see p.62. There are a number of other tier one and tier two terms in this cluster, as follows.

- **Tier one terms:** *as, at, during, now, of, on, together, when, while*

- **Tier two terms:** *at the same time, at this point, meanwhile, concurrently, in the meantime, nowadays, simultaneously*

When students encounter high-frequency words (or sight words) the teacher presents in the cluster format, they have the advantage of *referencing other words used in the same way*—thus increasing the number of linkages (that is, exposures) to the terms and the semantic clues as to their meanings.

Recommendation Number Two: Continue to Teach Unusual Words Prior to Reading New Passages

Many reading programs have lists of words students should be exposed to prior to reading new narrative and expository texts. This still makes good sense even when a school is using the approach to tier one, tier two, and tier three terms in this book. However, the previewed terms should not be given the same weight as the tier one and tier two terms before reading a passage since many of them might be low-frequency words. Rather, teachers should consider these prereading terms situationally important in that they are useful in understanding the passage students are about to read. But these words might not be important enough for instructional time beyond what is necessary to help students read the upcoming text.

Ensuring a Working Knowledge of Tier One and Tier Two Terms

Not only should the type of vocabulary guide instruction but also the level of depth of understanding intended as the outcome. It is quite easy to make the mistake of thinking that all vocabulary instruction should result in students acquiring a deep level of understanding of all terms. This, by definition, would require a fairly intensive instructional emphasis. While such intense instruction makes sense for tier three terms and perhaps some of the tier two terms (we address this in chapter 3, page 37), it does not make sense for any of the tier one and some of the tier two terms. Some, perhaps many, students might already have a basic understanding of tier one terms and the more frequent tier two terms.

Because of this, the instructional focus for tier one and some of the tier two terms should be ensuring that students have a working knowledge of the terms. There are two key components to this statement: *ensuring* and *working knowledge.* In this book, *ensuring* means the teacher has information about each student's knowledge of the tier one and selected tier two terms. If that information indicates a student understands specific tier one or tier two terms, no further instruction is necessary. *Working knowledge* means students have a general idea of what a word means. This would manifest as the student encountering the word in written or oral language and having enough understanding of the term that encountering it would add to (as opposed to detract from) the student's comprehension of what was written or spoken. This is a rather low threshold for understanding.

One might legitimately ask, "Why is the bar set so low for students' understanding of tier one and selected tier two terms?" The main reason is students will encounter the tier one terms (for sure) and some of the tier two terms (most likely) enough that, over time, they will develop a deep understanding of the terms. Another way of saying this is that teachers can rely on incidental learning as the primary form of knowledge development for the tier one terms and selected tier two terms.

Relying on Incidental Learning

When it comes to vocabulary development, *incidental learning* is much more powerful than might be obvious. For example, author Susan Carey (1978) noted students initially start learning a word by rather quickly associating a new term with some general meaning, even though that meaning is very general or vague. This is referred to as *fast mapping.* As students experience the word in the future, they add new characteristics to their understanding, as well as correct their previous misconceptions. This is referred to as *extended mapping,* which can go on indefinitely as a student has more and more encounters with a term. In effect, human beings are always learning about new words and words they are already familiar with, even though they are not aware of this. As Stahl (1999) noted, adults possess a surprising amount of information about words they have encountered—even words they think they don't know very well.

Extended mapping occurs as students encounter words multiple times. Of course, multiple encounters occur quite naturally with tier one terms and some of the tier two terms. One way to facilitate extended mapping is through the cluster approach in this book.

Using the Cluster Approach

As described in the introduction (page 1), all tier one and tier two terms are organized in semantic clusters. To illustrate, reconsider the following tier one and tier two terms for cluster 102, Bodies of Water.

- **Tier one terms:** *lake, ocean, puddle, river, sea, stream, bay, creek, pond*
- **Tier two terms:** *brook, cove, current, delta, gulf, inlet, marsh, outlet, rapids, strait, surf, swamp, tide, tributary, waterfall, waterline, bog, eddy, estuary, fjord, geyser, headwaters, lagoon, marshland, reef*

Assume students are not aware of the term *creek.* Even with one exposure to the term in class, they would probably encounter it enough for its meaning to solidify. The same might be said of some of the tier two terms in this cluster, depending on the students' environment. For example, if students live in any area near a lake, a stream, or an ocean, they might frequently encounter terms like *headwaters*, *eddy*, and *estuary*.

One of the more powerful instructional strategies to use with clusters is to emphasize the differences between terms. This might seem counterintuitive since the clusters are based on the similarities between terms. For example, all of the terms in cluster 102 are somehow related to bodies of water. This relationship provides students with an initial common reference point for all the terms in the cluster. But it is their *differences* within this general frame of reference that distinguishes the unique features of each term within the cluster. Some of the terms in cluster 102 are different types of large bodies of water (for example, *ocean*, *sea*); some are parts of large bodies of water (for example, *bay*, *cove*); and some are bodies of running water (for example, *creek*, *river*, *waterfall*), and so on. By providing opportunities to describe the differences in terms within a cluster, students will gradually learn the unique features of the terms in the cluster.

Implementing a Coordinated Schoolwide Plan

Ensuring all students have a working knowledge of the tier one and tier two terms in the student notebooks should be a coordinated schoolwide effort. This means the school creates a coordinated plan as opposed to having individual teachers identify which clusters to address and which resources to use.

A schoolwide plan's design should ensure all students have a working knowledge of tier one terms by at least grade 5, and a working knowledge of the tier two terms in the student notebook by grade 5. This can be done by having teachers at different grade levels identify those clusters their grade level will be responsible for. For example, first-grade teachers might be responsible for clusters 1–100, second-grade teachers would be responsible for clusters 101–200, and so on.

While this approach is very straightforward, I have found that administrators and teachers typically like to select the clusters they will be responsible for based on units they will be teaching. For example, third-grade teachers might collectively decide they will be responsible for teaching a unit on oceans. Collectively, those teachers might elect to include the following clusters in their instruction.

- **Cluster 70:** Sea Animals
- **Cluster 87:** Locations Near Water
- **Cluster 159:** Vehicles (Sea Transportation)
- **Cluster 296:** Locations For/Near Water (Manmade)
- **Cluster 309:** Shellfish (and Others)
- **Cluster 391:** Water-Related Directions

In this example, the teachers judged there are six clusters all pertaining to the unit on oceans. Under this model, teachers address each cluster (regardless of where it is placed chronologically) associated with oceans. Teachers then have students identify their competence levels on these vocabulary clusters as they move through the unit.

A similar approach is for teachers to simply use the supercluster structures. That is, teachers at each grade level examine the topics they will cover in the curriculum. They identify the clusters that correspond to those topics and then identify the supercluster. To illustrate, second-grade teachers might examine the various content they will teach throughout the year and determine their responsibility for the following superclusters as part of the instruction in those units.

- **Supercluster 6:** Time (2, 16, 24, 29, 52, 59, 79, 83, 126, 144, 233)
- **Supercluster 8:** Color (57, 415)
- **Supercluster 10:** Animals (32, 35, 64, 65, 70, 82, 95, 117, 155, 188, 189, 194, 309, 310, 341)
- **Supercluster 13:** Trees and Plants (36, 108, 192, 269, 421)
- **Supercluster 22:** Food and Eating (48, 51, 74, 86, 124, 136, 153, 162, 174, 176, 208, 222, 232, 246)
- **Supercluster 30:** Shapes (69, 99, 142, 193, 218, 270, 303, 326)

Working With the Folios for Each Cluster

When addressing a specific cluster, it is advisable to give a copy of the accompanying folio to each student. One of the first things students should do when working in a folio is to identify the terms they think they already know. Specifically, each folio starts with a list of tier one terms with a small box next to each. For cluster 79, Parts of a Day, those terms are the following.

☐ *day*	☐ *night*	☐ *midnight*
☐ *evening*	☐ *noon*	☐ *overnight*
☐ *hour*	☐ *second*	☐ *sundown*
☐ *minute*	☐ *tonight*	☐ *sunrise*
☐ *morning*	☐ *afternoon*	☐ *sunset*

Teachers then instruct students to check the box next to any term they already know. Of course, this initial self-assessment might be inaccurate, but even if students don't really know a word they check off (or do know a word they do not check off), some learning occurs simply by virtue of the fact that students have at least thought about the meaning of each term and made a judgement regarding their level of understanding of each term.

After students make their initial cursory evaluation of their understanding of each term, they should consider the visual representation of each term in the folio and the brief accompanying definition. To illustrate, consider the word *day* in figure I.4 (page 11). The folio visual representation is a calendar with a specific day circled. The folio also identifies the term as a noun and provides the definition: *A **day** is one period of twenty-four hours. There are seven **days** in a week.*

There is a section near the end of each folio that provides an extended definition of each term. In the case of the term *day*, that extended definition is: *A* day *is one period of twenty-four hours. There are seven* days *in a week. Here's how you could use* day *in a sentence: He had a busy* day *filled with work and errands.* A teacher might present these extended definitions to students verbally or simply have students read them if they require more information about the term. Finally, a video accompanies each folio. Each video repeats the visual representation in the folio but also includes an audio recording of the extended definition.

It is important to note that the definitions in the folios and videos are not the typical dictionary definitions. This is because dictionary definitions are not traditionally designed to teach the reader what terms mean. In fact, prior to internet-based dictionaries, dictionary definitions had to be relatively short to save space. This leads many literacy specialists to conclude that relying on dictionaries as the primary method of communicating the meaning of new words to students is not advisable because those definitions do not provide a rich source of semantic clues as to the words' meaning (McKeown, 1991, 1993; Miller & Gildea, 1987; Scott & Nagy, 1997; Stahl & Fairbanks, 1986). The folio definitions are very user friendly and similar to how a friend might explain a term to another friend. A useful resource is the Collins COBUILD online dictionary (https://collinsdictionary.com/us/dictionary/english) or hardcopy dictionary (Roehr & Carroll, 2010). A more in-depth explanation appears on pages 23–25.

In effect, there are three ways a student can access the definition of a term: (1) the folio representation with the brief definition, (2) the extended definition near the end of the folio, and (3) the video recording with a visual representation and orally presented extended definition. There are a variety of ways to use these three parallel resources.

One approach to using the folio resources is to provide students with time to go through the pictures and brief descriptions individually. Teachers would then organize students into small groups to discuss these meanings. As these groups interact, the teacher might remind team members to look at the extended definitions in the folios if they want more information about a particular word. It would also be at this point that the teacher engages students in discussions about the differences between words.

Teachers can also use the video-based representations and definitions in a variety of ways. For example, the teacher might elect to show a video to the entire class. Certainly ELs and students without strong language backgrounds should view the videos. Students who need the simultaneous input of the visual representation of the word and the audio presentation of the extended definition might view these folios individually or in small, homogenous groups.

Each folio also contains two Check Your Understanding activities. To illustrate, figures 1.2 and 1.3 (page 24) contain the two activities for cluster 79, Parts of a Day.

Answers to all the Check Your Understanding activities appear at the end of each folio. Teachers might have students complete these activities on their own and then go over the answers with the whole class or small groups. Again, this is a good time to for teachers to emphasize the differences in word meanings.

By the time students receive information about the meaning and use of the words in a cluster, and they have gone through the activities to check their understanding, they should have a strong sense of their level of knowledge about each term.

Addressing the Challenge Words

Each cluster in the *Building Basic Vocabulary* student notebook also lists selected tier two terms or *challenge words* in the folios. Students should not master tier one terms before they attempt the tier two terms. Indeed, my recommendation is that students consider *all* challenge words in each cluster. However, the folios do not provide any instructional resources for tier two terms. This notwithstanding, the cluster approach provides a rich semantic environment for students to glean meaning about challenge words. To illustrate, consider cluster 64, Cats/Dogs. Tier one terms in that cluster are *cat, dog, doggie, fox, lion, tiger, wolf, bulldog, collie.*

Tier two terms in the student notebook for this cluster include *beagle, cougar, coyote, greyhound, hyena, Labrador, leopard, panther, pug, puma.* Again, students should start by identifying those challenge words they feel like they already know. For those terms they are unfamiliar with, students might look up the meaning of the words in a hardcopy or internet-based dictionary.

Directions: Match each word to the correct description. One description will not be used.

Word		Description
1. _____ morning	a.	The time when the sun sets; also known as sunset
2. _____ noon	b.	A period of twenty-four hours
3. _____ hour	c.	The part of the day between the time when people usually wake up and noon
4. _____ tonight	d.	Through the whole night or at some point during the night
5. _____ sundown	e.	A period of sixty seconds
6. _____ day	f.	Twelve o'clock in the middle of the day
7. _____ midnight	g.	A period of sixty minutes
8. _____ evening	h.	Twelve o'clock in the middle of the night
1. _____ afternoon	i.	The time in the evening when the sun goes down; also known as sundown
2. _____ overnight	j.	The part of each day between the end of the afternoon and the time you go to bed
3. _____ minute	k.	A few seconds
4. _____ sunrise	l.	One of the sixty parts a minute is divided into
5. _____ night	m.	The part of each day that begins at lunchtime and ends around six o'clock
6. _____ sunset	n.	The time in the morning when the sun first appears in the sky
7. _____ second	o.	The part of each day when the sun has set and it is dark outside
	p.	The evening of today

Figure 1.2: Check Your Understanding activity A for cluster 79.

As mentioned previously, I typically recommend that students use the Collins COBUILD (Roehr & Carroll, 2010) dictionary (online or hardcopy), which uses definitions that resemble how one person might explain a word to another person. For example, consider the following dictionary definitions adapted from Collins COBUILD (Roehr & Carroll, 2010) for some of the challenge words for cluster 64.

- A **beagle** is a small hound with a smooth coat, short legs, and drooping ears, used in hunting small game.

- A **cougar** is a wild member of the cat family. Cougars have brownish-gray fur and live in mountain regions of North and South America.

- A **coyote** is a small wolf which lives in the plains of North America.

- A **greyhound** is a dog with a thin body and long, thin legs, which can run very fast. Greyhounds sometimes run in races people bet on.

Directions: Circle the correct answer.

Questions	a	b	c
1. How many seconds are in a minute?	7	24	60
2. How many minutes are in an hour?	30	60	120
3. How many hours are in a day?	24	12	6
4. How many days are in a week?	1	7	24
5. Which happens earliest?	morning	night	noon
6. Which happens latest?	noon	night	morning
7. Which happens second?	morning	afternoon	evening
8. Which happens last?	evening	morning	afternoon
9. Which refers to the evening of today?	evening	night	tonight
10. Which happens during the day?	overnight	midnight	noon
11. Which happens during the night?	morning	midnight	noon
12. Which happens in the morning?	sunrise	sunset	sundown
13. Which happens throughout the night?	sunrise	overnight	day
14. Which happens in the evening?	noon	sunrise	sundown
15. Which two words mean the same thing?	sunrise and sundown	sundown and sunset	sunrise and sunset

Figure 1.3: Check Your Understanding activity B for cluster 79.

- A **hyena** is an animal that looks like a dog and makes a sound similar to a human laugh. Hyenas live in Africa and Asia.

- A **Labrador** or **Labrador retriever** is a type of large dog with short, thick black or gold hair.

- A **leopard** is a type of large, wild cat with yellow fur and black spots. Leopards live in Africa and Asia.

- A **panther** is a large, wild animal, usually black, that belongs to the cat family.

- A **pug** is a small, fat, short-haired dog with a flat face.

- A **puma** is a wild animal with brownish-gray fur that belongs to the cat family. Pumas live in mountain regions of North and South America.

Each of these definitions are nontechnical, and each term in the Collins COBUILD online dictionary provides multiple pictures and more detailed print information.

Students working in small groups can discuss the challenge terms they know and don't know. From this group interaction, students should garner enough information to acquire a rough approximation of what the words mean. It is important to remember that students will encounter even the tier two terms listed in the student notebook frequently enough for them to experience multiple exposures, which will help reinforce and shape students' understanding of these terms.

As mentioned previously, the student notebook does not include all the tier two terms. Specifically, there are 2,889 tier two terms in the student notebook, and 5,120 tier two terms in appendix A (page 61) of this book. There are a number of ways teachers might address the issue of the tier two words in appendix A, but not listed in the student notebook.

- Ignore the tier two terms not listed, and rely on incidental learning for students to make connections.

- Present the extra tier two terms to interested students.

- Select some of the unaddressed tier three terms in appendix A and treat them with the same level of direct instruction as the subject-matter tier three terms.

Encouraging Students to Record Information Using Their Notebooks

When students are done using the folios and video recordings for a specific cluster, they should go to their student notebooks as soon as possible and evaluate themselves on each word in the folio using the scale in figure 1.4.

Understanding Level	Descriptor
4	I understand even more about the term than I was taught.
3	I understand the term, and I'm not confused about any part of what it means.
2	I'm a little uncertain about what the term means, but I have a general idea.
1	I'm very uncertain about the term. I really don't understand what it means.

Source: Adapted from Marzano & Pickering, 2005.
Figure 1.4: Scale for self-evaluation of understanding of terms.

The student notebook has a section for each word where students can assess themselves and find some clues regarding each word's meaning. Figure 1.5 (page 26) depicts the section of the student notebook for cluster 79, Parts of a Day, in which a student has evaluated herself and recorded clues to the meaning of some words.

Note that in this particular example (see figure 1.5), the student has scored herself on all tier one and tier two terms and recorded information that helps her remember what certain words mean. In some cases, the student drew arrows connecting words that mean about the same thing. In other cases, the student wrote in words or phrases to remind herself of the word's meaning. In some cases, the student provided a symbol or picture to remind her of the word's meaning. These arrows, pictures, symbols, and written reminders help students remember what they learned about new terms.

Periodically, the teacher should have students go back to their notebooks and identify terms they scored themselves a 2 or 1 with the intention of updating those scores. If students find terms they still would rate themselves a 2 or 1, the teacher might provide time for them to gather information about the terms via

day	④3 2 1		evening	4③2 1	
hour	④3 2 1		minute	④3 2 1	
morning	④3 2 1		night	④3 2 1	
noon	④3 2 1		second	④3 2 1	
tonight	④3 2 1		afternoon	④3 2 1	
midnight	④3 2 1		overnight	4③2 1	
(sundown)	④3 2 1 ←		sunrise	④3 2 1	
sunset	④3 2 1				
CHALLENGE WORDS					
(dawn)	4③2 1		(daybreak)	4 3 2 1	
(dusk)	4③2 1	before night	(instant)	4 3②1	quick
midday	4 3 2①	afternoon	(moment)	4 3②1	
nightfall	4 3②1	sun goes down	noontime	4 3②1	lunch
twilight	4 3 2①	stars come out	workday	4 3②1	my dad

Source: Marzano, 2018a, pp. 49–50.

Figure 1.5: Cluster 79 in a student notebook example.

interactions with other students, using the internet, or both. As the teacher addresses new clusters, students should repeat this process of evaluating themselves and recording information that reminds them of the meaning of words difficult for them.

Ideally, teachers should allow and encourage students to work on tier one and tier two terms in their notebooks outside of school. This also means teachers should allow students to take their notebooks home. It is also best if students have internet access to the online resources outside of school. This requires students know the login information and have access to the internet.

With these resources in place, students can examine clusters of their choice on their own time independently or with help from family members and friends. To illustrate, assume that a student is on cluster 61, Communication (Presentation of Information). Also assume the student is interested in weather. The student might find clusters with weather-related terms like the following.

- **Cluster 226:** Wind and Storms
- **Cluster 307:** Natural Catastrophes
- **Cluster 406:** Clouds

In effect, students might identify any clusters of interest to them and work through the folios on their own by initially scoring each word in the folio, watching the video, reading the short or extended definitions, and engaging in the Check Your Understanding activities.

Badging Milestones in Tier One and Tier Two Development

One of the more powerful things schools can and should do to monitor and celebrate students' progress through the clusters is to provide badges for various levels of mastery. One simple approach follows.

- **Bronze badge:** 100 clusters
- **Silver badge:** 200 clusters
- **Gold badge:** 300 clusters
- **Platinum badge:** All 420 clusters

When students have recorded self-evaluation scores of 3 or 4 on the tier one and tier two words in one hundred clusters from their student notebooks, they have reached the *bronze level*. When they have recorded self-evaluations for tier one and tier two terms in two hundred clusters, they have reached the *silver level*, and so on. It's important to note that these clusters do not have to be sequential. For example, a student might earn bronze status by demonstrating scores of 3 or 4 on the words in clusters 1–62; 70–82; 89; 100–125.

Variations on the badging include the following.

- Badging separately for tier one and tier two terms
- Requiring scores of 3 or 4 on a majority of the terms (for example, 80 percent) within a cluster (as opposed to all terms) as the criterion for mastering a cluster

Summary

This chapter focused on a schoolwide approach to ensuring students have a working knowledge of all tier one terms and selected tier two terms by the time they enter middle school. For many students, direct instruction of tier one terms will not be necessary because students might already know them and, even if they don't, a brief exposure will suffice to provide a foundation for incidental learning. This is also probably the case for some tier two terms. One of the first steps necessary for an elementary schoolwide approach is to procure the appropriate resources. Recommended resources include the following.

- This book, *Teaching Basic, Advanced, and Academic Vocabulary: A Comprehensive Framework for Elementary Instruction,* for each teacher

- The student notebook *Building Basic Vocabulary: Tracking My Progress* (Marzano, 2018a) for each student

- Student and teacher access to the online tool (which includes folios and video recordings for each cluster)

Another important step is for educators to identify which clusters they will address at each grade level. There are multiple options for doing this, some of which incorporate tier one and tier two vocabulary into units of instruction taught at specific grade levels.

A strong recommendation from this chapter is to give students badges that signify and celebrate each student's progress through the clusters.

CHAPTER 2

Tier One and Tier Two Terms for Individual Students

While it is true that the whole-class approach described in chapter 1 (page 17) will suffice for the vast majority of students, some students may require more individualized attention. Specifically, students of poverty and ELs might require extra attention.

Students of Poverty

Students of poverty might have particular needs with tier one and tier two terms. Researchers William E. Nagy and Patricia A. Herman (1984) found that students from families of different socioeconomic status (SES) had consistent differences in the sizes of their vocabulary, and they could predict these differences by family income. Specifically, they estimated a 4,700-word difference in vocabulary size between high- and low-SES students (Nagy & Herman, 1984). Additionally, they estimated that mid-SES first graders had about 50 percent more words in their vocabulary than low-SES first graders (Nagy & Herman, 1984). In a paper presented at a meeting of the American Educational Research Association, Michael F. Graves and Wayne H. Slater (1987) found less dramatic differences. They estimated first graders from high-income backgrounds had vocabularies double the size of first graders from low-income families (Graves & Slater, 1987).

Authors Betty Hart and Todd R. Risley's (1995) study dramatized the differences in vocabulary knowledge between students can be traced back to SES. Hart and Risley (1995) estimated the differences in vocabulary development due to family SES for children between the ages of ten and thirty-six months and included three socioeconomic groups: (1) *welfare families*, (2) *working-class families*, and (3) *professional families*. (The reader should note the labels Hart and Risley, 1995, used to describe these groups would most likely not be appropriate in the 21st century due to negative connotations.) Hart and Risley (1995) estimated thirty-six-month-old children from welfare families had about 70 percent of the vocabulary of children from working-class families and only about 45 percent of the vocabulary of children from professional families. Hart and Risley (2003) also determined the reason for these differences—students from lower-income families were simply experiencing less words from verbal interactions than those from higher-income families:

> The average child on welfare was having half as much experience per hour (616 words per hour) as the average working-class child (1,251 words per hour) and less than one-third that of the average child in a professional family (2,153 words per hour). . . . In four years of such experience, an average child in a

professional family would have accumulated experience with almost 45 million words, an average child in
a working-class family would have accumulated experience with 26 million words, and an average child in
a welfare family would have accumulated experience with 13 million words. (p. 8)

Hart and Risley (2003) concluded students from families on welfare enter school having heard approximately thirty million fewer words than students from professional families. This finding is commonly referred to as "the 30 million word gap" (Hart & Risley, 2003, p. 4). This gap puts low-SES students at an immediate disadvantage and clearly in need of instruction on tier one and selected tier two terms.

English Learners

ELs represent another group of students who might require extra assistance regarding tier one and selected tier two terms. Child development experts Andrew Biemiller and Naomi Slonim (2001) explain that ELs beginning school have already learned from 5,000 to 7,000 words in their first language, but this does not transfer to their second language, which makes intuitive sense. While second-language learners might have well developed vocabularies in their first language, they typically do not have well developed vocabularies in their second language, regardless of their SES. University of Miami researchers Vivian M. Umbel, Barbara Z. Pearson, Maria C. Fernández, and D. K. Oller (1992) examined the receptive vocabulary of Hispanic ELs in Miami in both English and Spanish, and found that even ELs from middle- and high-SES families had poorly developed vocabularies in their second language. Coauthors Yvonne S. Freeman and David E. Freeman (2009) identified three categories of ELs: (1) those new to the United States (moved to the United States within the past year) but well prepared in the schools in their homeland; (2) those new to the United States but not well prepared in the schools in their homeland; and (3) those who have been in the United States for a long time and have succeeded in acquiring tier one and some tier two vocabulary but require help in tier three academic vocabulary. Freeman and Freeman (2009) explained that teachers should carefully consider these differences when designing direct vocabulary instruction.

Fortunately, direct vocabulary instruction can be very useful with ELs. Researchers Barry McLaughlin, Diane August, Catherine Snow, Maria Carlo, Cheryl Dressler, Claire White et al. (2000) examined the impact of direct vocabulary instruction on ELs and found the program closed the gap between ELs and native English speakers by 50 percent in measures of vocabulary knowledge and reading comprehension.

Using the Online Diagnostic Assessment

For students who require individual attention on the tier one and selected tier two terms, it is useful to employ the online diagnostic assessment (www.marzanoresources.com/resources/student-assessment). To use this assessment, individual students must have access to the online tool (www.marzanoresources.com /resources/building-basic-vocabulary). Multiple students can use the site at the same time, but each student must be on a separate device. Activate the online diagnostic assessment by clicking the Online version link to the right of Adaptive Student Assessment on the main page.

Students are presented with two forced-choice items, like the following (see figure 2.1) for cluster 1, Modals.

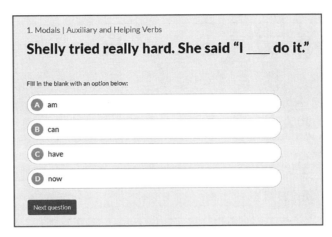

Figure 2.1: Sample online diagnostic assessment item for cluster 1, Modals.

Another feature of the online diagnostic assessment is that students do not necessarily have to read the items themselves. Rather, they can click on the play icon next to the prompt, and the program will read the items and alternatives accompanying each item.

An important feature of the online diagnostic assessment is that it does not assess each cluster simply because it would take too much time to do so. With 420 clusters in the student notebook, each with two items, a student relatively familiar with the tier one terms would have to complete 840 items to demonstrate his or her competence! The time needed to answer this many items would be prohibitive at best.

To make the online assessment more efficient, the program scores students' answers using a specific algorithm. The assessment starts with cluster 1 and presents two forced-choice items for terms in that cluster. If students answer both items correctly, they automatically jump to the items for cluster 25. If they answer both items for cluster 25 correctly, the students are directed to cluster 50, and so on. If both items are not answered correctly, students are moved down to the previous cluster, then to the next-previous cluster, and so on until the students answer both items in a cluster correctly.

Using the Hardcopy Diagnostic Assessment

There is also a hardcopy version of the diagnostic assessment. Activate the online diagnostic assessment by clicking the PDF version link to the right of Adaptive Student Assessment on the main page of the online tool (www.marzanoresources.com/resources/building-basic-vocabulary). It is also in appendix B (page 245). The hardcopy diagnostic assessment uses a different format, and to administer it, a teacher must interact one-to-one with a student. It basically requires the teacher to point to the pair of words for each cluster and ask the student to say the words and use them in a sentence. The pairs of words for the first one hundred clusters are depicted in table 2.1 (page 32). The teacher uses the same convention as the online diagnostic assessment (clusters are skipped if a student appears to recognize and understand both terms for a cluster). The specifics of the hardcopy diagnostic assessment are also in appendix B.

Table 2.1: Pairs of Words for Clusters 1–100

1	can will	2	during while	3	do have	4	am is
5	too with	6	they him	7	her its	8	what when
9	to at	10	to since	11	that which	12	how why
13	each either	14	good-bye maybe	15	more very	16	ready early
17	left right	18	almost enough	19	half less	20	far apart
21	forward backwards	22	outside indoors	23	under underneath	24	late afterward
25	where anywhere	26	top overhead	27	without instead	28	number dozen
29	Tuesday February	30	maybe allegedly	31	please hopefully	32	turkey ostrich
33	big tiny	34	any nobody	35	tadpole kitten	36	tree flower
37	corner edge	38	catch toss	39	climb lift	40	do use
41	own belong	42	we're they're	43	sad sorry	44	carry mail
45	happy celebrate	46	choice appoint	47	helmet glasses	48	breakfast dessert
49	point address	50	moon planet	51	drink chew	52	month decade
53	lullaby rhyme	54	ballet solo	55	care enjoy	56	person hero
57	blue green	58	best important	59	fast hurry	60	kindergarten classroom
61	say recite	62	glove sandal	63	run hike	64	dog lion
65	horse kangaroo	66	go travel	67	idea forget	68	student graduate
69	empty hollow	70	fish seal	71	read trace	72	truth mistake
73	foot spoonful	74	mix mustard	75	finger shoulders	76	leg ankle
77	show cartoon	78	cold hot	79	noon overnight	80	tooth tongue
81	he's here's	82	turtle dinosaur	83	today ancient	84	bell siren

85	I'll she'll	86	butter cheese	87	island coast	88	nurse doctor
89	win champion	90	air weather	91	kitchen hallway	92	rope glue
93	driveway drawbridge	94	aunt grandparent	95	caterpillar dragonfly	96	cup mug
97	row glide	98	pile bunch	99	deep tall	100	greet thank

Moving Through the Clusters

Once students have a starting place for the 420 clusters in the student notebook, they should move through the clusters using the online folios as their source of information. They should also use the student notebook. When using the folios, students would first identify those terms they think they know. Recall, this activity is simply to help students activate their prior knowledge about the terms in the cluster. The next step should be for students to go directly to the video recording that provides a representation of each word along with its extended definition. This, of course, is somewhat different from the whole-class approach. With that approach, the students first read the information about each term using the folio content. ELs and students of poverty identified as needing individual help, and who are working independently or in small homogenous groups, should consult the video-based information first. After students have watched the video, they might then look over the definitions in the folios to reinforce what they observed and heard in the video.

Next, students move to the Checking Your Understanding activities in the folio. They might complete these individually or in dyads or small groups since the answers for each activity are near the end of the folio.

Immediately after working in a cluster, students should move to their student notebook and record their self-evaluation scores for each word. It's also important for students to make notes or add drawings in the spaces provided to remind them of what the terms mean. It is very important for students receiving individual attention to also record information in the notebook to help them remember the meaning of new or challenging terms. For example, see cluster 82, Reptiles/Mythical Animals, in figure 2.2 (page 34).

Figure 2.2 represents the notebook entries for a specific EL regarding terms in cluster 82. Note the student recorded entries for a few terms in the cluster. It is important to recognize that some of these entries are written in Spanish, the student's native language. This it not only acceptable but also advisable. Using terms in students' native language to help them remember the meaning of a term in the target language they are learning provides a strong semantic connection between their native language to the new term.

Another consideration when working through the clusters is *backfilling*. The manner in which the diagnostic assessment works creates a need for students to occasionally examine words in clusters that come *before* the cluster the teacher has directed students to start with. As previously mentioned, the assessment jumps twenty-five clusters if students answer both items correctly. While this is an efficient way to identify a starting place for students, it can also introduce errors into the system. That is, once the system identifies his or her starting place, an individual student might not be familiar with all or even a majority of the terms in the skipped clusters. The best guard against this is to have students periodically *backfill* scores.

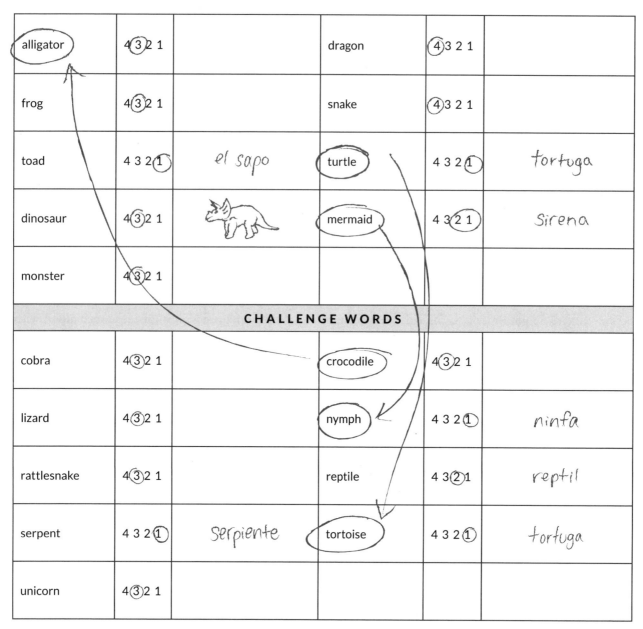

alligator	4 ③ 2 1		dragon	④ 3 2 1	
frog	4 ③ 2 1		snake	④ 3 2 1	
toad	4 3 2 ①	*el sapo*	turtle	4 3 2 ①	*tortuga*
dinosaur	④ 3 2 1		mermaid	4 3 ② 1	*Sirena*
monster	4 ③ 2 1				
CHALLENGE WORDS					
cobra	4 ③ 2 1		crocodile	4 ③ 2 1	
lizard	4 ③ 2 1		nymph	4 3 2 ①	*ninfa*
rattlesnake	4 ③ 2 1		reptile	4 3 ② 1	*reptil*
serpent	4 3 2 ①	*Serpiente*	tortoise	4 3 2 ①	*tortuga*
unicorn	4 ③ 2 1				

Figure 2.2: Sample notebook entry.

To illustrate backfilling, consider an individual student who starts at cluster 79 based on his or her online diagnostic assessment. That student will be making entries (as described earlier in this chapter and in chapter 3, page 37) in his or her notebook starting with cluster 79. Periodically, though, the teacher would provide time for the student to examine the words in each of the 78 clusters he or she skipped. This doesn't require much time—likely a few minutes or less per cluster. The student would start with cluster 1 and simply scan through the words, scoring him- or herself on each word using the self-assessment scale. For words the student assigns a score of 2 or 1, he or she would consult the video recording and folio information to obtain an initial understanding of the terms. The student would also record arrows, pictures, symbols, and verbal information to help remind him or her of the meaning and use of the terms.

Summary

This chapter addressed tier one and tier two vocabulary as it relates to individual students, including students of poverty and ELs. Students from both these groups might need one-to-one attention in addition to or in lieu of the whole-class activities used to help students move through the clusters. This approach involves having individual students take the online diagnostic assessment or hardcopy diagnostic assessment the teacher administers. These assessments provide a recommended cluster as a starting point for each student. With this approach, students first consult the video recordings and then go to the written (folio) activities. Also, students spend more time and energy recording reminders of what words mean in their student notebooks. It is recommended for students to periodically examine clusters that come *before* their starting cluster to ensure they have a chance to learn unfamiliar terms in those clusters. This process is referred to as *backfilling*.

CHAPTER 3

Teaching Tier Three Terms

Recall that tier three terms that are the focus of classroom instruction are subject-matter specific. As described in the introduction (page 1), researchers identified the tier three terms in appendix C (page 251) after a comprehensive analysis of standards (Dodson, 2019; Simms, 2017). There are 2,141 subject-specific tier three terms in appendix C that span grades K–5 for ELA, mathematics, science, and social studies. As with the tier one and tier two terms, these words are organized in clusters corresponding to topics that might be the focus of instruction. To illustrate, for fifth-grade mathematics, appendix C lists the following fourteen topics.

1. Multiplication and Division
2. Fraction Addition and Subtraction
3. Fraction Multiplication
4. Fraction Division
5. Decimal Place Values
6. Decimal Addition and Subtraction
7. Decimal Multiplication and Division
8. Exponents
9. Numerical Expressions
10. Numerical Patterns
11. Measurement Conversions
12. Volume
13. Two-Dimensional Figures
14. Coordinate Planes

Specific tier three terms are listed for each of these topics. For example, for the topic Coordinate Planes, the following terms are listed: *Cartesian coordinate plane, coordinates, ordered pair, origin, point, x-axis, x-coordinate, y-axis, y-coordinate, horizontal, vertical.*

It is important to note that some tier three terms are also on the tier one or tier two lists. For example, at the third-grade level, the word *sentence* is found under the ELA topic Generating Sentences. Terms under this topic are *complex sentence, compound sentence, simple sentence, linking word, subordinating conjunction.* The word *sentence* also appears as a tier one term in cluster 238, Words, Phrases, and Sentences, along with the following terms: *word, adjective, adverb, noun, verb.* It is clear that the expectation for understanding the word *sentence* is much greater when it is a subject-matter tier three term. This chapter discusses teaching tier three terms effectively, drawing from Marzano et al.'s (2015) book, *Vocabulary for the New Science Standards.*

The Need for Direct Instruction

With tier one and some of the tier two terms, educators can rely on incidental learning because students will encounter these terms so frequently. If students have just a cursory exposure to the terms the folios provide, the video recordings, student self-evaluations, and representations in the student notebook, they will have a very good chance of internalizing these terms over time. However, with tier three terms and the less-frequent tier two terms, the teacher cannot rely on incidental learning. Rather, the teacher must explicitly teach and reinforce these terms.

As with tier one and tier two terms, the tier three terms in this book are organized into semantic clusters referred to as *measurement topics*. In a series of other works, my colleagues and I (Marzano, 2006, 2010b, 2018b) described how teachers should embed these terms in proficiency scales like figure 3.1 depicts.

Teachers can use the scale in figure 3.1 to plan instruction and assessment regarding the topic Coordinate Planes. The score 3.0 content articulates the learning goals for this topic. This involves graphing points on a coordinate plane and using a coordinate plane to solve problems. The score 4.0 content requires students to go above and beyond the learning goals and usually involves some application of knowledge. Score 2.0 content contains basic vocabulary, basic understandings, and basic processes necessary to accomplish the goal of score 3.0 in the proficiency scale. More pertinent to the topic of this book, the score 2.0 of the proficiency scale contains the tier three vocabulary terms important to the topic Coordinate Planes. As mentioned in the introduction (page 1), educators should teach all tier three terms in the context of specific subject-matter topics. Stated differently, educators should *not* teach tier three terms in isolation.

As described previously, teachers might determine there is also a need for instruction on some tier two terms. Recall that the student notebook only contains 2,889 of the 5,160 tier two terms, leaving 2,271 terms unaddressed. I recommend individual teachers or all teachers in a school operating as a team identify some of these unaddressed tier two terms they wish to directly teach, along with the subject-specific tier three terms. Relative to this, it is important to note there are some clusters in appendix A (page 61) comprised totally of tier three terms. These are clusters 421–444. The words in these clusters (along with selected tier two terms from other clusters) might be added to the list of terms for which a teacher provides direct instruction.

Direct instruction can take many forms. In a number of works (Marzano, 2004, 2010b; Marzano & Pickering, 2005; Marzano & Simms, 2013), I described six steps that incorporate research-based elements of effective vocabulary instruction. Those six steps are as follows.

1. Provide a description, an explanation, or an example of the new term.
2. Ask students to restate the description, explanation, or example in their own words.
3. Ask students to construct a picture, symbol, or graphic representing the term or phrase.
4. Periodically engage students in activities that help them add to their knowledge of the terms to which they have previously been exposed.
5. Periodically ask students to discuss the terms with one another.
6. Periodically involve students in games that allow them to play with terms.
(Marzano et al., 2015)

Let's consider each of these in some depth.

4.0	The student will: Investigate the effects of performing simple mathematical operations on *x*- and *y*-coordinates (for example, when given the ordered pair [1, 2] identify the ordered pairs that would result if the coordinates were both multiplied by 2 or 3, plot the results and draw a line to connect each set of points, then use the graph to predict what might happen if the coordinates were both multiplied by 7, 10, or 15).
3.5	In addition to score 3.0 performance, partial success at score 4.0 content
3.0	The student will: Graph points on a coordinate plane (for example, when given a set of ordered pairs, graph the pairs as points on a coordinate plane). Use a coordinate plane to solve problems (for example, when given a coordinate plane in which the x-axis represents the numbered avenues of a city and the y-axis represents numbered streets, and when given that a person at the corner of Second Avenue and Fourth Street walks four blocks north, three blocks east, and one block south, identify the person's final location and then determine the shortest possible route they could have taken).
2.5	No major errors or omissions regarding score 2.0 content, and partial success at score 3.0 content
2.0	The student will recognize or recall specific vocabulary (for example, Cartesian coordinate plane, coordinates, graph, horizontal, ordered pair, origin, point, vertical, *x*-axis, *x*-coordinate, *y*-axis, *y*-coordinate). The student will perform basic processes such as: • Explain that the location of a point on a coordinate plane can be specified by identifying the values on the *x*- and *y*-axes with which the point aligns. • Identify the *x*- and *y*-coordinates of a given point on a coordinate plane. • Explain that a point can be plotted on a coordinate plane by beginning at the origin and first counting along the *x*-axis until reaching the value that corresponds to the point's *x*-coordinate, then counting upward until reaching the location that aligns with the value on the *y*-axis that corresponds to the point's *y*-coordinate. • Draw lines to connect points on a coordinate plane. • Explain that the horizontal or vertical distance between two points on a coordinate plane can be determined by counting the units between the points. For example, when given a graph of the points (4, 6) and (4, 10), the distance between the points can be determined by counting how many units (4) it takes to move from one point to the other. • Perform movements on a coordinate plane. For example, when given the starting point (2, 1) and the directions "move up 4 units, right 5 units, and down 3 units," perform the movements and identify the point (7, 2) as the resulting location. • Translate movements on a coordinate plane into operations on a set of coordinates. For example, when given the starting point (3, 2) explain that the directions "move down 1 and right 3" are performed by subtracting 1 from the *y*-coordinate and adding 3 to the *x*-coordinate.
1.5	Partial success at score 2.0 content, and major errors or omissions regarding score 3.0 content
1.0	With help, partial success at score 2.0 content and score 3.0 content
0.5	With help, partial success at score 2.0 content but not at score 3.0 content
0.0	Even with help, no success

Figure 3.1: Proficiency scale for the fifth-grade mathematics topic Coordinate Planes.

Step 1: Provide a Description, an Explanation, or an Example of the New Term

The first step in this six-step process involves providing students with information that allows them to form a rudimentary, but memorable, understanding of the new tier three terms. This can occur in three ways: a description, an explanation, or an example of the new term.

Provide a Description

When providing a description, the teacher presents information similar to the type online and hardcopy Collins COBUILD dictionaries (Roehr & Carroll, 2010) provide, as discussed in chapter 1 (pages 22–23). Again, these dictionaries are a great source for teachers seeking help with constructing initial descriptions of tier three terms and selected tier two terms. Table 3.1 provides some examples.

Table 3.1: Descriptions From Collins COBUILD Dictionary (Roerhr & Carroll, 2010)

mass	*Mass* is the amount of physical matter that something contains. *Pluto and Triton have nearly the same size, mass, and density.*
molecule	A *molecule* is the smallest amount of a chemical substance that can exist by itself. *When hydrogen and oxygen molecules combine, the reaction produces heat and water.*
organism	An *organism* is a living thing. *We study very small organisms such as bacteria.*
ratio	A *ratio* is a relationship between two things when it is expressed in numbers or amounts. *The adult-to-child ratio is one to six.*

Source: Adapted from Marzano et al., 2015, p. 17.

To illustrate how teachers might use the COBUILD dictionary (Roehr & Carroll, 2010) definitions, teachers seeking to describe *ratio* to their classes would start by consulting the following definition.

> A *ratio* is a relationship between two things when it is expressed in numbers or amounts. For example, if there are ten boys and thirty girls in a room, the ratio of boys to girls is 1:3, or one to three.

Teachers might then change or augment this definition to suit the needs of their particular students. For example, because students are very familiar with the problem of too many deer in their rural county, a teacher might change the description of *ratio* to the following.

> A ratio is a relationship between two things when it is expressed in numbers or amounts. For example, if there are 300 deer and only two wolves in a specific area, the ratio of wolves to deer is 1:150.

Provide an Explanation

What constitutes an effective explanation of a word varies depending on what kind of word it is. Vocabulary learning experts Joseph R. Jenkins and Robert Dixon (1983) identified four general types of explanations for a new term. These four types are differentiated by the nature of the term and the familiarity students have with the term.

1. The new term has a simple synonym with which students are familiar or can explain in very concrete ways. For example, the term *typhoon* has the synonym *hurricane* with which many students are familiar. Students can explain the term *ice* as frozen water.

2. The new term has a simple synonym, but students are not familiar with the synonym. For example, the term *combustible* is synonymous with the term *flammable* but students might not understand this synonym.

3. The new term does not have a simple synonym, but students have background knowledge they can easily relate to the term. For example, the term *population* has no obvious direct synonym but most students would understand the concept of people in a specific group, like the population of a city or school.

4. The new term does not have a simple synonym and students do not have relevant background knowledge from which to draw. For example, the term *cryosphere* refers to areas on Earth where water only occurs in its solid, frozen form. Unless students have seen pictures or video footage of polar regions, they will have no experiential base to understand this concept.

If a new term fits into the first or third categories, providing an explanation is fairly easy. The teacher either provides a known synonym, a brief concrete explanation, or a more detailed explanation that relates to students' background knowledge. However, if the term falls into the second or fourth categories, explanations will need to be more complex and will probably involve the introduction of new knowledge necessary to learn the term.

Effective explanations for new terms also take on different characteristics depending on the term's *part of speech* (Stahl, 1999). Marzano et al. (2015) provided practical illustrations of explanations for nouns, verbs, and modifiers.

Explaining Nouns

Nouns are typically either concrete (*precipitation, pollen, oxygen*) or abstract (*interdependence, equilibrium, extinction*). The easiest way to explain concrete nouns is to describe their characteristics, as in the following examples.

- *Precipitation* is any sort of moisture that falls from the sky, such as rain, snow, sleet, or hail.
- *Pollen* is the yellow dust found inside flowers and blossoms on plants.
- *Oxygen* is a clear gas humans need to breathe to survive.

Abstract nouns can be more difficult to describe and are better suited for examples. To illustrate, explaining *interdependence* is challenging, particularly for K–2 students. It is very useful to involve students in activities that provide them with concrete experiences regarding abstract nouns. For example, a teacher might have students play a game that requires them to work together and then explain that the game requires them to exhibit interdependence.

Explaining Verbs

Verbs typically refer to actions and therefore are amenable to teachers simply describing those actions. For example, a teacher might explain that *absorbing* means something is soaking up something else. It is often best to explain verbs in the context of specific nouns. While explaining the term *absorb*, the teacher might point out that only certain things can absorb other things. The teacher would then provide examples like the following.

- The plant absorbed the sun's energy.

- The layer of sand absorbed the contamination.

One effective way teachers can emphasize this point is to provide students with sentence frames for the verb *absorb* like the following.

The _____ absorbed the _____.

As students fill in nouns that make sense in this frame, the teacher helps them make connections between the verb and specific types of associated nouns.

Explaining Modifiers (Adjectives and Adverbs)

When explaining adjectives and adverbs, it is useful to engage in two types of explanatory activities. The first is to simply describe the concept behind the term. For an adjective such as magnetic, the teacher might say, "When something is *magnetic*, it attracts other objects." Second, the teacher can provide sentences that exemplify the term, such as the following.

- There was a magnetic attraction between the magnet and the paperclip.

- The Earth has a magnetic field around it.

- Running an electric current through the coil produced a magnetic force.

The same approach can be applied to *adverbs*, such as *jointly*. The teacher might begin by explaining that *jointly* means two things perform an action together, usually with equal responsibility. The teacher would also provide examples such as the following.

- There are just the two brothers, and they both own the house jointly. They are very close.

- The military operation was conducted jointly by the Navy and the Marines.

Provide an Example

Examples are probably the most powerful way of describing new terms and teachers should use them whenever possible. Consider the noun *interdependence.* To explain this, the teacher might present examples of groups of interdependent animals, such as the gelada monkey and walia ibex in the Ethiopian Highlands, who work together to protect themselves from wolf predation.

Depending on the time available, teachers can concretely provide examples during class. For instance, after describing and explaining a term such as *conduction* (when heat is transferred from one substance to another through direct contact), a teacher can engage students in demonstrations, such as the following.

- Heating a pot on a stove
- Touching a metal spoon sitting in a pot of boiling water
- Laying under a heated blanket
- Picking up a mug of hot coffee

Step 2: Ask Students to Restate the Description, Explanation, or Example in Their Own Words

During step 2 of the effective vocabulary instruction six-step process, the teacher asks students to restate the teacher's description, explanation, or example. This is because the act of creating their own version of what a new term means forces students to think about the term in depth and helps anchor the term in memory.

Teachers should give students wide latitude in constructing their descriptions, explanations, and examples, and also encourage students to draw from their own experiences as they do so. For example, a student might describe the term *atmosphere* as: "When the space shuttle re-enters the atmosphere, the friction from the air creates heat, making the shuttle look like it is on fire." Another student might say, "When I ride in an airplane, I climb through different layers of the atmosphere."

Both of these student-generated constructions are legitimate responses, even though one is more detailed than the other. As long as students' constructions do not include any major errors, misconceptions, or omissions, teachers should honor their personalized descriptions, explanations, and examples. During later steps in the process, students will return to these descriptions, explanations, and examples to revise and refine them.

To execute step 2, students must record their restated descriptions, explanations, and examples. There are many forms such restatements can take. Marzano et al. (2015) recommended a format involving the following components.

- The new term
- The academic subject associated with the term, if applicable (for example, science or mathematics)
- The category or measurement topic associated with the term (for example, Biogeology or Conservation of Matter)
- The student's current level of understanding of the term (for example, 4, 3, 2, or 1)
- The student's description, explanation, and example of the term
- The student's visual depiction of the term (see step 3, page 45)
- Words related to the term, such as synonyms or antonyms

Figure 3.2 (page 44) depicts how this might look.

With the tier one and tier two terms, students should rate their level of understanding for each term using the following scale.

4: I understand even more about the term than I was taught.

3: I understand the term, and I'm not confused about any part of what it means.

2: I'm a little uncertain about what the term means, but I have a general idea.

1: I'm very uncertain about the term. I really don't understand what it means.

Students' initial familiarity with a word may lead them to rate their initial understanding of a term at level 2 or 1. Teachers should expect this since students have not yet had very many exposures to the term or many opportunities to practice using it in various contexts. As they engage in activities, discussions, and games during steps 4–6, students' understanding of the term should deepen and increase.

Term:		
Subject:	Topic or category:	Level of understanding: 1 2 3 4
Description in words:		Synonyms:
		Antonyms:
Picture:		

Source: Marzano & Simms, 2013, p. 21.

Figure 3.2: Recording page for tier three terms.

*Visit **MarzanoResources.com/reproducibles** for a free reproducible version of this figure.*

One important decision teachers must make is whether students should complete, save, and store these pages in three-ring binders. These binders would contain tier three terms and selected tier two terms. As they complete steps 2 and 3 for a word, students would put the pages in their binders. The binders would have dividers for various sections, such as mathematics, science, ELA, and social studies. Students should also create a section for tier two words the teacher directly taught them. This section might be called *Challenge Words*. I also recommend students also have a section called *My Words* in their vocabulary binders. In this section, students would record any words that capture their interest, whether those words relate to academic subjects or not (Marzano & Pickering, 2005).

Instead of placing the recorded page for every word in their binders, another option is to have students save the recording pages for only those words they are having difficulty with or words the teacher wants them to continually update their understanding of.

Still another option is not to have binders for tier three and selected tier two terms. Rather, after students fill out a recording page, they would have the option of keeping it or returning it to the teacher to recycle.

Probably, the most promising option (done in tandem with those previously described) is to create an electronic classroom tier three and selected tier two vocabulary binder. The class binder might reside on a common drive like Google. The teacher could store selected students' recording pages so any student might access them at any time. Additionally, the teacher might create one class recording page for each term and update this page with input from the class as it re-examines words in steps 4, 5, or 6 of the six-step process.

Step 3: Ask Students to Construct a Picture, Symbol, or Graphic Representing the Term or Phrase

This step is a corollary to step 2 (in which students articulate their own version of what the new term means). The only difference is they do so using a nonlinguistic modality. There are at least five ways a student might approach this step.

1. Sketch the actual object.

2. Sketch a symbol for the term.

3. Sketch an example of the term.

4. Sketch a cartoon or vignette with a character using the term.

5. Sketch a graphic for the term.

Collectively, these types of recordings are called *nonlinguistic representations*. Figure 3.3 (page 46) depicts these five ways.

Marzano et al. (2015) noted that even with these five methods, some students may still have trouble with this step, especially if they don't see themselves as being proficient at drawing or art. Other students might spend too much time during this step, drawing overly detailed or elaborate pictures. Still others might argue that their linguistic descriptions are adequate and nonlinguistic representations are redundant.

To address these issues, teachers can model all the different appropriate nonlinguistic representation methods. Teachers might also incorporate multimedia graphics, videos, animations, or previous students' pictures into their examples of appropriate visual depictions.

Step 4: Periodically Engage Students in Activities That Help Them Add to Their Knowledge of the Terms to Which They Have Previously Been Exposed

Teachers should execute steps 1, 2, and 3 of the six-step process in order, with the teacher introducing a term (step 1) and students representing it linguistically (step 2) and nonlinguistically (step 3). Teachers should *not* execute steps 4, 5, and 6, in order nor should they do these steps for each new term. The purpose of steps 4, 5, and 6 are to provide multiple exposures to the tier three terms and selected tier two terms *after* students obtain an initial understanding of the them through steps 1, 2, and 3. Each of these steps involves the teachers introducing multiple terms to students. Each new exposure to previously introduced terms provides an opportunity for students to deepen their knowledge of the terms. I recommend students have an opportunity to engage in at least one of these steps at least once per week. Of the three, step 4 is the most diverse and robust. The various ways students can engage in step 4 include comparing and contrasting, classifying, creating metaphors, creating analogies, and examining root words and affixes.

Method	Term	Picture
1. Sketch the actual object. *If a term is concrete and easy to depict, simply sketch a picture of it.*	Punnett square	
2. Sketch a symbol for the term. *If a term is abstract, sketch a symbol that represents the term.*	Fahrenheit	
3. Sketch an example of the term. *If a term is abstract, sketch an example of the term.*	organism	
4. Sketch a cartoon or vignette with a character using the term. *If a term is abstract, use speech bubbles to show how a character in a cartoon might use the term.*	terrestrial	
5. Sketch a graphic for the term. *If a term is abstract, sketch a graphic that depicts the meaning of the term.*	proliferation	

Source: Adapted from Marzano & Simms, 2013.

Figure 3.3: Five methods for nonlinguistic representation.

Visit **MarzanoResources.com/reproducibles** *for a free reproducible version of this figure.*

Comparing and Contrasting

Comparing and contrasting activities are easy to execute and can be quite informative in terms of deepening students' knowledge of terms. Sentence stems like the following are particularly useful to this end.

_____and _____ are similar because they both:

* _____

* _____

_____and _____ are different because:

* _____is _____, while _____is _____

* _____is _____, while _____is _____

To illustrate the use of sentence stems, consider what a student comparing the terms *atom* and *molecule* might say.

Atoms and molecules are similar because they both:

* Are present in all objects and living things

* Are invisible to the naked eye

Atoms and molecules are different because:

* Atoms are the smallest particles that still have the properties of an element, while molecules are made up of two or more atoms

Venn diagrams are another structure students can use for comparing and contrasting. Here, differences are written in individual circles and similarities in the area where the circles overlap. Figure 3.4 shows how this might manifest when comparing *abiotic* and *biotic*.

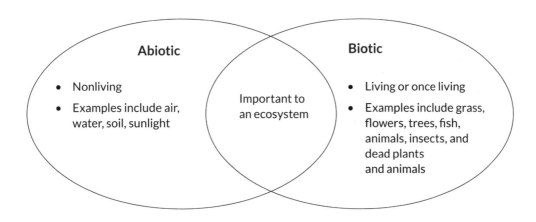

Source: Marzano et al., 2015, p. 29.

Figure 3.4: Venn diagram comparing *abiotic* and *biotic*.

A close relative of the Venn diagram is the *double bubble diagram*. With these diagrams, students again compare two terms by identifying their shared and unique characteristics. In figure 3.5, a student has compared the terms *hydrogen* and *helium*.

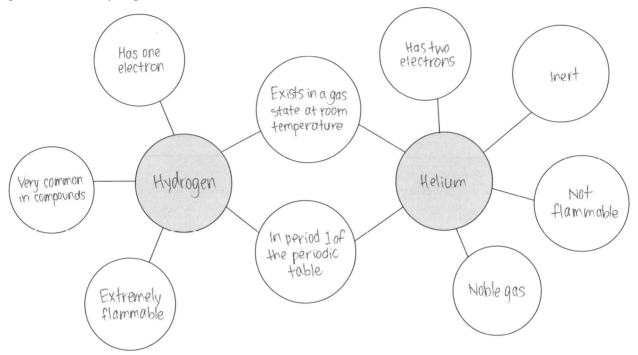

Source: Marzano et al., 2015, p. 29.
Figure 3.5: Double bubble diagram comparing *hydrogen* and *helium*.

Shared characteristics appear in bubbles that connect to both terms, while unique characteristics appear in bubbles that connect to only one of the terms.

When students compare and contrast three or more items, they can use a *comparison matrix*. Figure 3.6 depicts a comparison matrix for the terms *proton*, *neutron*, and *electron*.

When using the comparison matrix, students write the terms at the top of each column, and the terms' attributes (size, location, charge, and number) in each row. To complete the matrix, students fill in information about the identified attributes for each term and summarize their similarities and differences. Students record these summaries in the Conclusions cell at the bottom of the matrix.

Classifying

In its most basic form, *classifying* involves grouping terms into categories. *Classifying activities* can fall anywhere on a continuum from structured to open-ended. The most structured form of classifying involves teachers selecting the vocabulary terms to be classified and the categories students will use to sort them. For example, a teacher might present students with the following list of terms and two categories: *Elements* and *Chemical Compounds*.

hydrogen	chloride	sodium hydroxide
helium	calcium chloride	oxygen
carbon	chlorine	nitrogen
carbon dioxide	sodium	iron
ammonium		

	Proton	Neutron	Electron
Size	Smaller than an atom (subatomic), but larger than an electron; about the same size as a neutron	Smaller than an atom (subatomic), but larger than an electron; about the same size as a proton	Smaller than an atom (subatomic), a proton, and a neutron
Location	In the nucleus of an atom	In the nucleus of an atom	Outside the nucleus of an atom
Charge	Positively charged	Not charged	Negatively charged
Number	Determines the atomic number of the atom's element	Determines the isotope of an element	Determines how an atom forms ionic bonds with other atoms
Conclusions:	Protons, neutrons, and electrons are all subatomic particles. Electrons are the smallest of the three, while protons and neutrons are about the same size. Protons and neutrons are both found in the nucleus of an atom, but electrons are outside the atom's nucleus. Protons and electrons are similar because they both carry charges but different because protons are positively charged and electrons are negatively charged. Neutrons are different from both protons and electrons because they do not carry a charge. The number of each type of subatomic particle in an atom determines its atomic number (protons), its isotope (neutrons), and how it forms ionic bonds with other atoms (electrons).		

Source: Marzano et al., 2015, p. 30.

Figure 3.6: Comparison matrix for *proton*, *neutron*, and *electron*.

Teachers then ask students to sort each term into the appropriate category and explain their reasoning.

A more open-ended approach would involve the teacher presenting students with a list of terms and asking them to identify or create their own categories. Teachers would require students to defend their selected categories and explain why they put specific terms into specific categories.

Creating Metaphors

Metaphors involve relating two terms to each other on an abstract or nonliteral level. For example, the expression "life is a roller coaster" does not *literally* refer to riding a roller coaster at an amusement park. Rather, the metaphor is intended to make a connection between one aspect of being on a roller coaster—going up and down—with life's propensity to have high points and low points. Identifying abstract connections requires students to think deeply about the meaning of terms. Marzano et al. (2015) provided the following example of how metaphors might help students deepen their understanding of science terminology:

> A science teacher might ask students to create metaphors for a specific term, such as *DNA*. One student might say that "DNA is a barcode" because it contains a lot of information in a small space. Another student might say "DNA is a blueprint" because it contains instructions for synthesizing proteins. These two responses illustrate one of the most important aspects of asking students to create metaphors: explaining one's reasoning. Students should always include a "because" statement after their metaphors. One way to help students generate metaphors and explain their reasoning is to use a sentence stem, such as:
>
> _____ is/are _____
> because _____. (p. 31)

Teachers can heighten the complexity of metaphors by having students describe a number of abstract relationships between two terms. Figure 3.7 depicts an example of this.

Focus Term (Tenor): *immune system*	General Descriptors	Related Term (Vehicle): *personal bodyguard*
• Protects the body against damage • Fights against microorganisms • Fights against cancer • Doesn't attack our own cells • Responds to millions of different kinds of pathogens • Remembers pathogens it has encountered before and deals with them more efficiently during subsequent infections (acquired immunity)	• Prevents damage • Fights against outside invaders • Fights against inside invaders • Knows who is a friend • Knows what to do in lots of different situations • Has a good memory	• Keeps you from getting hurt • Keeps strangers from hurting you • Keeps people who claim to be friends from hurting you • Can sense who is a friend and who is an enemy • Experienced • Smart

Source: Adapted from Marzano et al., 2015, p. 31.

Figure 3.7: Metaphor matrix.

With complex metaphors, the teacher provides the term, which is the focus of the metaphor and technically called the *tenor*. In this case, the tenor in the metaphor is *immune system*. The teacher also provides the term *personal bodyguard*, which represents the item for which abstract relationships exist. This term is technically referred to as the *vehicle*. Students then have to describe multiple, reasonable abstract relationships between the tenor and the vehicle in the General Descriptors column (see figure 3.7).

Creating Analogies

An *analogy* articulates relationships between pairs of terms. For example, *Slow is to fast as cold is to hot.* The relationship of slow to fast is that slow involves little speed whereas fast involves a great deal of speed. The relationship between cold and hot is that cold involves low temperature while hot involves a high temperature. Even though speed and temperature are not related, the fact that the pairs share a common relationship of the *degree* of something creates the analogical relationship.

As with comparing and contrasting, and creating metaphors, teachers can provide sentence stems to help students create analogies. There are several different types of sentence stems a teacher might use, including the following examples.

- **Provide one pair of terms and ask students to generate the second pair:**

    Photosynthesis is to plant cells as ＿＿＿＿＿＿＿ is to ＿＿＿＿＿＿＿.

- **Provide the first term of each pair and ask students to generate a second term for each pair:**

    Photosynthesis is to ＿＿＿＿＿＿＿ as eating is to ＿＿＿＿＿＿＿.

- **Provide the second term of each pair and ask students to generate a first term for each pair:**

    ＿＿＿＿＿＿＿ is to plant cells as ＿＿＿＿＿＿＿ is to animal cells.

Alternatively, the teacher could use a visual analogy diagram such as the one in figure 3.8 to help students organize their analogies.

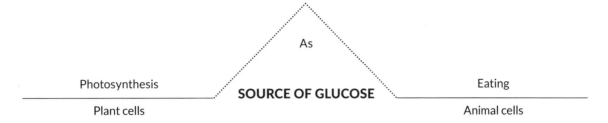

Source: Marzano et al., 2015, p. 32.
Figure 3.8: Visual analogy diagram.

To use the *visual analogy diagram*, students fill in one pair of terms on the left side of the diagram and the corresponding pair of terms on the right side of the diagram. Students also describe the relationship by writing a word or phrase under the peak in the middle of the diagram.

Examining Affixes and Root Words

Marzano et al. (2015) recommended activities requiring students to examine affixes and roots in step 4 of the six-step process. William Nagy, Virginia Berninger, Robert Abbott, Katherine Vaughan, and Karin Vermeulen (2003) found that students' understanding of word parts and how words are constructed strongly correlated with their vocabulary knowledge. However, based on the research of Marilyn J. Adams (1990), they caution against teaching word parts to students who are still learning to read. This is because the segmentation of a word into syllables does not always match the segmentation of a word into word parts. For example, a student would probably try to segment the word *endothermic* into syllables (en-do-ther-mic) to decode it, but the morphological segmentation for this word is different (endo-therm-ic). This could be confusing to a reader. For confident readers who have reached a level of automaticity with decoding longer words, however, understanding root words and affixes can help them remember words they have learned and figure out the meaning of unfamiliar terms. Stahl (2005) further added:

> A discussion of word parts should become an integral part of word-learning instruction. Discussions that include stories about word origins and derivations can stir interest in learning more about language—that is, build word consciousness. Stories that help children to see and understand how similarities in word spellings may show similarities in meaning, may solidify and expand their word knowledge. For example, the seemingly dissimilar words *loquacious*, *colloquium*, and *elocution* all come from the root word *loq*, meaning "to talk." Knowing this connection may make it easier for children to remember the words. (p. 111)

Students should address all prefixes, suffixes, and root words. *Prefixes* come at the beginning of a word and typically add to or change the meaning of the root word to which they are attached. *Suffixes* come at the end of a word and typically affect the root word's part of speech. Prefixes and suffixes are collectively referred to as *affixes*. Root words are often based on Greek or Latin and carry specific meanings.

Affixes

English language affixes are too numerous and diverse to be of much use instructionally. However, Thomas G. White, Joanne Sowell, and Alice Yanagihara (1989) operationalized the teaching of affixes by identifying the most frequently used prefixes and suffixes in English. They discovered that 97–99 percent of words with affixes use one of about twenty prefixes and suffixes (see table 3.2, page 52).

Table 3.2: Frequently Occurring Prefixes and Suffixes

Prefix	Percentage of All Prefixed Words	Suffix	Percentage of All Suffixed Words
un-	26	-s, -es	31
re-	14	-ed	20
in-, im-, ir-, il- (meaning "not")	11	-ing	14
dis-	7	-ly	7
en-, em-	4	-er, -or (indicating agency)	4
non-	4	-ion, -tion, -ation, -ition	4
in-, im- (meaning "in" or "into")	4	-ible, -able	2
over- (meaning "too much")	3	-al, -ial	1
mis-	3	-y	1
sub-	3	-ness	1
pre-	3	-ity, -ty	1
inter-	3	-ment	1
fore-	3	-ic	1
de-	2	-ous, -eous, -ious	1
trans-	2	-en	1
super-	1	-er (indicating comparison)	1
semi-	1	-ive, -ative, -itive	1
anti-	1	-ful	1
mid-	1	-less	1
under- (meaning "too little")	1	-est	1

Source: Adapted from Marzano et al., 2015, p. 33; White et al., 1989, pp. 303–304.

The affixes in table 3.2 become even more useful when one realizes that of these twenty affixes, "the top-three prefixes are used in 51 percent of all prefixed words and the top-three suffixes are used in 65 percent of all suffixed words" (Marzano et al., 2015, p. 34). Based on these findings, White and his colleagues (1989) recommended that affix instruction should focus on prefixes and affixes people most frequently use. Table 3.3 shows a series of lessons to facilitate such instruction.

Table 3.3: Recommended Sequences for Teaching Affixes

Teaching Prefixes	Teaching Suffixes
Lesson 1: Present examples and nonexamples of words with prefixes (*unkind* and *refill* have prefixes [*un-* and *re-*]; *uncle* and *reason* do not have prefixes).	**Lesson 1:** Present examples and nonexamples of words with suffixes (*employee* and *natural* have suffixes [*-ee* and *-al*]; *bee* and *charcoal* do not).
Lesson 2: Explain and give examples of the negative meanings of *un-* and *dis-* ("not" as in *unlike* and *disagree*).	**Lesson 2:** Present words with suffixes whose spellings do not change when the suffix is added (such as *monkeys, foxes, walking, higher, jumped, softly, laughable, comical,* and *windy*).
Lesson 3: Explain and give examples of the negative meanings of *in-, im-,* and *non-* ("not" as in *incompetent, impossible,* and *nonconforming*).	**Lesson 3:** Illustrate each of the three major spelling changes that can occur with suffixes—
Lesson 4: Explain and give examples of both meanings of *re-* ("again" as in *rebuild* or *revise* and "back" as in *recover* or *relapse*).	• Consonant blending (*bigger, running, skipped, sunny*)
Lesson 5: Address the less common meanings of *un-* and *dis-* ("do the opposite" as in *unbutton* or *disown*) and *in-* and *im-* ("in" or "into" as in *inquire* or *implant*).	• Change from *y* to *i* (*married, skies, happily, classifiable, filthiness*)
Lesson 6: Explain and give examples of *en-* and *em-* ("in" or "into" as in *encircle* and *embrace*), *over-* ("above" or "beyond" as in *overreact*), and *mis-* ("bad" or "wrong" as in *mistrust* or *mistrial*).	• Deleted silent e (*riding, gated, baker, advisable, natural, wheezy*)
	Lesson 4: Provide examples of inflectional endings (*-s, -es, -ed, -ing*) and derivational suffixes (*-ly, -er, -ion, -able, -al, -y, -ness*).

Source: Adapted from White et al., 1989, p. 34.

The left column of table 3.3 briefly outlines lessons that focus on the most frequently used prefixes (*un-, re-, in-, im-, dis-, en-, em-, non-, over-,* and *mis-*). The right side are brief outlines of lessons that focus on the most frequent suffixes (*-s, -es, -ed, -ing, -ly, -er, -ion, -able, -al, -y,* and *-ness*) as well as derivational suffixes to words.

Root Words

Many English words have Greek or Latin roots, and this is particularly the case with tier three terms. As noted in Marzano et al. (2015):

> Knowing root words helps students discern the meaning of unknown words, but root words are extremely numerous and no rigorous studies have been done to identify which roots are most useful for students. Several authors have compiled lists of common Greek and Latin roots (Fry, Kress, & Fountoukidis, 2000; Marzano, 2004; Padak, Newton, Rasinski, & Newton, 2008; Rasinski, Padak, Newton, & Newton, 2007; Stahl, 1999). (pp. 34–35)

Marzano et al. (2015) provided root words particularly applicable to science. Finally, the internet also offers many resources for exploring root words and affixes, including the following.

Online Etymology Dictionary (*www.etymonline.com*)—This site allows you to type in any part of a word (affix, root, or word) and see its origin, root words, and other words related to it.

English-Word Information (https://wordinfo.info)—This site allows you to type in a word and see information about its language of origin, what family of root words it belongs to, and how it is commonly used.

Merriam-Webster YouTube Channel (*www.youtube.com/user/MerriamWebsterOnline*)—This site provides two-minute videos featuring editors from Merriam-Webster discussing the etymology, roots, and correct usage of various English words (for example, *octopuses* vs. *octopi, healthy* vs. *healthful*). (p. 36)

As students engage in step 4 activities, they should periodically return to their vocabulary binders or recording pages to update and add to previous entries. This might include updating their linguistic or nonlinguistic descriptions or adding additional examples or nonexamples.

Step 5: Periodically Ask Students to Discuss the Terms With One Another

Step 5 focuses on extending students' vocabulary knowledge by interacting with their peers. These peer discussions directly and indirectly help students make semantic connections between new terms and their background knowledge. According to Stahl and Nagy (2006), collaborating with their peers during these discussions gives students the benefit of a larger body of background knowledge.

Step 5 activities can be quite informal and spontaneous, such as having students work in dyads or triads during specific activities. Students might make note of where they agree and disagree about specific terms. They might reconcile disagreements by consulting the internet, asking the teacher, or consulting with other students.

At a more structured level, Elfrieda H. Hiebert and Gina N. Cervetti (2012) suggested that students work together to articulate semantic relationships. They suggested a number of types of semantic relationships including the following (Marzano et al., 2015):

- Semantic classes (*eggs* are in the category of *food*)
- Words that commonly occur together (*dozen* is often paired with *eggs*)
- Superordination (*sedimentary* refers to a type of *rock*)
- Synonym (*glittering* and *sparkling* have roughly the same meaning)
- Part-whole (a *branch* is part of a *tree*)
- Instrumentality (a *broom* is used to sweep the *floor*)
- Theme (*hospital* and *nurse* are both medical-related terms)

To help students identify such semantic relationships, teachers might use the following prompts.

- What category does this word belong to?
- What other words are commonly associated with this word?
- Does this word represent a type of something? If so, what?
- What is a synonym for this word?
- Does this word represent part of something? If so, what?
- Does this word represent something that causes something else? If so, what is caused?
- Is this word part of some larger theme? If so, what is the theme and what are some other words that belong with that theme?

Perhaps the most robust type of step 5 activity is to have students work in groups to create semantic maps (Marzano et al., 2015). To start, the teacher chooses a word to be the focus of the activity—for example, *endangered species*. The teacher then asks students to generate a list of words associated with the focus term. For *endangered species*, students might come up with the following list.

extinct	*whaling*	*disease*
rhino	*whales*	*reproduction*
sea turtle	*deforestation*	*natural selection*
panda	*climate change*	*extant*
bald eagle	*habitat destruction*	*zoos*
poachers	*pollution*	*legislation*
hunting	*fur*	*Endangered Species Act*
ivory	*invasive species*	*conservation*
blubber	*encroachment*	*preservation*

Next students identify categories and organize the various terms. These categories are represented as circles or nodes in the *semantic map* with other words forming spokes around those nodes. Figure 3.9 depicts this. Students generated five categories for the terms they listed in figure 3.9: (1) *animals*, (2) *causes*, (3) *solutions*, (4) *degrees*, and (5) *products* from endangered species. They connected each term to the appropriate category. In some cases, a term is related to a category through another term; for example, *encroachment, climate change, deforestation,* and *pollution* are all types of *habitat destruction*, which is one cause of *endangered species*.

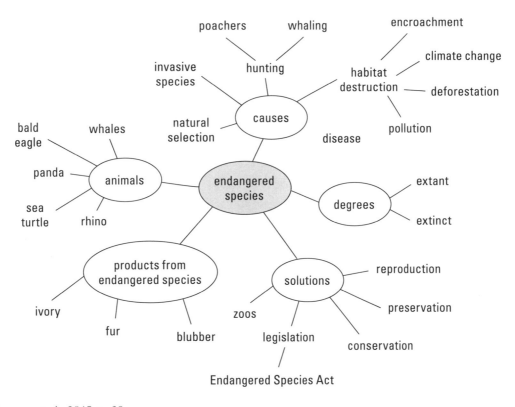

Figure 3.9: Semantic map for *endangered species*.

Once students complete their semantic maps, they should explain them. If students worked individually, each might explain his or her map to a partner. If students worked in groups, they might pair with another group to explain their maps.

Step 6: Periodically Involve Students in Games That Allow Them to Play With Terms

Step 6 emphasizes word play. Camille L. Z. Blachowicz and Peter Fisher (2012) explain that *word play* has a number of positive characteristics including motivation; it requires students to think metacognitively about words and to be actively involved with words, and it represents a form of practice with words. Jennifer I. Berne and Camille L. Z. Blachowicz (2008) surveyed seventy-two educators and found word play to be one of the top-three most commonly cited effective practices for increasing students' vocabulary.

Word play does not need to be complex or time consuming. Blachowicz and Fisher (2012) noted that it can be as simple as sharing puns or jokes. For example, consider sharing the following quips with students (Marzano et al., 2015).

- Never trust an *atom*; they make up everything.

- The other day I made a chemistry joke, but I got no *reaction*.

- I bet *Earth* makes fun of all the other planets for having no life.

- Two *atoms* were walking down the sidewalk and suddenly one slipped off the curb and said, "Oh no, I've lost my *electron*!" The other atom said, "Are you sure?" and the first atom replied, "Yes, I'm *positive*!"

- I would make a science joke, but all the good ones *argon*.

More formal word games can last a single class period or be extended to last for an entire unit. Marzano et al. (2015) described a number of vocabulary games reading experts developed that can be played for step 6. The following are a number of recommended games from *Vocabulary for the New Science Standards* (Marzano et al., 2015). See the recommended sources for each game to obtain complete directions.

Alphabet Antonyms

In this Blachowicz and Fisher (2008) game for middle and high school students, each student writes down a number of vocabulary words that all begin with the same letter. For example, for the letter *e*, a particular student might choose: *Earth, Earth materials, earthquake, ecosystem,* and *erosion.* Then he or she writes an antonym for each word, as in the following.

- *Earth—space*
- *Earth materials—living matter*
- *Earthquake—still tectonic plates*
- *Ecosystem—dysfunctional natural community*
- *Erosion—accretion*

The student then presents only the antonyms to the class (that is, *space, living matter, still tectonic plates, dysfunctional natural community, accretion*). The class tries to guess the correct antonyms, all of which will start with the same letter—in this case *e.*

Classroom Feud

In this Lindsay Carleton and Robert J. Marzano (2010) game for all grade levels and modeled after the television game show *Family Feud*, students work in teams to answer questions about vocabulary terms. Teams earn points by correctly answering the questions.

Create a Category

In this Carleton and Marzano (2010) game for upper-elementary through high school students, students work together to categorize a list of terms in a limited amount of time. Teams receive points based on how quickly they create categories and the utility of their categories.

Definition, Shmefinition

In this Carleton and Marzano (2010) game for upper-elementary through high school students, students try to identify the correct description of a vocabulary term out of a group of student-invented definitions.

Digital Vocabulary Field Trip

This Bridget Dalton and Dana L. Grisham (2011) game is designed for upper-elementary through high school students. Using an online program like TrackStar (http://trackstar.4teachers.org), teachers collect and annotate a series of websites that pertain to a vocabulary term or group of terms. Students then explore the websites to answer a series of teacher-designed questions.

Draw Me

Modeled after the game Pictionary™, this Marzano and Pickering (2005) game for all grade levels involves one student drawing pictures of terms in a predetermined category. Other students on the same team try to guess the word depicted as quickly as possible.

Magic Letter, Magic Word

In this Carleton and Marzano (2010) game for elementary and middle school students, students try to identify the vocabulary term (beginning or ending with the "magic letter") that is the correct response to a teacher-provided clue.

Motor Imaging

In this Ula Price Casale (1985) game for all grade levels, students create gestures that represent the meaning of vocabulary terms. For example, for the phrase *subduction zone*, students might hold their hands out in front of them—palms down, parallel to the floor—and then slowly move them toward each other. When the sides of their hands meet, they let one slide under the other to signify one tectonic plate sliding under another tectonic plate.

Name It!

In this Carleton and Marzano (2010) game for lower-elementary students, the teacher presents students with photographs. Students the use vocabulary terms to express what they see in various photographs.

Name That Category

In this Marzano and Pickering (2005) game for upper-elementary through high school students, the teacher provides a secret list of categories, and a designated student tries to help his teammates guess each category by naming vocabulary terms that fit in the category. As soon as his or her team guesses one category, the clue-giver starts naming terms in the next category. The first team to name all the categories correctly wins the game.

Opposites Attract

In this Carleton and Marzano (2010) game for elementary students, students work together to pair vocabulary terms with their antonyms. Students obtain points based on how quickly they can match terms and antonyms.

Possible Sentences

In this Stahl (2005) game for middle and high school students, the teacher selects six to eight words that students are not likely to know and four to six words that students are likely to know. Using this list, students create sentences, each of which must contain at least two words from the list. The teacher displays these sentences, and students discuss whether each one is correct, incorrect, or partially correct and modify them as needed.

Puzzle Stories

In this Carleton and Marzano (2010) game for upper-elementary and middle school students, students construct a puzzle and then use vocabulary terms to describe the scene depicted in the puzzle.

Root Relay

In this Judith A. Scott, Tatiana F. Miller, and Susan Leigh Flinspach (2012) game for upper-elementary and middle school students, teams construct words using an array of prefixes, suffixes, and root words written on separate cards. One student from each team runs to the assortment of affixes and roots, selects one, and brings it back to his team. The next student does the same. The first team to form a complete word wins.

Secret Language

In this Ula C. Manzo and Anthony V. Manzo (2008) game for upper-elementary through high school students, two students try to communicate the meaning of a vocabulary term to the class by using it in context over the course of a day or class period. At the end of the designated time period, the class tries to guess what the secret word was and explain its meaning.

Sentence Stems

In this Beck and colleagues (2002) game for middle and high school students, the teacher creates a sentence stem that requires students to explain the vocabulary term in order to complete it. For example, "*Percolation* is the stage of the water cycle when . . ." or "*Naturalistic observation* is different from *analog observation* because . . ."

Silly Questions

In this McKeown and colleagues (1985) game for middle and high school students, students answer questions created by combining two vocabulary terms, such as "Can a *backbone* be a *muscle?* Why or why not?" "Would a *proton* be in *equilibrium?* Why or why not?" and so on.

Talk a Mile a Minute

In this Marzano and Pickering (2005) game for upper-elementary through high school students, the teacher prepares individual cards with a category at the top and a list of terms from that category beneath, as shown in figure 3.10.

Conservation of Matter		
product	properties	phase change
chemical	dissolve	substance

Source: Marzano et al., 2015, p. 45.

Figure 3.10: Sample card for Talk a Mile a Minute.

The teacher designates one member of each team the "talker" and passes a card to this student. The teacher starts a timer and, similar to the games Taboo and Catch Phrase, the talker tries to get his or her teammates to say each word in the list without saying any of the other words on the card or in the heading.

Two of a Kind

In this Carleton and Marzano (2010) game for elementary school students, students match up synonyms, homonyms, or antonyms. Using a memory-style format, students turn over cards with vocabulary terms written on them. The teacher provides students with the synonym, homonym, or antonym, and students try to remember which card has a match.

Vocabulary Charades

In this Marzano and Pickering (2005) game for all grade levels, students try to guess which vocabulary term their teammate is acting out.

Vocab Vids

In this Dalton and Grisham (2011) game for middle and high school students, students create sixty-second videos that exemplify the meaning of a vocabulary term. Teachers periodically show the videos and then students describe what they have learned.

What Is the Question?

In this *Jeopardy!*-like Carleton and Marzano (2010) game for upper-elementary through high school students, students have to come up with questions that describe teacher-provided vocabulary terms.

Where Am I?

In this Carleton and Marzano (2010) game for all grade levels, students give clues to help a student guess his or her "secret location." In this game, vocabulary terms refer to a specific place, such as *polar ice caps* or *wetland*.

Which One Doesn't Belong?

In this Carleton and Marzano (2010) game for all grade levels, students try to identify the vocabulary term that doesn't belong with the three other words in a group.

Who Am I?

In this Carleton and Marzano (2010) game for upper-elementary through high school students, students give clues to help a selected student guess his or her "secret identity." All vocabulary terms refer to a specific person, such as *Isaac Newton* or *Antoine Lavoisier*.

Word Associations

In this Beck and colleagues (2002) game for middle and high school students, the teacher provides students with words and phrases and asks students to figure out which vocabulary term goes with which word or phrase. For example, if students had already learned *chloroplast, magnification, organism,* and *chromosome,* the teacher might ask, "Which word goes with *photosynthesis?*" or "Which word goes with *DNA?*" Students then explain the relationships behind their answers.

Word Harvest

In this Carleton and Marzano (2010) game for lower-elementary school students, students "pick" words off of a construction paper tree or bush and sort them into baskets with different category labels.

Wordle

In this Dalton and Grisham (2011) game for upper-elementary through high school students, teachers use this electronic tool (www.wordle.com) to help students create visual representations of various vocabulary terms. When a block of text is pasted into the tool, Wordle produces a "word cloud" with high-frequency words from the passage appearing larger and low-frequency words appearing smaller. Students can manipulate the way the cloud looks and which words are included using different colors and configurations.

Word Wizzle

In this Scott and colleagues (2012) game for middle and high school students, students make contrasting statements about words based on a rule. For example, for the rule *properties of light* a student might say:

- "I like *intensity* but not *mass*."
- "I like *frequency* but not *density*."
- "I like *wavelength* but not *melting point*."
- "I like *speed* but not *boiling point*."

The class tries to figure out the rule using the fewest clues possible.

Summary

This chapter addressed direct instruction on subject-matter tier three terms relative to ELA, mathematics, science, and social studies. The case was also made that teachers might also select some of the tier two terms in appendix A (but not in the student notebook) as the focus of direct instruction, along with subject-area tier three terms.

Direct instruction should include six steps.

1. Provide a description, an explanation, or an example of the new term.
2. Ask students to restate the description, explanation, or example in their own words.
3. Ask students to construct a picture, symbol, or graphic representing the term or phrase.
4. Periodically engage students in activities that help them add to their knowledge of the terms to which they have previously been exposed.
5. Periodically ask students to discuss the terms with one another.
6. Periodically involve students in games that allow them to play with terms. (Marzano et al., 2015)

Teachers should use steps 1–3 with each word they directly instruct. One decision the school as a whole (or individual teachers) should make is whether students will record their responses to steps 2 and 3 in a binder, or whether students will simply record these on sheets not collected into a binder.

Do not apply steps 4–6 to individual terms, but rather to *groups of terms*. The steps provide opportunities for students to review and revise what they learned about terms as a result of steps 1, 2, and 3. Students should experience at least one of these first three steps at least once a week.

APPENDIX A

This appendix contains 420 clusters of semantically related tier one and tier two terms. The clusters are listed in order of how basic they are. Tier one terms are listed in bold; tier two terms within a cluster are not in bold. Each word is accompanied by an index of basicness that ranges from 1 (most basic) to 5 (least basic). For the most part, this index is based on word frequency with 1 indicating the highest frequency words and 5 indicating the lowest frequency words within this set of words. These index scores are referred to as *Importance* scores. As mentioned in the introduction (page 5), all words with an index of 3 or below are considered tier one terms. Those words with an index of 4 or 5 are considered tier two terms. Each word is also coded as to its part of speech. Finally, this appendix also contains twenty-four clusters (numbered 421–444) that do not contain any tier one terms but are populated by tier two terms only. With each cluster are listed related clusters. Each group of related clusters represents a supercluster as described in chapter 1 (page 17).

1. Modals
Related Clusters: 3, 4, 342, 411

Word	Importance	Part of Speech
can	1	verb
cannot	1	verb
could	1	verb
may	1	verb
might	1	verb
must	1	verb
shall	1	verb
should	1	verb
will	1	verb
would	1	verb
ought	4	verb
used to	4	verb

2. Relationship Markers (Concurrent Action)
Related Clusters: 16, 24, 29, 52, 59, 79, 83, 126, 144, 233

Word	Importance	Part of Speech
as	1	conjunction
at	1	preposition
during	1	preposition
now	1	adverb
of	1	preposition
on	1	preposition
together	1	adverb
when	1	adverb
while	1	noun

Word	Importance	Part of Speech
at the same time	4	adverb
at this point	4	adverb
meanwhile	4	noun
concurrently	5	adverb
in the meantime	5	adverb
nowadays	5	noun
simultaneously	5	adverb

3. Primary Auxiliary Verbs
Related Clusters: 1, 4, 342, 411

Word	Importance	Part of Speech
did	1	verb
do	1	verb
does	1	verb
doing	1	verb
done	1	verb
had	1	verb
has	1	verb
have	1	verb

4. Auxiliary Verbs
Related Clusters: 1, 3, 342, 411

Word	Importance	Part of Speech
am	1	verb
are	1	verb
be	1	verb
been	1	verb
is	1	verb
was	1	verb
were	1	verb
being	2	verb

5. Relationship Markers (Addition)
Related Clusters: 27, 252, 299

Word	Importance	Part of Speech
and	1	conjunction
of	1	preposition
too	1	adverb
with	1	preposition
as well	4	adverb
as well as	4	conjunction
further	4	adverb
in addition	4	adverb
moreover	4	adverb
namely	4	adverb
likewise	5	adverb

6. Pronouns/Reflexive Pronouns
Related Clusters: 7, 8, 11, 12, 34

Word	Importance	Part of Speech
he	1	pronoun
him	1	pronoun
I	1	pronoun
it	1	pronoun
me	1	pronoun
myself	1	pronoun
she	1	pronoun
them	1	pronoun
they	1	pronoun
us	1	pronoun
we	1	pronoun
you	1	pronoun
herself	2	pronoun
himself	2	pronoun
yourself	3	pronoun
itself	4	pronoun
oneself	4	pronoun
ourselves	4	pronoun
thee	4	pronoun
themselves	4	pronoun
thou	4	pronoun
thy	4	pronoun

7. Possessive Pronouns
Related Clusters: 6, 8, 11, 12, 34

Word	Importance	Part of Speech
her	1	pronoun
hers	1	pronoun
its	1	pronoun
mine	1	pronoun
my	1	pronoun
our	1	pronoun
their	1	pronoun
your	1	pronoun
yours	1	pronoun
his	2	pronoun
ours	2	pronoun
theirs	2	pronoun

8. Interrogative Pronouns
Related Clusters: 6, 7, 11, 12, 34

Word	Importance	Part of Speech
what	1	pronoun
when	1	pronoun
where	1	pronoun
which	1	pronoun
whichever	4	pronoun

9. Direction To and From
Related Clusters: 17, 20, 21, 22, 23, 25, 26, 37, 49, 390, 430

Word	Importance	Part of Speech
at	1	preposition
from	1	preposition
to	1	preposition
bound for	4	verb
hither	5	adverb

10. Cause/Effect (Relationship Markers)
Related Cluster: 273

Word	Importance	Part of Speech
because	1	conjunction
by	1	preposition
for	1	preposition
from	1	preposition
if	1	conjunction
since	1	preposition
so	1	adverb
then	1	adverb
to	1	preposition
because of	2	preposition
if only	4	conjunction
if … then	4	conjunction
in that case	4	conjunction
now that	4	conjunction
on account of	4	preposition
so that	4	adverb

Word	Importance	Part of Speech
therefore	4	adverb
thus	4	adverb
until . . . then	4	adverb
when . . . then	4	conjunction
where . . . there	4	conjunction
whereas	4	conjunction
accordingly	5	adverb
as a consequence	5	conjunction
as a result	5	conjunction
consequently	5	adverb
else	5	adjective
for all that	5	conjunction
for as much	5	conjunction
for the fact that	5	conjunction
hence	5	adverb
hereby	5	adverb
herein	5	adverb
hereupon	5	adverb
herewith	5	adverb
in that	5	conjunction
lest	5	conjunction
thereby	5	adverb
whereby	5	conjunction
wherefore	5	adverb
whereupon	5	conjunction

11. Relative Pronouns
Related Clusters: 6, 7, 8, 12, 34

Word	Importance	Part of Speech
that	1	pronoun
which	1	pronoun
who	1	pronoun
whom	4	pronoun

12. Indefinite/Interrogative Adverbs
Related Clusters: 6, 7, 8, 11, 34

Word	Importance	Part of Speech
how	1	pronoun
why	1	pronoun
somehow	4	pronoun
someway	4	pronoun
whenever	4	pronoun
wherever	4	pronoun

13. Specifiers
Related Clusters: 15, 18, 19, 28, 33, 73, 130, 327, 373, 374

Word	Importance	Part of Speech
a	1	article
an	1	article
each	1	adjective
every	1	adjective
no	1	adverb
that	1	pronoun
the	1	article

continued →

Word	Importance	Part of Speech
these	1	pronoun
this	1	pronoun
those	1	pronoun
either	2	pronoun

14. Exclamations
Related Clusters: 61, 100, 105, 177, 198, 207, 255, 345, 346, 383

Word	Importance	Part of Speech
ah	1	interjection
aha	1	interjection
bye	1	interjection
gee	1	interjection
good-bye	1	interjection
ha	1	interjection
hello	1	interjection
hey	1	interjection
hi	1	interjection
ho	1	interjection
maybe	1	adverb
no	1	adverb
oh	1	interjection
ok	1	interjection
okay	1	adjective
ooh	1	interjection
yes	1	adverb
goodnight	2	interjection

Word	Importance	Part of Speech
wow	2	interjection
ay	4	interjection
aye	4	interjection
beware	4	verb
bravo	4	interjection
farewell	4	interjection
howdy	4	interjection
hurrah	4	interjection
ugh	4	interjection
alas	5	interjection

15. Intensifiers
Related Clusters: 13, 18, 19, 28, 33, 73, 130, 327, 373, 374

Word	Importance	Part of Speech
more	1	adjective
most	1	adjective
much	1	adjective
so	1	adverb
such	1	adjective
sure	1	adjective
too	1	adverb
very	1	adverb
well	1	adverb
badly	3	adverb
a great deal	4	adverb
absolute(ly)	4	adjective

Word	Importance	Part of Speech
altogether	4	adverb
by far	4	adverb
complete(ly)	4	adjective
deeply	4	adverb
highly	4	adverb
in all respects	4	adverb
intense	4	adjective
perfectly	4	adverb
quite	4	adverb
totally	4	adverb
ultimately	4	adverb
widely	4	adverb
dynamic	5	adjective
extreme	5	adjective
utmost	5	adjective

16. Relationship Markers
Related Clusters: 2, 24, 29, 52, 59, 79, 83, 126, 144, 233

Word	Importance	Part of Speech
already	1	adverb
early	1	adjective
fresh	1	adjective
new	1	adjective
ready	1	adjective
since	1	adverb
young	2	adjective
ago	3	adjective
lately	3	adverb

Word	Importance	Part of Speech
as yet	4	adverb
at first	4	adverb
before now	4	adverb
before that	4	adverb
current	4	adverb
due	4	adjective
former	4	adjective
initial	4	adjective
modern	4	adjective
now that	4	conjunction
original	4	adjective
precede	4	verb
previous	4	adjective
recent	4	adjective
so far	4	adverb
source	4	noun
until then	4	adverb
beforehand	5	adverb
heretofore	5	adverb
hitherto	5	adverb

17. Directions
Related Clusters: 9, 20, 21, 22, 23, 25, 26, 37, 49, 390, 430

Word	Importance	Part of Speech
left	1	adjective
right	1	adjective
east	2	noun
north	2	noun

continued ➡

Word	Importance	Part of Speech
south	2	noun
west	2	noun
midwest	4	noun
northeast	4	noun
northeastern	4	adjective
northern	4	adjective
northward	4	adjective
northwest	4	noun
southeast	4	noun
southeastern	4	adjective
southern	4	adjective
southland	4	noun
southward	4	adjective
southwest	4	noun
starboard	4	noun
western	4	adjective
westward	4	adjective

18. Diminishers

Related Clusters: 13, 15, 19, 28, 33, 73, 130, 327, 373, 374

Word	Importance	Part of Speech
almost	1	adverb
enough	1	adjective
just	1	adjective
only	1	adjective
hardly	2	adverb
alone	3	adverb

Word	Importance	Part of Speech
mostly	3	adverb
nearly	3	adverb
simply	3	adverb
a bit	4	adverb
a little	4	adverb
adequate	4	adjective
as good as	4	adverb
at least	4	adverb
barely	4	adverb
in part	4	adverb
in particular	4	adverb
kind of	4	adverb
mainly	4	adverb
moderate	4	adjective
more or less	4	adverb
overall	4	adjective
practically	4	adverb
precisely	4	adverb
probable	4	adjective
purely	4	adverb
quite	4	adverb
rather	4	adverb
scarcely	4	adverb
slightly	4	adverb
somewhat	4	adverb
sort of	4	adverb
specifically	4	adverb
sufficient	4	adjective
sufficiently	4	adverb

Word	Importance	Part of Speech
mere	5	adjective
particularly	5	adverb
to some extent	5	adverb

19. Amounts

Related Clusters: 13, 15, 18, 28, 33, 73, 130, 327, 373, 374

Word	Importance	Part of Speech
all	1	adjective
another	1	adjective
both	1	pronoun
few	1	adjective
half	1	noun
less	1	adjective
little	1	adjective
lot	1	adjective
many	1	adjective
more	1	adjective
most	1	adjective
none	1	pronoun
only	1	adjective
other	1	adjective
pair	1	noun
two	1	noun
whole	2	adjective
amount	3	noun
couple	3	noun
extra	3	adjective
plenty	3	noun
several	3	noun

Word	Importance	Part of Speech
single	3	noun
twice	3	adverb
additional	4	adjective
capacity	4	noun
decrease	4	verb
double	4	noun
entire	4	adjective
exceed	4	verb
excess	4	noun
increase	4	noun
lack	4	noun
least	4	adjective
leftover	4	noun
lone	4	adjective
numerous	4	adjective
outnumber	4	verb
partial	4	adjective
particular	4	adjective
plural	4	adjective
quantity	4	noun
remainder	4	noun
sole	4	adjective
spare	4	adjective
stub	4	noun
surplus	4	noun
unit	4	noun
volume	4	noun
abundant	5	adjective
ample	5	adjective
binary	5	adjective

continued →

Word	Importance	Part of Speech
deduct	5	verb
lush	5	adjective
majority	5	noun
mate	5	noun
scarcity	5	noun
sparse	5	adjective
supplement	5	noun
twain	5	noun

20. Distances
Related Clusters: 9, 17, 21, 22, 23, 25, 26, 37, 49, 390, 430

Word	Importance	Part of Speech
along	1	preposition
away	1	adverb
beside	1	preposition
between	1	preposition
by	1	preposition
close	1	adjective
far	1	adverb
near	1	preposition
past	1	preposition
toward	1	preposition
apart	3	adverb
aside	3	adverb
beyond	3	preposition
nearby	3	adjective
opposite	3	adjective
outer	3	adjective

Word	Importance	Part of Speech
abroad	4	adverb
closeness	4	noun
contact	4	noun
distant	4	adjective
homeward	4	adverb
local	4	adjective
overseas	4	adverb
remote	4	adjective
yonder	4	adverb
abreast	5	adverb
adjacent	5	adjective
nigh	5	adverb
outlying	5	adjective
vicinity	5	noun

21. Front/Middle/Back
Related Clusters: 9, 17, 20, 22, 23, 25, 26, 37, 49, 390, 430

Word	Importance	Part of Speech
ahead	1	adverb
back	1	noun
behind	1	preposition
end	1	noun
forward	1	adjective
front	1	noun
middle	1	adjective
center	2	noun
last	2	adjective
ahead of	3	adverb

Word	Importance	Part of Speech
among	3	preposition
backward	3	adjective
backwards	3	adverb
rear	3	noun
background	4	noun
central	4	adjective
core	4	noun
forth	4	adverb
hind	4	adjective
intermediate	4	adjective
medium	4	noun
midst	4	noun
midway	4	adverb
fore	5	adjective
fro	5	adverb
obverse	5	adjective

22. In/Out
Related Clusters: 9, 17, 20, 21, 23, 25, 26, 37, 49, 390, 430

Word	Importance	Part of Speech
across	1	preposition
in	1	preposition
inside	1	noun
into	1	preposition
out	1	adverb
outside	1	noun
through	1	preposition
enter	2	verb

Word	Importance	Part of Speech
outdoors	2	noun
indoor	3	noun
indoors	3	noun
throughout	3	preposition
within	3	adverb
exterior	4	adjective
inland	4	adjective
inner	4	adjective
interior	4	adjective
inward	4	adjective
outward	4	adjective
overboard	4	adverb
embark	5	verb
external	5	adjective
internal	5	adjective

23. Down/Under
Related Clusters: 9, 17, 20, 21, 22, 25, 26, 37, 49, 390, 430

Word	Importance	Part of Speech
below	1	preposition
bottom	1	noun
down	1	preposition
low	1	adjective
under	1	preposition
beneath	2	preposition
underneath	2	preposition
downhill	3	noun
downstairs	3	noun

continued →

downward	3	adverb
downwind	4	adverb
underfoot	4	noun
underground	4	noun
undergrowth	4	noun

24. Relationship Markers (Subsequent Action)
Related Clusters: 2, 16, 29, 52, 59, 79, 83, 126, 144, 233

Word	Importance	Part of Speech
before	1	preposition
late	1	adjective
next	1	adjective
soon	1	adverb
then	1	adverb
until	1	preposition
afterward	3	adverb
afterwards	3	adverb
later	3	adjective
latter	3	adjective
after that	4	adverb
eventual	4	adjective
in the end	4	adverb
tardy	4	adjective
henceforth	5	adverb
hereafter	5	adverb

25. Locations (Nonspecific)
Related Clusters: 9, 17, 20, 21, 22, 23, 26, 37, 49, 390, 430

Word	Importance	Part of Speech
here	1	adverb
there	1	adverb
where	1	adverb
nowhere	2	noun
somewhere	2	noun
anywhere	3	noun
someplace	3	noun
all over	4	adjective
elsewhere	4	adverb

26. Up/On
Related Clusters: 9, 17, 20, 21, 22, 23, 25, 37, 49, 390, 430

Word	Importance	Part of Speech
above	1	preposition
high	1	adjective
off	1	preposition
on	1	preposition
over	1	preposition
tip	1	noun
top	1	noun
up	1	preposition
onto	2	preposition
upon	2	preposition
aboard	3	adverb
overhead	3	adjective
upright	3	adjective

Word	Importance	Part of Speech
upside-down	3	noun
upstairs	3	noun
upward	3	adjective
atop	4	preposition
peak	4	noun
summit	4	noun
upland	4	adjective
upper	4	adjective
pinnacle	5	noun

27. Relationship Markers (Contrast)
Related Clusters: 5, 252, 299

Word	Importance	Part of Speech
but	1	conjunction
else	1	adjective
not	1	adverb
or	1	conjunction
still	1	conjunction
than	1	conjunction
without	1	preposition
yet	2	conjunction
against	3	preposition
compare	3	verb
either	3	conjunction
except	3	preposition
instead	3	adverb
neither	3	conjunction

Word	Importance	Part of Speech
unless	3	conjunction
whether	3	conjunction
although	4	conjunction
anyhow	4	adverb
anyway	4	adverb
contrast	4	verb
however	4	adverb
in comparison	4	conjunction
nevertheless	4	adverb
nor	4	conjunction
otherwise	4	adverb
though	4	conjunction
whereas	4	conjunction
alternatively	5	adverb
at any rate	5	conjunction
despite	5	preposition
in any case	5	conjunction
in any event	5	conjunction
neither . . . nor	5	conjunction
nonetheless	5	conjunction
notwithstanding	5	preposition
on the other hand	5	conjunction
regardless of	5	conjunction
versus	5	preposition

28. Numbers

Related Clusters: 13, 15, 18, 19, 33, 73, 130, 327, 373, 374

Word	Importance	Part of Speech
eight	1	noun
five	1	noun
four	1	noun
nine	1	noun
one	1	noun
seven	1	noun
six	1	noun
ten	1	noun
three	1	noun
two	1	noun
zero	1	noun
eighteen	2	noun
eighty	2	noun
eleven	2	noun
fifteen	2	noun
fifty	2	noun
first	2	noun
forty	2	noun
fourteen	2	noun
hundred	2	noun
nineteen	2	noun
ninety	2	noun
number	2	noun
numeral	2	noun
second	2	noun
seventeen	2	noun

Word	Importance	Part of Speech
seventy	2	noun
sixteen	2	noun
sixty	2	noun
thirteen	2	noun
thirty	2	noun
thousand	2	noun
twelve	2	noun
twenty	2	noun
billion	3	noun
decimal	3	noun
dozen	3	noun
million	3	noun
ninth	3	adjective
seventh	3	adjective
sixth	3	adjective
tenth	3	adjective
third	3	adjective
data	4	noun
digit	4	noun
fourscore	4	noun
integer	4	noun
nineteenth	4	adjective
seventeenth	4	adjective
sixteenth	4	adjective
sixtieth	4	adjective
thirteenth	4	adjective
thousandth	4	adjective
trillion	4	noun
triple	4	noun

Word	Importance	Part of Speech
twelfth	4	adjective
twentieth	4	adjective
triad	5	noun
trice	5	noun

29. Days and Months
Related Clusters: 2, 16, 24, 52, 59, 79, 83, 126, 144, 233

Word	Importance	Part of Speech
April	2	noun
August	2	noun
December	2	noun
February	2	noun
Friday	2	noun
January	2	noun
July	2	noun
June	2	noun
March	2	noun
May	2	noun
Monday	2	noun
November	2	noun
October	2	noun
Saturday	2	noun
September	2	noun
Sunday	2	noun
Thursday	2	noun
Tuesday	2	noun
Wednesday	2	noun

30. Attitudinals (Lack of Truth/Doubt)
Related Clusters: 31, 285, 369, 431, 439, 440

Word	Importance	Part of Speech
maybe	1	adverb
possibly	3	adverb
allegedly	4	adverb
perhaps	4	adverb
supposedly	4	adverb
seemingly	5	adverb

31. Attitudinals (Other)
Related Clusters: 30, 285, 369, 431, 439, 440

Word	Importance	Part of Speech
please	1	adverb
hopefully	3	adverb
preferably	4	adverb

32. Birds
Related Clusters: 35, 64, 65, 70, 82, 95, 117, 155, 188, 189, 194, 309, 310, 341

Word	Importance	Part of Speech
bird	2	noun
chicken	2	noun
crow	2	noun
duck	2	noun
eagle	2	noun
fowl	2	noun

continued →

Word	Importance	Part of Speech
goose	2	noun
hen	2	noun
jay	2	noun
owl	2	noun
parrot	2	noun
robin	2	noun
rooster	2	noun
turkey	2	noun
bluebird	4	noun
canary	4	noun
crane	4	noun
cuckoo	4	noun
dodo	4	noun
dove	4	noun
falcon	4	noun
gull	4	noun
hawk	4	noun
heron	4	noun
hummingbird	4	noun
lark	4	noun
mockingbird	4	noun
oriole	4	noun
ostrich	4	noun
parakeet	4	noun
peacock	4	noun
pelican	4	noun
penguin	4	noun
pheasant	4	noun
pigeon	4	noun

Word	Importance	Part of Speech
quail	4	noun
raven	4	noun
seagull	4	noun
sparrow	4	noun
swan	4	noun
vulture	4	noun
woodpecker	4	noun
wren	4	noun
albatross	5	noun
cock	5	noun
drake	5	noun
finch	5	noun
gander	5	noun
mallard	5	noun
partridge	5	noun
starling	5	noun

33. Size and Weight

Related Clusters: 13, 15, 18, 19, 28, 73, 130, 327, 373, 374

Word	Importance	Part of Speech
big	1	adjective
giant	2	adjective
great	2	adjective
huge	2	adjective
large	2	adjective
little	2	adjective
small	2	adjective

Word	Importance	Part of Speech
tiny	2	adjective
enormous	3	adjective
gigantic	3	adjective
jumbo	3	adjective
bulk	4	adjective
grand	4	adjective
immense	4	adjective
mammoth	4	adjective
massive	4	adjective
medium	4	adjective
miniature	4	adjective
monstrous	4	adjective
vast	4	adjective
compact	5	adjective
petite	5	adjective
wee	5	adjective

34. Indefinite Pronouns
Related Clusters: 6, 7, 8, 11, 12

Word	Importance	Part of Speech
any	1	pronoun
each	1	pronoun
enough	1	pronoun
nothing	1	pronoun
some	1	pronoun
nobody	2	pronoun
anybody	3	pronoun
anyone	3	pronoun
no one	3	pronoun

Word	Importance	Part of Speech
somebody	3	pronoun
someone	3	pronoun
something	3	pronoun
anything	4	pronoun
whoever	4	pronoun

35. Baby Animals
Related Clusters: 32, 64, 65, 70, 82, 95, 117, 155, 188, 189, 194, 309, 310, 341

Word	Importance	Part of Speech
bunny	2	noun
calf	2	noun
cub	2	noun
kitten	2	noun
pup	2	noun
puppy	2	noun
tadpole	2	noun
chick	4	noun
colt	4	noun
fawn	4	noun
yearling	4	noun

36. Vegetation (General)
Related Clusters: 108, 192, 269, 421

Word	Importance	Part of Speech
bush	2	noun
flower	2	noun
plant	2	noun
tree	2	noun

continued →

Word	Importance	Part of Speech
vegetation	2	noun
weed	2	noun
oasis	4	noun
shrub	4	noun
underbrush	4	noun
arbor	5	noun
flora	5	noun
photosynthesis	5	noun

37. Boundaries

Related Clusters: 9, 17, 20, 21, 22, 23, 25, 26, 49, 390, 430

Word	Importance	Part of Speech
corner	2	noun
edge	2	noun
limit	2	noun
margin	2	noun
side	2	noun
border	4	noun
brim	4	noun
horizon	4	noun
perimeter	4	noun
ridge	4	noun
rim	4	noun
verge	4	noun
bounds	5	noun
brink	5	noun
flank	5	noun

38. Tossing and Catching

Related Clusters: 39, 40, 44, 66, 141, 147, 169, 170, 182, 199, 215, 216, 247, 280, 281, 282, 283, 300, 301, 302, 322, 338, 403

Word	Importance	Part of Speech
catch	2	verb
pass	2	verb
throw	2	verb
toss	2	verb
cast	4	verb
chuck	4	verb
flick	4	verb
fling	4	verb
flip	4	verb
heave	4	verb
pitch	4	verb
hurl	5	verb
snag	5	verb
thrust	5	verb

39. Ascending Motion

Related Clusters: 38, 40, 44, 66, 141, 147, 169, 170, 182, 199, 215, 216, 247, 280, 281, 282, 283, 300, 301, 302, 322, 338, 403

Word	Importance	Part of Speech
climb	2	verb
lift	2	verb
raise	2	verb
order	3	noun

rank	3	verb
rise	3	verb
arise	4	verb
blastoff	4	noun
hoist	4	verb
load	4	verb
mount	4	verb
pry	4	verb
rate	4	verb
ascend	5	verb
elevate	5	verb

40. The Act of Occurring

Related Clusters: 38, 39, 44, 66, 141, 147, 169, 170, 182, 199, 215, 216, 247, 280, 281, 282, 283, 300, 301, 302, 322, 338, 403

Word	Importance	Part of Speech
do	1	verb
use	2	verb
happen	3	verb
occur	3	verb
apply	4	verb
function	4	verb
react	4	verb
reaction	4	noun
undergo	4	verb
commit	5	verb

41. Ownership/Possession

Related Clusters: 89, 148, 171, 184, 426

Word	Importance	Part of Speech
belong	2	verb
have	2	verb
own	2	verb
possess	3	verb
custody	4	noun
maintain	4	verb
occupy	4	verb
ownership	4	noun
possession	4	noun
property	4	noun
heirloom	5	noun
monopoly	5	noun

42. Contractions (Are)

Related Clusters: 81, 85, 150, 235, 274

Word	Importance	Part of Speech
they're	2	contraction
we're	2	contraction
you're	2	contraction

43. Sadness

Related Clusters: 45, 55, 291, 292, 293, 311, 312, 313, 378, 379, 380, 381, 416, 417, 422, 427, 428

Word	Importance	Part of Speech
sad	2	adjective
sorry	2	adjective
unhappy	2	adjective

continued →

Word	Importance	Part of Speech
contrite	4	adjective
discomfort	4	noun
forlorn	4	adjective
gloom	4	noun
grief	4	noun
heartache	4	noun
letdown	4	noun
loneliness	4	noun
miserable	4	adjective
mourn	4	verb
pitiful	4	adjective
pout	4	verb
sorrow	4	noun
suffer	4	verb
sulk	4	verb
dismay	5	noun
doldrums	5	noun
misery	5	noun
remorse	5	noun
repent	5	verb
woe	5	noun

44. Giving and Taking

Related Clusters: 38, 39, 40, 66, 141, 147, 169, 170, 182, 199, 215, 216, 247, 280, 281, 282, 283, 300, 301, 302, 322, 338, 403

Word	Importance	Part of Speech
bring	2	verb
carry	2	verb
deliver	2	verb
get	2	verb
give	2	verb
mail	2	verb
move	2	verb
place	2	verb
present	2	verb
put	2	verb
return	2	verb
send	2	verb
set	2	verb
take	2	verb
bear	3	verb
remove	3	verb
airmail	4	verb
deposit	4	verb
export	4	verb
fetch	4	verb
furnish	4	verb
homecoming	4	noun
import	4	verb
provide	4	verb
relay	4	verb

Word	Importance	Part of Speech
rid	4	verb
ship	4	verb
supply	4	verb
transplant	4	verb
trundle	4	verb
bestow	5	verb
dispatch	5	verb
eliminate	5	verb
retrieve	5	verb
shuttle	5	verb
transfer	5	verb

45. Fun and Joy
Related Clusters: 43, 55, 291, 292, 293, 311, 312, 313, 378, 379, 380, 381, 416, 417, 422, 427, 428

Word	Importance	Part of Speech
fun	2	noun
glad	2	adjective
happy	2	adjective
joke	2	noun
jolly	2	adjective
joy	2	noun
merry	2	adjective
play	2	verb
please	2	verb
silly	2	adjective
celebrate	3	verb
happiness	3	noun

Word	Importance	Part of Speech
humor	3	noun
joyful	3	adjective
amuse	4	verb
cheerful	4	adjective
coddle	4	verb
delight	4	verb
entertain	4	verb
frolic	4	verb
gag	4	noun
glee	4	adjective
jest	4	noun
jubilant	4	adjective
playful	4	adjective
pleasure	4	noun
riddle	4	noun
antic	5	noun
mirth	5	noun
pamper	5	verb
wisecrack	5	noun

46. Choice
Related Clusters: 67, 132, 137, 154, 225, 249, 277, 347, 348, 349, 384

Word	Importance	Part of Speech
choice	2	noun
choose	2	verb
decide	2	verb
judge	2	verb
pick	2	verb

continued →

select	2	verb
appoint	3	verb
sort	3	verb
assign	4	verb
decision	4	noun
dedicate	4	verb
judgment	4	noun
weed	4	verb
discriminate	5	verb
verdict	5	noun

47. Things Worn on the Head
Related Clusters: 62, 125, 129, 145, 178, 212, 224, 263, 354, 435

Word	Importance	Part of Speech
cap	2	noun
glasses	2	noun
hat	2	noun
helmet	2	noun
hood	2	noun
mask	2	noun
sunglasses	2	noun
crown	3	noun
bonnet	4	noun
goggles	4	noun
headdress	4	noun
spectacles	4	noun
turban	4	noun
veil	4	noun
visor	4	noun
beret	5	noun
tiara	5	noun

48. Types of Meals
Related Clusters: 51, 74, 86, 124, 136, 153, 162, 174, 176, 208, 222, 232, 246

Word	Importance	Part of Speech
breakfast	2	noun
dinner	2	noun
lunch	2	noun
meal	2	noun
picnic	2	noun
supper	2	noun
treat	2	noun
dessert	3	noun
banquet	4	noun
buffet	4	noun
chow	4	noun
feast	4	noun
refreshment	4	noun

49. Location (General)
Related Clusters: 9, 17, 20, 21, 22, 23, 25, 26, 37, 390, 430

Word	Importance	Part of Speech
address	2	noun
direction	2	noun
place	2	noun
point	2	noun
position	2	noun
spot	2	noun
location	3	noun
altitude	4	noun
axis	4	noun

destination	4	noun
distance	4	noun
niche	4	noun
whereabouts	4	noun

50. Bodies in Space
Related Clusters: 114, 139, 168, 267, 362, 363, 398

Word	Importance	Part of Speech
moon	2	noun
sky	2	noun
star	2	noun
sun	2	noun
universe	2	noun
world	2	noun
meteor	3	noun
planet	3	noun
space	3	noun
asteroid	4	noun
celestial	4	adjective
comet	4	noun
constellation	4	noun
eclipse	4	noun
galaxy	4	noun
globe	4	noun
Jupiter	4	noun
lunar	4	adjective
Mars	4	noun
Mercury	4	noun
Neptune	4	noun
Pluto	4	noun

Word	Importance	Part of Speech
satellite	4	noun
Saturn	4	noun
solar	4	adjective
stratosphere	4	noun
Uranus	4	noun
Venus	4	noun
cosmos	5	noun
stellar	5	adjective

51. Eating and Drinking
Related Clusters: 48, 74, 86, 124, 136, 153, 162, 174, 176, 208, 222, 232, 246

Word	Importance	Part of Speech
bite	2	verb
drink	2	verb
eat	2	verb
feed	2	verb
sip	2	verb
swallow	2	verb
chew	3	verb
devour	4	verb
dine	4	verb
gargle	4	verb
gnaw	4	verb
gorge	4	verb
guzzle	4	verb
munch	4	verb
nibble	4	verb
consume	5	verb

52. Periods of Time

Related Clusters: 2, 16, 24, 29, 59, 79, 83, 126, 144, 233

Word	Importance	Part of Speech
age	2	noun
fall	2	noun
generation	2	noun
month	2	noun
season	2	noun
summer	2	noun
week	2	noun
weekend	2	noun
winter	2	noun
year	2	noun
century	3	noun
decade	3	noun
spring	3	noun
weekday	3	noun
autumn	4	noun
cycle	4	noun
millennium	4	noun
period	4	noun
semester	4	noun
term	4	noun
duration	5	noun
interval	5	noun
perennial	5	adjective
yule	5	noun

53. Poems and Songs

Related Clusters: 71, 112, 138, 248, 256, 279, 319, 320

Word	Importance	Part of Speech
lullaby	2	noun
music	2	noun
poem	2	noun
rhyme	2	noun
song	2	noun
measure	3	noun
anthem	4	noun
ballad	4	noun
carol	4	noun
hymn	4	noun
lyric	4	noun
score	4	noun
staff	4	noun
stanza	4	noun
suite	4	noun
ditty	5	noun
limerick	5	noun
meter	5	noun
psalm	5	noun
refrain	5	noun
serenade	5	noun

54. Music and Dance
Related Clusters: 77, 239, 244

Word	Importance	Part of Speech
dance	2	noun
music	2	noun
ballet	3	noun
melody	3	noun
orchestra	3	noun
solo	3	noun
accent	4	noun
concert	4	noun
duet	4	noun
flat	4	noun
jig	4	noun
minuet	4	noun
musical	4	noun
octave	4	noun
opera	4	noun
polka	4	noun
rhythm	4	noun
round	4	noun
scale	4	noun
treble	4	noun
tune	4	noun
waltz	4	noun
conduct	5	verb
float	5	verb
interval	5	noun
jazz	5	noun
meter	5	noun

Word	Importance	Part of Speech
pantomime	5	noun
presto	5	noun
range	5	noun
register	5	noun
rest	5	noun
stave	5	noun
swing	5	noun
symphony	5	noun
unison	5	noun

55. Caring and Trust
Related Clusters: 43, 45, 291, 292, 293, 311, 312, 313, 378, 379, 380, 381, 416, 417, 422, 427, 428

Word	Importance	Part of Speech
believe	2	verb
care	2	noun
enjoy	2	verb
like	2	verb
love	2	verb
forgive	3	verb
want	3	verb
admiration	4	noun
admire	4	verb
adore	4	verb
affection	4	noun
appreciate	4	verb
approve	4	verb
depend	4	verb

continued →

Word	Importance	Part of Speech
favor	4	noun
fond	4	adjective
gratitude	4	noun
pardon	4	verb
prefer	4	verb
privilege	4	noun
regard	4	verb
regret	4	verb
rely	4	verb
respect	4	noun
support	4	verb
value	4	noun
entrust	5	verb
mania	5	noun
romance	5	noun
vouch	5	verb

56. People (General Names)
Related Clusters: 94, 111, 203, 204, 205, 206, 227, 317, 330, 343, 344, 382, 432, 444

Word	Importance	Part of Speech
human	2	noun
individual	2	noun
people	2	noun
person	2	noun
hero	3	noun
self	3	noun
being	4	noun
chap	4	noun

character	4	noun
folk	4	noun
heroine	4	noun
highness	4	noun
majesty	4	noun
mankind	4	noun

57. Color
Related Cluster: 415

Word	Importance	Part of Speech
black	2	noun
blue	2	noun
brown	2	noun
color	2	noun
gold	2	noun
gray	2	noun
green	2	noun
orange	2	noun
pink	2	noun
purple	2	noun
red	2	noun
white	2	noun
yellow	2	noun
blonde	3	noun
colorful	3	adjective
silver	3	noun
beige	4	noun
brunette	4	noun
buff	4	noun
colorless	4	adjective

Word	Importance	Part of Speech
dapple	4	noun
hazel	4	noun
hue	4	noun
lavender	4	noun
maroon	4	noun
pigment	4	noun
roan	4	noun
scarlet	4	noun
tan	4	noun
tangerine	4	noun
taupe	4	noun
vermilion	4	noun
violet	4	noun
amber	5	noun
azure	5	noun
chromatic	5	adjective
crimson	5	noun
ecru	5	noun
indigo	5	noun
iridescent	5	adjective
livid	5	adjective
magenta	5	noun
mauve	5	noun
russet	5	noun
tawny	5	noun
towhead	5	noun

58. Importance and Value
Related Clusters: 72, 243, 368

Word	Importance	Part of Speech
best	2	adjective
better	2	adjective
dear	2	adjective
fine	2	adjective
good	2	adjective
important	2	adjective
perfect	2	adjective
outstanding	3	adjective
super	3	adjective
useful	3	adjective
absolute	4	adjective
adequate	4	adjective
base	4	noun
basic	4	adjective
dandy	4	adjective
desirable	4	adjective
elementary	4	adjective
essence	4	noun
essential	4	adjective
excellent	4	adjective
fabulous	4	adjective
fantastic	4	adjective
impressive	4	adjective
magnificent	4	adjective
main	4	adjective
major	4	adjective
marvelous	4	adjective
memorable	4	adjective

continued ➡

Word	Importance	Part of Speech
miraculous	4	adjective
necessary	4	adjective
positive	4	adjective
practical	4	adjective
precious	4	adjective
primary	4	adjective
prime	4	adjective
regal	4	adjective
remarkable	4	adjective
spectacular	4	adjective
splendid	4	adjective
sufficient	4	adjective
superb	4	adjective
superior	4	adjective
supreme	4	adjective
terrific	4	adjective
tremendous	4	adjective
urgent	4	adjective
usable	4	adjective
valuable	4	adjective
value	4	noun
vital	4	adjective
wonderful	4	adjective
worth	4	noun
acute	5	adjective
crucial	5	adjective
crux	5	noun
delightful	5	adjective
fundamental	5	adjective
invaluable	5	adjective

Word	Importance	Part of Speech
noteworthy	5	adjective
sublime	5	adjective
worthwhile	5	adjective

59. Speed
Related Clusters: 2, 16, 24, 29, 52, 79, 83, 126, 144, 233

Word	Importance	Part of Speech
fast	2	adjective
hurry	2	verb
quick	2	adjective
race	2	noun
rush	2	verb
slow	2	adjective
speed	2	noun
sudden	2	adjective
dash	3	verb
slowdown	3	noun
abrupt	4	adjective
automatic	4	adjective
automatically	4	adverb
brief	4	adjective
brisk	4	adjective
bustle	4	verb
charge	4	verb
decelerate	4	verb
fuss	4	noun
gradual	4	adjective
haste	4	noun

Word	Importance	Part of Speech
immediate	4	adjective
instant	4	adjective
jiffy	4	noun
pace	4	noun
rapid	4	adjective
scoot	4	verb
speedy	4	adjective
spontaneous	4	adjective
swift	4	adjective
tempo	4	noun
accelerate	5	verb
fleet	5	adjective
flurry	5	noun
frenzy	5	noun
headlong	5	adverb
helter-skelter	5	adverb
hustle	5	verb
offhand	5	adverb
presto	5	adverb
prompt	5	adjective
scurry	5	verb
velocity	5	noun
whisk	5	verb

60. Places Related to Learning/Experimentation
Related Clusters: 106, 121, 190, 210, 321, 324, 335, 364, 365, 366, 399, 400

Word	Importance	Part of Speech
kindergarten	2	noun
library	2	noun
museum	2	noun
school	2	noun
classroom	3	noun
schoolroom	3	noun
campus	4	noun
college	4	noun
lab	4	noun
laboratory	4	noun
planetarium	4	noun
schoolhouse	4	noun
university	4	noun
academy	5	noun
gallery	5	noun
seminary	5	noun

61. Communication (Presentation of Information)
Related Clusters: 14, 100, 105, 177, 198, 207, 255, 345, 346, 383

Word	Importance	Part of Speech
describe	2	verb
explain	2	verb
present	2	verb
say	2	verb

continued →

Word	Importance	Part of Speech
state	2	verb
tell	2	verb
brag	3	verb
inform	3	verb
mention	3	verb
recite	3	verb
advertise	4	verb
announce	4	verb
boast	4	verb
claim	4	verb
declare	4	verb
demonstrate	4	verb
detail	4	noun
exclaim	4	verb
exhibit	4	verb
express	4	verb
media	4	noun
notify	4	verb
preach	4	verb
pronounce	4	verb
refer	4	verb
acquaint	5	verb
allude	5	verb
broadcast	5	verb
clarify	5	verb
convey	5	verb
indicate	5	verb
specify	5	verb

Word	Importance	Part of Speech
stress	5	verb
telecast	5	noun
telegraph	5	noun
testify	5	verb
transmit	5	verb
utter	5	verb
vouch	5	verb

62. Things Worn on the Hands/Feet

Related Clusters: 47, 125, 129, 145, 178, 212, 224, 263, 354, 435

Word	Importance	Part of Speech
boot	2	noun
glove	2	noun
mittens	2	noun
shoe	2	noun
skate	2	noun
sock	2	noun
stocking	2	noun
sandal	3	noun
slipper	3	noun
mitt	4	noun
moccasin	4	noun
garter	5	noun

63. Walking/Running
Related Clusters: 308, 339, 408, 409

Word	Importance	Part of Speech
dance	2	verb
march	2	verb
run	2	verb
skip	2	verb
step	2	verb
trip	2	verb
walk	2	verb
hike	3	verb
limp	3	verb
stumble	3	verb
tiptoe	3	verb
trot	3	verb
hobble	4	verb
jog	4	verb
lope	4	verb
pace	4	verb
plod	4	verb
romp	4	verb
saunter	4	verb
scamper	4	verb
shamble	4	verb
shuffle	4	verb
stagger	4	verb
stride	4	verb
stroll	4	verb
strut	4	verb
swagger	4	verb
trudge	4	verb

Word	Importance	Part of Speech
waddle	4	verb
amble	5	verb
gait	5	verb
prance	5	verb
promenade	5	verb
ramble	5	verb
toddle	5	verb
tread	5	verb

64. Cats/Dogs
Related Clusters: 32, 35, 65, 70, 82, 95, 117, 155, 188, 189, 194, 309, 310, 341

Word	Importance	Part of Speech
cat	2	noun
dog	2	noun
doggie	2	noun
fox	2	noun
lion	2	noun
tiger	2	noun
wolf	2	noun
bulldog	3	noun
collie	3	noun
beagle	4	noun
bloodhound	4	noun
canine	4	noun
cougar	4	noun
coyote	4	noun
dingo	4	noun
greyhound	4	noun

continued →

Word	Importance	Part of Speech
hound	4	noun
leopard	4	noun
mutt	4	noun
panther	4	noun
poodle	4	noun
pug	4	noun
puma	4	noun
spaniel	4	noun
terrier	4	noun
watchdog	4	noun
wildcat	4	noun
bobcat	5	noun
hyena	5	noun
jackal	5	noun
Labrador	5	noun
puss	5	noun

65. Land Animals (General)
Related Clusters: 32, 35, 64, 70, 82, 95, 117, 155, 188, 189, 194, 309, 310, 341

Word	Importance	Part of Speech
bear	2	noun
cow	2	noun
deer	2	noun
donkey	2	noun
elephant	2	noun
giraffe	2	noun
horse	2	noun
lamb	2	noun

Word	Importance	Part of Speech
pig	2	noun
pony	2	noun
rabbit	2	noun
sheep	2	noun
bat	3	noun
bull	3	noun
kangaroo	3	noun
moose	3	noun
raccoon	3	noun
reindeer	3	noun
skunk	3	noun
zebra	3	noun
anteater	4	noun
antelope	4	noun
ass	4	noun
badger	4	noun
bronco	4	noun
buffalo	4	noun
burro	4	noun
camel	4	noun
caribou	4	noun
cattle	4	noun
cottontail	4	noun
doe	4	noun
elk	4	noun
ferret	4	noun
gazelle	4	noun
hare	4	noun
hedgehog	4	noun
hippopotamus	4	noun

Word	Importance	Part of Speech
hog	4	noun
jackass	4	noun
llama	4	noun
mare	4	noun
mink	4	noun
mole	4	noun
mule	4	noun
mustang	4	noun
opossum	4	noun
ox	4	noun
pinto	4	noun
platypus	4	noun
rhinoceros	4	noun
sow	4	noun
stag	4	noun
stallion	4	noun
steer	4	noun
stud	4	noun
weasel	4	noun
yak	4	noun
bison	5	noun
polecat	5	noun
ram	5	noun
steed	5	noun
wombat	5	noun

66. Coming/Going (General)

Related Clusters: 38, 39, 40, 44, 141, 147, 169, 170, 182, 199, 215, 216, 247, 280, 281, 282, 283, 300, 301, 302, 322, 338, 403

Word	Importance	Part of Speech
go	1	verb
come	2	verb
leave	2	verb
travel	2	verb
visit	2	verb
wander	2	verb
appear	3	verb
approach	3	verb
arrive	3	verb
depart	3	verb
disappear	3	verb
exit	3	verb
journey	3	verb
proceed	3	verb
access	4	verb
advance	4	verb
adventure	4	noun
departure	4	noun
dissolve	4	verb
expedition	4	noun
hitchhike	4	verb
migrate	4	verb
migration	4	noun
oncoming	4	adjective
roam	4	verb

continued →

Word	Importance	Part of Speech
sightseeing	4	noun
stray	4	verb
tour	4	verb
vanish	4	verb
voyage	4	noun
withdraw	4	verb
headway	5	noun
progress	5	noun
retreat	5	verb

Word	Importance	Part of Speech
reflection	4	noun
amnesia	5	noun
concept	5	noun
conscience	5	noun
contemplate	5	verb
ponder	5	verb
reckon	5	verb
recollect	5	verb
visualize	5	verb

67. Memory/Thought (General)

Related Clusters: 46, 132, 137, 154, 225, 249, 277, 347, 348, 349, 384

Word	Importance	Part of Speech
forget	2	verb
idea	2	noun
remember	2	verb
think	2	verb
thought	2	noun
wonder	2	verb
imagine	3	verb
memory	3	noun
concentrate	4	verb
consider	4	verb
imagination	4	noun
meditate	4	verb
memorize	4	verb
recall	4	verb

68. Students and Teachers

Related Clusters: 88, 146, 167, 173, 229, 236, 257, 264, 265, 266, 297, 333, 334, 355, 356, 357, 358, 359, 360, 361, 392, 393, 394, 395, 396, 397, 436

Word	Importance	Part of Speech
principal	2	noun
student	2	noun
teacher	2	noun
graduate	3	noun
pupil	3	noun
schoolteacher	3	noun
adviser	4	noun
bookworm	4	noun
counselor	4	noun
freshman	4	noun
instructor	4	noun
professor	4	noun
tutor	4	noun

dean	5	noun
mentor	5	noun
sophomore	5	noun

69. Emptiness and Fullness
Related Clusters: 99, 142, 193, 218, 270, 303, 326

Word	Importance	Part of Speech
empty	2	noun
fill	2	verb
full	2	adjective
hollow	3	adjective
deflate	4	verb
exhaust	4	verb
null	4	adjective
stuff	4	verb
swollen	4	adjective
vacant	4	adjective
void	4	adjective
deplete	5	verb
fraught	5	adjective

70. Sea Animals
Related Clusters: 32, 35, 64, 65, 82, 95, 117, 155, 188, 189, 194, 309, 310, 341

Word	Importance	Part of Speech
fish	2	noun
seal	2	noun
whale	2	noun
salmon	3	noun

Word	Importance	Part of Speech
shark	3	noun
tuna	3	noun
bass	4	noun
carp	4	noun
catfish	4	noun
cod	4	noun
dolphin	4	noun
flounder	4	noun
guppy	4	noun
herring	4	noun
minnow	4	noun
porpoise	4	noun
sardine	4	noun
smelt	4	noun
snapper	4	noun
swordfish	4	noun
trout	4	noun
walrus	4	noun
hammerhead	5	noun

71. Writing, Drawing, and Reading
Related Clusters: 53, 112, 138, 248, 256, 279, 319, 320

Word	Importance	Part of Speech
color	2	verb
copy	2	verb
draw	2	verb
paint	2	verb

continued →

Word	Importance	Part of Speech
print	2	verb
read	2	verb
scribble	2	verb
sign	2	verb
spell	2	verb
write	2	verb
handwriting	3	noun
misspell	3	verb
publish	3	verb
skim	3	verb
trace	3	verb
underline	3	verb
abbreviate	4	verb
browse	4	verb
doodle	4	verb
draft	4	verb
illustrate	4	verb
indent	4	verb
penmanship	4	noun
proofread	4	verb
punctuate	4	verb
rewrite	4	verb
scan	4	verb
scrawl	4	verb
shorthand	4	noun
sketch	4	verb
watercolor	4	noun
calligraphy	5	noun
etch	5	verb

Word	Importance	Part of Speech
jot	5	verb
legible	5	adjective
stencil	5	verb

72. Right and Wrong
Related Clusters: 58, 243, 368

Word	Importance	Part of Speech
correct	2	adjective
just	2	adjective
real	2	adjective
right	2	adjective
true	2	adjective
truth	2	noun
wrong	2	adjective
error	3	noun
fair	3	adjective
fault	3	adjective
honest	3	adjective
mistake	3	noun
acceptable	4	adjective
accurate	4	adjective
actual	4	adjective
appropriate	4	adjective
blunder	4	noun
candid	4	adjective
crime	4	noun
decent	4	adjective
false	4	adjective
flaw	4	noun

Word	Importance	Part of Speech
genuine	4	adjective
honesty	4	noun
honorable	4	adjective
illegal	4	adjective
incorrect	4	adjective
innocent	4	adjective
justice	4	noun
lapse	4	adjective
legal	4	adjective
precise	4	adjective
proper	4	adjective
realistic	4	adjective
relevant	4	adjective
satisfactory	4	adjective
suitable	4	adjective
apt	5	adjective
authentic	5	adjective
eligible	5	adjective
moral	5	adjective
sin	5	noun
valid	5	adjective
wholesome	5	adjective

73. Units of Measurement
Related Clusters: 13, 15, 18, 19, 28, 33, 130, 327, 373, 374

Word	Importance	Part of Speech
foot	2	noun
gallon	2	noun
grade	2	noun
inch	2	noun
mile	2	noun
pound	2	noun
quart	2	noun
yard	2	noun
mouthful	3	noun
spoonful	3	noun
tablespoon	3	noun
bushel	4	noun
cupful	4	noun
degree	4	noun
gram	4	noun
handful	4	noun
liter	4	noun
meter	4	noun
metric	4	adjective
ounce	4	noun
pinch	4	noun
pint	4	noun
teaspoonful	4	noun
ton	4	noun
mil	5	noun
volt	5	noun
watt	5	noun

74. Ingredients Used to Make Food
Related Clusters: 48, 51, 86, 124, 136, 153, 162, 174, 176, 208, 222, 232, 246

Word	Importance	Part of Speech
dough	2	noun
flour	2	noun
gravy	2	noun
mix	2	noun
pepper	2	noun
salt	2	noun
sauce	2	noun
sugar	2	noun
catsup	3	noun
mayonnaise	3	noun
mustard	3	noun
batter	4	noun
cinnamon	4	noun
garlic	4	noun
graham	4	noun
shortening	4	noun
spice	4	noun
starch	4	noun
vinegar	4	noun
yeast	4	noun
cloves	5	noun
ginger	5	noun
herb	5	noun
ingredient	5	noun
nutmeg	5	noun
parsley	5	noun

75. Limbs
Related Clusters: 76, 80, 115, 140, 157, 160, 191, 213, 336, 437

Word	Importance	Part of Speech
arm	2	noun
elbow	2	noun
finger	2	noun
hand	2	noun
thumb	2	noun
shoulders	3	noun
wrist	3	noun
armpit	4	noun
forearm	4	noun
knuckle	4	noun
nails	4	noun
palm	4	noun
biceps	5	noun
cuticle	5	noun

76. Legs and Feet
Related Clusters: 75, 80, 115, 140, 157, 160, 191, 213, 336, 437

Word	Importance	Part of Speech
feet	2	noun
foot	2	noun
knee	2	noun
leg	2	noun
toe	2	noun
ankle	3	noun
heel	3	noun

Word	Importance	Part of Speech
arch	4	noun
shank	4	noun
shin	4	noun
thigh	4	noun
crotch	5	noun

77. Movies and Plays
Related Clusters: 54, 239, 244

Word	Importance	Part of Speech
act	2	verb
cartoon	2	noun
film	2	noun
movie	2	noun
show	2	noun
stage	2	noun
comedy	3	noun
play	3	noun
background	4	noun
drama	4	noun
perform	4	verb
plot	4	noun
preview	4	noun
program	4	noun
rehearsal	4	noun
scene	4	noun
setting	4	noun
skit	4	noun
audition	5	noun
cinema	5	noun

Word	Importance	Part of Speech
climax	5	noun
matinee	5	noun
scenery	5	noun
vaudeville	5	noun

78. Temperature
Related Clusters: 220, 376, 414, 442

Word	Importance	Part of Speech
cold	2	adjective
heat	2	noun
hot	2	adjective
temperature	2	noun
warm	2	adjective
chill	3	noun
cool	3	adjective
arctic	4	adjective
temperate	4	adjective
thermal	4	adjective
warmth	4	noun
Celsius	5	noun
Centigrade	5	noun
Fahrenheit	5	noun
frigid	5	adjective
lukewarm	5	adjective

79. Parts of a Day

Related Clusters: 2, 16, 24, 29, 52, 59, 83, 126, 144, 233

Word	Importance	Part of Speech
day	2	noun
evening	2	noun
hour	2	noun
minute	2	noun
morning	2	noun
night	2	noun
noon	2	noun
second	2	noun
tonight	2	noun
afternoon	3	noun
midnight	3	noun
overnight	3	adjective
sundown	3	noun
sunrise	3	noun
sunset	3	noun
dawn	4	noun
daybreak	4	noun
dusk	4	noun
instant	4	noun
midday	4	noun
moment	4	noun
nightfall	4	noun
noonday	4	noun
noontime	4	noun
workday	4	noun
twilight	5	noun

80. Throat and Mouth

Related Clusters: 75, 76, 115, 140, 157, 160, 191, 213, 336, 437

Word	Importance	Part of Speech
gum	2	noun
mouth	2	noun
teeth	2	noun
throat	2	noun
tooth	2	noun
voice	2	noun
jaw	3	noun
lip	3	noun
tongue	3	noun
fang	4	noun
windpipe	4	noun
bicuspid	5	noun
molar	5	noun
oral	5	adjective

81. Contractions (Is)

Related Clusters: 42, 85, 150, 235, 274

Word	Importance	Part of Speech
he's	2	contraction
I'm	2	contraction
it's	2	contraction
she's	2	contraction
that's	2	contraction
there's	2	contraction
here's	3	contraction
what's	3	contraction
where's	3	contraction
how's	4	contraction

82. Reptiles/Mythical Animals

Related Clusters: 32, 35, 64, 65, 70, 95, 117, 155, 188, 189, 194, 309, 310, 341

Word	Importance	Part of Speech
alligator	2	noun
dragon	2	noun
frog	2	noun
snake	2	noun
toad	2	noun
turtle	2	noun
dinosaur	3	noun
mermaid	3	noun
monster	3	noun
cobra	4	noun
crocodile	4	noun
lizard	4	noun
rattlesnake	4	noun
reptile	4	noun
tortoise	4	noun
unicorn	4	noun
nymph	5	noun
serpent	5	noun

83. Time (Relative)

Related Clusters: 2, 16, 24, 29, 52, 59, 79, 126, 144, 233

Word	Importance	Part of Speech
old	2	adjective
past	2	noun
present	2	noun
today	2	noun

Word	Importance	Part of Speech
tomorrow	2	noun
yesterday	2	noun
ancient	3	adjective
future	3	noun
history	3	noun
someday	3	noun
antique	4	noun
childhood	4	noun
eternity	4	noun
historic	4	adjective
primitive	4	adjective
puberty	4	noun
youth	4	noun
heirloom	5	noun
medieval	5	adjective
relic	5	noun

84. Sound-Producing Devices

Related Clusters: 103, 156, 165, 175

Word	Importance	Part of Speech
alarm	2	noun
bell	2	noun
horn	2	noun
phone	2	noun
doorbell	3	noun
siren	3	noun
telephone	3	noun
chime	4	noun
earphone	4	noun

continued →

Word	Importance	Part of Speech
gong	4	noun
loudspeaker	4	noun
sonar	4	noun
firebox	5	noun

85. Contractions (Will)
Related Clusters: 42, 81, 150, 235, 274

Word	Importance	Part of Speech
he'll	2	contraction
I'll	2	contraction
she'll	2	contraction
they'll	2	contraction
we'll	3	contraction
you'll	3	contraction
there'll	4	contraction
what'll	4	contraction

86. Dairy Products
Related Clusters: 48, 51, 74, 124, 136, 153, 162, 174, 176, 208, 222, 232, 246

Word	Importance	Part of Speech
butter	2	noun
cheese	2	noun
egg	2	noun
yolk	2	noun
cream	3	noun
margarine	3	noun
curd	5	noun

87. Locations Near Water
Related Clusters: 101, 102, 127, 296, 352, 353, 391, 424

Word	Importance	Part of Speech
beach	2	noun
island	2	noun
coast	3	noun
shore	3	noun
mainland	4	noun
peninsula	4	noun
pier	4	noun
riverbank	4	noun
seashore	4	noun
waterfront	4	noun
isthmus	5	noun
lakeside	5	noun
riverside	5	noun
shoreline	5	noun
strand	5	noun

88. Medical Occupations
Related Clusters: 68, 146, 167, 173, 229, 236, 257, 264, 265, 266, 297, 333, 334, 355, 356, 357, 358, 359, 360, 361, 392, 393, 394, 395, 396, 397, 436

Word	Importance	Part of Speech
dentist	2	noun
nurse	2	noun
doctor	3	noun
dentistry	4	noun
physician	4	noun

Word	Importance	Part of Speech
surgeon	4	noun
intern	5	noun
therapist	5	noun

89. Losing/Winning
Related Clusters: 41, 148, 171, 184, 426

Word	Importance	Part of Speech
loss	2	noun
winner	2	noun
champion	3	noun
defeat	3	verb
win	3	verb
accomplishment	4	noun
conquer	4	verb
conquest	4	noun
dominant	4	adjective
dominate	4	verb
downfall	4	noun
excel	4	verb
overcome	4	verb
overthrow	4	verb
success	4	noun
triumph	4	verb
overrun	5	verb
overtake	5	verb
prevail	5	verb
subdue	5	verb
triumphant	5	adjective
victor	5	noun

90. Nature and Weather (General)
Related Clusters: 226, 307, 375, 406

Word	Importance	Part of Speech
air	2	noun
weather	2	noun
nature	3	noun
atmosphere	4	noun
climate	4	noun
environment	4	noun

91. Rooms
Related Clusters: 113, 123, 134, 217, 284

Word	Importance	Part of Speech
basement	2	noun
bathroom	2	noun
cellar	2	noun
closet	2	noun
garage	2	noun
hall	2	noun
kitchen	2	noun
nursery	2	noun
room	2	noun
bedroom	3	noun
doorway	3	noun
hallway	3	noun
playroom	3	noun
porch	3	noun
aisle	4	noun
attic	4	noun

continued →

Word	Importance	Part of Speech
balcony	4	noun
ballroom	4	noun
chamber	4	noun
cloakroom	4	noun
corridor	4	noun
den	4	noun
entrance	4	noun
lobby	4	noun
loft	4	noun
pantry	4	noun
parlor	4	noun
stateroom	4	noun
veranda	4	noun
washroom	4	noun
threshold	5	noun

92. Fasteners

Related Clusters: 96, 118, 119, 163, 242, 254, 275, 276, 314, 315, 316, 419, 420

Word	Importance	Part of Speech
chain	2	noun
glue	2	noun
key	2	noun
lock	2	noun
nail	2	noun
needle	2	noun
pin	2	noun
rope	2	noun
string	2	noun

Word	Importance	Part of Speech
cable	3	noun
knot	3	noun
screw	3	noun
shoelace	3	noun
strap	3	noun
bolt	4	noun
chord	4	noun
clamp	4	noun
clothespin	4	noun
cord	4	noun
handcuff	4	noun
hinge	4	noun
keyhole	4	noun
lasso	4	noun
latch	4	noun
padlock	4	noun
peg	4	noun
shoestring	4	noun
slot	4	noun
spike	4	noun
staple	4	noun
tack	4	noun
tether	4	noun
thong	4	noun
thumbtack	4	noun
twine	4	noun
lariat	5	noun
rivet	5	noun

93. Things You Travel On

Related Clusters: 97, 120, 128, 159, 234, 318, 331

Word	Importance	Part of Speech
alley	2	noun
bridge	2	noun
driveway	2	noun
highway	2	noun
path	2	noun
railroad	2	noun
road	2	noun
sidewalk	2	noun
street	2	noun
track	2	noun
trail	2	noun
avenue	3	noun
freeway	3	noun
mall	3	noun
racetrack	3	noun
ramp	3	noun
route	3	noun
tunnel	3	noun
airfield	4	noun
airstrip	4	noun
chute	4	noun
course	4	noun
detour	4	noun
drawbridge	4	noun
intersection	4	noun
lane	4	noun
pass	4	noun
passage	4	noun

Word	Importance	Part of Speech
passageway	4	noun
pathway	4	noun
rail	4	noun
railway	4	noun
runway	4	noun
waterway	4	noun
way	4	noun
airway	5	noun
blacktop	5	noun
boulevard	5	noun
bypass	5	noun
byway	5	noun
causeway	5	noun
crossroad	5	noun
parkway	5	noun
seaway	5	noun
span	5	noun

94. Family Relationships

Related Clusters: 56, 111, 203, 204, 205, 206, 227, 317, 330, 343, 344, 382, 432, 444

Word	Importance	Part of Speech
aunt	2	noun
brother	2	noun
dad	2	noun
family	2	noun
father	2	noun
granny	2	noun
ma	2	noun

continued →

Word	Importance	Part of Speech
mama	2	noun
mom	2	noun
mother	2	noun
papa	2	noun
parent	2	noun
sister	2	noun
son	2	noun
uncle	2	noun
cousin	3	noun
daughter	3	noun
grandparent	3	noun
husband	3	noun
mammy	3	noun
nephew	3	noun
niece	3	noun
sibling	3	noun
wife	3	noun
ancestor	4	noun
bride	4	noun
groom	4	noun
heir	4	noun
household	4	noun
offspring	4	noun
spouse	4	noun
domo	5	noun
guardian	5	noun
maternal	5	noun
patriarch	5	noun
pedigree	5	noun
ward	5	noun

95. Insects

Related Clusters: 32, 35, 64, 65, 70, 82, 117, 155, 188, 189, 194, 309, 310, 341

Word	Importance	Part of Speech
ant	2	noun
bee	2	noun
bug	2	noun
butterfly	2	noun
caterpillar	2	noun
fly	2	noun
insect	2	noun
ladybug	2	noun
spider	2	noun
worm	2	noun
bumblebee	3	noun
cockroach	3	noun
flea	3	noun
grasshopper	3	noun
mosquito	3	noun
moth	3	noun
slug	3	noun
wasp	3	noun
beetle	4	noun
centipede	4	noun
cricket	4	noun
dragonfly	4	noun
hornet	4	noun
housefly	4	noun
larva	4	noun
millipede	4	noun
mite	4	noun

Word	Importance	Part of Speech
parasite	4	noun
pupa	4	noun
silkworm	4	noun
termite	4	noun
yellow jacket	4	noun
arachnid	5	noun
drone	5	noun
firefly	5	noun
gnat	5	noun
katydid	5	noun
leech	5	noun
lice	5	noun
mantis	5	noun

96. Cooking and Eating Utensils
Related Clusters: 92, 118, 119, 163, 242, 254, 275, 276, 314, 315, 316, 419, 420

Word	Importance	Part of Speech
bowl	2	noun
cup	2	noun
dish	2	noun
fork	2	noun
glass	2	noun
knife	2	noun
pan	2	noun
plate	2	noun
pot	2	noun
spoon	2	noun
chopsticks	3	noun

Word	Importance	Part of Speech
mug	3	noun
opener	3	noun
tablespoon	3	noun
teaspoon	3	noun
tray	3	noun
casserole	4	noun
crock	4	noun
kettle	4	noun
ladle	4	noun
platter	4	noun
saucer	4	noun
scoop	4	noun
sieve	4	noun
silverware	4	noun
skillet	4	noun
spatula	4	noun
teacup	4	noun
teapot	4	noun
tong	4	noun
chinaware	5	noun
goblet	5	noun
stein	5	noun

97. Vehicles (Actions/Characteristics)
Related Clusters: 93, 120, 128, 159, 234, 318, 331

Word	Importance	Part of Speech
drive	2	verb
passenger	2	noun
ride	2	verb
row	2	verb
sail	2	verb
cruise	3	verb
glide	3	verb
aviation	4	noun
horsepower	4	noun
launch	4	verb
marine	4	noun
naval	4	adjective
navigate	4	verb
transport	4	verb
aerial	5	adjective
airborne	5	adjective

98. General Names for Groups
Related Clusters: 200, 258, 298, 401

Word	Importance	Part of Speech
gather	2	noun
group	2	noun
pile	2	noun
sequence	2	noun
bunch	3	noun

Word	Importance	Part of Speech
classify	3	verb
collect	3	verb
list	3	noun
organize	3	verb
stack	3	noun
arrange	4	verb
array	4	noun
assemble	4	verb
assortment	4	noun
bale	4	noun
batch	4	noun
blend	4	noun
bundle	4	noun
chronology	4	noun
clump	4	noun
cluster	4	noun
collection	4	noun
compound	4	noun
curriculum	4	noun
directory	4	noun
file	4	noun
heap	4	noun
invoice	4	noun
kit	4	noun
medley	4	noun
menu	4	noun
mixture	4	noun
network	4	noun
roster	4	noun

Word	Importance	Part of Speech
schedule	4	noun
series	4	noun
sheaf	4	noun
stock	4	noun
summarize	4	verb
table	4	noun
wad	4	noun
web	4	noun
aggregate	5	noun
alloy	5	noun
hybrid	5	noun
muster	5	noun
spectrum	5	noun
swath	5	noun

Word	Importance	Part of Speech
shallow	3	adjective
thick	3	adjective
width	3	noun
broad	4	adjective
deepen	4	verb
dense	4	adjective
dimension	4	noun
extend	4	verb
layer	4	noun
measurement	4	noun
scale	4	noun
thickness	4	noun
trim	4	verb
stature	5	noun
tier	5	noun

99. Dimensionality

Related Clusters: 69, 142, 193, 218, 270, 303, 326

Word	Importance	Part of Speech
deep	2	adjective
height	2	noun
length	2	noun
long	2	adjective
short	2	adjective
size	2	noun
tall	2	adjective
thin	2	adjective
wide	2	adjective
depth	3	noun
narrow	3	adjective

100. Communication (Positive Information)

Related Clusters: 14, 61, 105, 177, 198, 207, 255, 345, 346, 383

Word	Importance	Part of Speech
agree	2	verb
bless	2	verb
greet	2	verb
pray	2	verb
thank	2	verb
welcome	2	verb
compliment	3	verb
cooperate	3	verb
encourage	3	verb

continued →

Word	Importance	Part of Speech
praise	3	verb
apology	4	noun
assure	4	verb
awe	4	verb
blessing	4	noun
charm	4	verb
congratulate	4	verb
congratulations	4	noun
flatter	4	verb
inspire	4	verb
participate	4	verb
prayer	4	noun
soothe	4	verb
teamwork	4	noun
tribute	4	noun
worship	4	verb
acknowledge	5	verb
credit	5	verb

Word	Importance	Part of Speech
rainbow	3	noun
raindrop	3	noun
rainfall	3	noun
snowball	3	noun
snowman	3	noun
steam	3	noun
drizzle	4	noun
fluid	4	noun
frost	4	noun
glacier	4	noun
iceberg	4	noun
mist	4	noun
moisture	4	noun
precipitation	4	noun
sleet	4	noun
slush	4	noun
snowdrift	4	noun
snowfall	4	noun
vapor	4	noun
aqua	5	noun
floe	5	noun

101. Forms of Water/Liquid
Related Clusters: 87, 102, 127, 296, 352, 353, 391, 424

Word	Importance	Part of Speech
ice	2	noun
rain	2	noun
snow	2	noun
water	2	noun
hail	3	noun
icicle	3	noun
liquid	3	noun

102. Bodies of Water
Related Clusters: 87, 101, 127, 296, 352, 353, 391, 424

Word	Importance	Part of Speech
lake	2	noun
ocean	2	noun
puddle	2	noun
river	2	noun

Word	Importance	Part of Speech
sea	2	noun
stream	2	noun
bay	3	noun
creek	3	noun
pond	3	noun
brook	4	noun
cove	4	noun
current	4	noun
delta	4	noun
gulf	4	noun
inlet	4	noun
marsh	4	noun
outlet	4	noun
rapids	4	noun
strait	4	noun
surf	4	noun
swamp	4	noun
tide	4	noun
tributary	4	noun
waterfall	4	noun
waterline	4	noun
bog	5	noun
eddy	5	noun
estuary	5	noun
fjord	5	noun
geyser	5	noun
headwaters	5	noun
lagoon	5	noun
marshland	5	noun
reef	5	noun

103. Noises (General)
Related Clusters: 84, 156, 165, 175

Word	Importance	Part of Speech
hear	2	verb
listen	2	verb
loud	2	adjective
noise	2	noun
quiet	2	adjective
sound	2	noun
aloud	3	adverb
calm	3	adjective
echo	3	noun
silence	3	noun
silent	3	adjective
clamor	4	noun
clatter	4	noun
commotion	4	noun
earshot	4	noun
harsh	4	adjective
hoarse	4	adjective
hush	4	noun
peal	4	noun
pitch	4	noun
racket	4	noun
serene	4	adjective
shrill	4	adjective
stillness	4	noun
tone	4	noun
trill	4	noun
audio	5	noun
blare	5	noun
crescendo	5	noun

continued →

Word	Importance	Part of Speech
eavesdrop	5	noun
harken	5	verb
intensity	5	noun
lull	5	noun
tranquil	5	adjective

104. Money and Goods
Related Clusters: 109, 116, 122, 201, 214

Word	Importance	Part of Speech
cent	2	noun
coin	2	noun
dollar	2	noun
money	2	noun
penny	2	noun
quarter	2	noun
cash	3	noun
check	3	noun
dime	3	noun
nickel	3	noun
pound	3	noun
ticket	3	noun
capital	4	noun
coupon	4	noun
fund	4	noun
payroll	4	noun
postage	4	noun
receipt	4	noun
shilling	4	noun
souvenir	4	noun

Word	Importance	Part of Speech
stock	4	noun
wealth	4	noun
currency	5	noun
finance	5	noun
guinea	5	noun
merchandise	5	noun
token	5	noun

105. Communication (General)
Related Clusters: 14, 61, 100, 177, 198, 207, 255, 345, 346, 383

Word	Importance	Part of Speech
speak	2	verb
speech	2	noun
talk	2	verb
chat	3	verb
discuss	3	verb
statement	3	noun
brainstorm	4	verb
comment	4	verb
communicate	4	verb
declaration	4	noun
dialogue	4	noun
discussion	4	noun
jabber	4	verb
lecture	4	noun
lisp	4	noun
powwow	4	verb
proposal	4	noun

Word	Importance	Part of Speech
remark	4	verb
sermon	4	noun
talkative	4	adjective
testimony	4	noun
blab	5	verb
converse	5	verb
drawl	5	verb
eloquent	5	adjective
fluent	5	adjective
negotiate	5	verb
proclamation	5	noun
verbal	5	adjective
vocal	5	adjective

106. Places Related to Protection/Incarceration
Related Clusters: 60, 121, 190, 210, 321, 324, 335, 364, 365, 366, 399, 400

Word	Importance	Part of Speech
cage	2	noun
cave	2	noun
shelter	2	noun
fort	3	noun
jail	3	noun
blockhouse	4	noun
cell	4	noun
dugout	4	noun
dungeon	4	noun
firehouse	4	noun

fortress	4	noun
garrison	4	noun
haven	4	noun
outpost	4	noun
prison	4	noun
pueblo	4	noun
stockade	4	noun
acropolis	5	noun
bunker	5	noun
quarantine	5	noun
stronghold	5	noun

107. Building and Repairing
Related Clusters: 164, 181, 251, 268, 325, 367

Word	Importance	Part of Speech
find	2	verb
fix	2	verb
make	2	verb
build	3	verb
develop	3	verb
prepare	3	verb
produce	3	verb
repair	3	verb
shape	3	verb
adjust	4	verb
constitute	4	verb
construct	4	verb
construction	4	noun
create	4	verb
establish	4	verb

continued →

Word	Importance	Part of Speech
forge	4	verb
form	4	verb
generate	4	verb
glaze	4	verb
install	4	verb
manufacture	4	verb
modify	4	verb
mold	4	verb
orient	4	verb
pave	4	verb
preserve	4	verb
process	4	verb
qualify	4	verb
rebuild	4	verb
restore	4	verb
rehabilitate	5	verb

108. Trees/Bushes (Parts)
Related Clusters: 36, 192, 269, 421

Word	Importance	Part of Speech
branch	2	noun
leaf	2	noun
twig	2	noun
bark	3	noun
limb	3	noun
stump	3	noun
bough	4	noun
knothole	4	noun

Word	Importance	Part of Speech
latex	4	noun
resin	4	noun
rubber	4	noun
sap	4	noun
stem	4	noun
sticker	4	noun
thorn	4	noun
treetop	4	noun
wicker	4	noun
foliage	5	noun
pith	5	noun

109. Places Where Money and Goods Are Kept
Related Clusters: 104, 116, 122, 201, 214

Word	Importance	Part of Speech
bank	2	noun
safe	2	noun
purse	3	noun
wallet	3	noun
account	4	noun
billfold	4	noun
commerce	4	noun
handbag	4	noun
pocketbook	4	noun
vault	4	noun
mint	5	noun
strongbox	5	noun

110. Actions Helpful to Humans
Related Clusters: 161, 250, 260

Word	Importance	Part of Speech
behave	2	verb
help	2	verb
save	2	verb
heal	3	verb
improve	3	verb
protect	3	verb
advantage	4	noun
aid	4	verb
assist	4	verb
benefit	4	noun
cure	4	verb
defend	4	verb
enrich	4	verb
foster	4	verb
guide	4	verb
nourish	4	verb
promote	4	verb
recover	4	verb
recycle	4	verb
relieve	4	verb
rescue	4	verb
revive	4	verb
sake	4	noun
stead	4	noun
accommodate	5	verb
avail	5	verb

Word	Importance	Part of Speech
behalf	5	noun
contribute	5	verb
escort	5	verb
fend	5	verb
refresh	5	verb

111. Females
Related Clusters: 56, 94, 203, 204, 205, 206, 227, 317, 330, 343, 344, 382, 432, 444

Word	Importance	Part of Speech
girl	2	noun
lady	2	noun
woman	2	noun
female	3	noun
housewife	3	noun
schoolgirl	3	noun
dame	4	noun
hostess	4	noun
lass	4	noun
mistress	4	noun
spinster	4	noun
squaw	4	noun
tomboy	4	noun
widow	4	noun
belle	5	noun
madam	5	noun
mademoiselle	5	noun

112. Things to Write On/With
Related Clusters: 53, 71, 138, 248, 256, 279, 319, 320

Word	Importance	Part of Speech
brush	2	noun
card	2	noun
crayon	2	noun
ink	2	noun
page	2	noun
paper	2	noun
pen	2	noun
pencil	2	noun
blackboard	3	noun
chalk	3	noun
chalkboard	3	noun
loose-leaf	3	noun
notebook	3	noun
paintbrush	3	noun
ballpoint	4	noun
pastel	4	noun
press	4	noun
scrapbook	4	noun
tablet	4	noun
typewriter	4	noun
parchment	5	noun
ream	5	noun
scroll	5	noun

113. Furniture
Related Clusters: 91, 123, 134, 217, 284

Word	Importance	Part of Speech
bed	2	noun
bench	2	noun
chair	2	noun
crib	2	noun
desk	2	noun
drawer	2	noun
seat	2	noun
table	2	noun
bookcase	3	noun
couch	3	noun
counter	3	noun
cradle	3	noun
cupboard	3	noun
playpen	3	noun
sofa	3	noun
stool	3	noun
altar	4	noun
armchair	4	noun
bleacher	4	noun
bunk	4	noun
cabinet	4	noun
cot	4	noun
furniture	4	noun
hutch	4	noun
mat	4	noun
mattress	4	noun
nook	4	noun

Word	Importance	Part of Speech
pulpit	4	noun
tabletop	4	noun
throne	4	noun
wheelchair	4	noun
bureau	5	noun
decor	5	noun
hammock	5	noun
pew	5	noun

114. Areas of Land
Related Clusters: 50, 139, 168, 267, 362, 363, 398

Word	Importance	Part of Speech
land	2	noun
lot	2	noun
place	2	noun
region	2	noun
area	3	noun
location	3	noun
territory	3	noun
zone	3	noun
acre	4	noun
clearing	4	noun
frontier	4	noun
plot	4	noun
site	4	noun
surface	4	noun
terrain	4	noun
tropics	4	noun

Word	Importance	Part of Speech
domain	5	noun
mantle	5	noun
outback	5	noun
premises	5	noun

115. Head and Face
Related Clusters: 75, 76, 80, 140, 157, 160, 191, 213, 336, 437

Word	Importance	Part of Speech
cheek	2	noun
chin	2	noun
face	2	noun
head	2	noun
brain	3	noun
forehead	3	noun
mind	3	noun
skull	4	noun
countenance	5	noun
ego	5	noun

116. Money-Related Characteristics
Related Clusters: 104, 109, 122, 201, 214

Word	Importance	Part of Speech
free	2	noun
poor	2	adjective
poverty	2	noun
rich	2	adjective

continued →

Word	Importance	Part of Speech
broke	3	noun
cheap	3	adjective
expensive	3	adjective
costly	4	adverb
humble	4	noun
luxury	4	noun
needy	4	adjective
posh	4	noun
royal	4	adjective
wasteful	4	adjective

117. Actions Related to Animals

Related Clusters: 32, 35, 64, 65, 70, 82, 95, 155, 188, 189, 194, 309, 310, 341

Word	Importance	Part of Speech
fish	2	verb
fly	2	verb
hunt	2	verb
trap	2	verb
buck	3	verb
gallop	3	verb
soar	3	verb
sting	3	verb
bareback	4	adjective
graze	4	verb
horseback	4	adverb
snare	4	verb
stampede	4	verb
swarm	4	verb

118. Appliances

Related Clusters: 92, 96, 119, 163, 242, 254, 275, 276, 314, 315, 316, 419, 420

Word	Importance	Part of Speech
oven	2	noun
radio	2	noun
stove	2	noun
television	2	noun
furnace	3	noun
heater	3	noun
refrigerator	3	noun
icebox	4	noun
microwave	4	noun
phonograph	4	noun
radiator	4	noun
stereo	4	noun
griddle	5	noun
kiln	5	noun
wireless	5	adjective

119. Tools (General)

Related Clusters: 92, 96, 118, 163, 242, 254, 275, 276, 314, 315, 316, 419, 420

Word	Importance	Part of Speech
hammer	2	noun
saw	2	noun
shovel	2	noun
tool	2	noun
drill	3	noun
rake	3	noun
screwdriver	3	noun

Word	Importance	Part of Speech
tweezers	3	noun
chisel	4	noun
crowbar	4	noun
device	4	noun
hoe	4	noun
implement	4	noun
instrument	4	noun
jack	4	noun
jigsaw	4	noun
lever	4	noun
pitchfork	4	noun
pliers	4	noun
resource	4	noun
sandpaper	4	noun
shim	4	noun
wedge	4	noun
sledge	5	noun
spade	5	noun
utensil	5	noun
wrench	5	noun

120. Vehicles (Air Transportation)

Related Clusters: 93, 97, 128, 159, 234, 318, 331

Word	Importance	Part of Speech
balloon	2	noun
helicopter	2	noun
kite	2	noun
plane	2	noun

Word	Importance	Part of Speech
rocket	2	noun
aircraft	3	noun
airline	3	noun
airplane	3	noun
spacecraft	3	noun
airliner	4	noun
blimp	5	noun
jetliner	5	noun

121. Places to Live

Related Clusters: 60, 106, 190, 210, 321, 324, 335, 364, 365, 366, 399, 400

Word	Importance	Part of Speech
castle	2	noun
home	2	noun
hotel	2	noun
house	2	noun
hut	2	noun
apartment	3	noun
motel	3	noun
palace	3	noun
tent	3	noun
cabin	4	noun
cottage	4	noun
habitat	4	noun
homestead	4	noun
igloo	4	noun
inn	4	noun
lodge	4	noun
manor	4	noun

continued →

Word	Importance	Part of Speech
mansion	4	noun
suite	4	noun
teepee	4	noun
wigwam	4	noun
barracks	5	noun
bungalow	5	noun
chalet	5	noun
dormitory	5	noun
estate	5	noun
hovel	5	noun
shanty	5	noun
villa	5	noun

122. Actions Related to Money and Goods

Related Clusters: 104, 109, 116, 201, 214

Word	Importance	Part of Speech
buy	2	verb
pay	2	verb
sale	2	noun
sell	2	verb
spend	2	verb
bet	3	verb
earn	3	verb
owe	3	verb
purchase	3	verb
afford	4	verb
bargain	4	noun
budget	4	noun

Word	Importance	Part of Speech
deal	4	noun
discount	4	noun
donate	4	verb
invest	4	verb
lease	4	verb
market	4	noun
repay	4	verb
scrimp	4	verb
subscribe	4	verb
auction	5	noun
insure	5	verb
peddle	5	verb
ransom	5	noun
redeem	5	verb
render	5	noun
retail	5	noun
splurge	5	verb
wholesale	5	noun

123. Parts of a Home

Related Clusters: 91, 113, 134, 217, 284

Word	Importance	Part of Speech
door	2	noun
floor	2	noun
roof	2	noun
stairs	2	noun
wall	2	noun
window	2	noun
ceiling	3	noun

Word	Importance	Part of Speech
chimney	3	noun
doorstep	3	noun
stair	3	noun
staircase	3	noun
stairway	3	noun
banister	4	noun
mantel	4	noun
pane	4	noun
sill	4	noun
smokestack	4	noun
spire	4	noun
steeple	4	noun
stile	4	noun
vent	4	noun
awning	5	noun
baseboard	5	noun
dormer	5	noun
eaves	5	noun
flue	5	noun
hearth	5	noun
lattice	5	noun
stovepipe	5	noun
wicket	5	noun

124. Foods That Are Prepared
Related Clusters: 48, 51, 74, 86, 136, 153, 162, 174, 176, 208, 222, 232, 246

Word	Importance	Part of Speech
bread	2	noun
bun	2	noun
cereal	2	noun
chips	2	noun
cracker	2	noun
crust	2	noun
hamburger	2	noun
hotdog	2	noun
jelly	2	noun
pancake	2	noun
pizza	2	noun
salad	2	noun
sandwich	2	noun
snack	2	noun
toast	2	noun
biscuit	3	noun
coleslaw	3	noun
loaf	3	noun
macaroni	3	noun
muffin	3	noun
noodle	3	noun
oatmeal	3	noun
omelet	3	noun
pretzel	3	noun
spaghetti	3	noun
taco	3	noun

continued →

Word	Importance	Part of Speech
tortilla	3	noun
waffle	3	noun
mush	4	noun
porridge	4	noun
flapjack	5	noun
gruel	5	noun
lasagna	5	noun
watercress	5	noun

125. Pants, Shirts, and Skirts
Related Clusters: 47, 62, 129, 145, 178, 212, 224, 263, 354, 435

Word	Importance	Part of Speech
belt	2	noun
diaper	2	noun
dress	2	noun
jeans	2	noun
pajamas	2	noun
pants	2	noun
pocket	2	noun
shirt	2	noun
skirt	2	noun
apron	3	noun
bathrobe	3	noun
nightgown	3	noun
robe	3	noun
shorts	3	noun
sweater	3	noun
tights	3	noun

Word	Importance	Part of Speech
blouse	4	noun
gown	4	noun
jersey	4	noun
overalls	4	noun
petticoat	4	noun
pinafore	4	noun
pullover	4	noun
slacks	4	noun
trousers	4	noun
vest	4	noun
cardigan	5	noun
dungarees	5	noun
kimono	5	noun

126. Frequency and Duration
Related Clusters: 2, 16, 24, 29, 52, 59, 79, 83, 144, 233

Word	Importance	Part of Speech
long	1	adjective
never	1	adverb
often	1	adverb
once	1	adverb
sometimes	2	adjective
always	3	adverb
anymore	3	adverb
awhile	3	adverb
daily	3	adjective
ever	3	adverb
forever	3	adverb

Word	Importance	Part of Speech
frequent	3	adjective
hourly	3	adverb
rare	3	adjective
regular	3	adjective
repeat	3	noun
seldom	3	adverb
twice	3	adverb
usual	3	adjective
weekly	3	adjective
annual	4	adjective
common	4	adjective
constant	4	noun
continue	4	verb
continuous	4	adjective
customary	4	adjective
general	4	adjective
habitual	4	adjective
infrequent	4	adjective
irregular	4	adjective
longtime	4	adjective
momentary	4	adjective
nightly	4	adverb
occasional	4	adjective
permanent	4	adjective
rehearse	4	verb
temporary	4	adjective
consecutive	5	adjective
eternal	5	adjective
persist	5	verb
sporadic	5	adjective

127. Water/Liquid (Related Actions)
Related Clusters: 87, 101, 102, 296, 352, 353, 391, 424

Word	Importance	Part of Speech
boil	2	verb
dive	2	verb
drain	2	verb
drip	2	verb
float	2	verb
melt	2	verb
pour	2	verb
sink	2	verb
spill	2	verb
splash	2	verb
stir	2	verb
swim	2	verb
wet	2	adjective
bubble	3	noun
dribble	3	verb
flush	3	verb
freeze	3	verb
leak	3	verb
slick	3	adjective
slippery	3	adjective
soak	3	verb
spray	3	verb
sprinkle	3	verb
squirt	3	verb
trickle	3	verb
absorb	4	verb

continued →

Word	Importance	Part of Speech
damp	4	adjective
defrost	4	verb
dissolve	4	verb
drench	4	verb
drift	4	verb
drown	4	verb
evaporate	4	verb
flow	4	verb
gush	4	verb
humid	4	adjective
moist	4	adjective
moisten	4	verb
ooze	4	verb
overflow	4	verb
penetrate	4	verb
ripple	4	verb
secrete	4	verb
seep	4	verb
slosh	4	verb
snorkel	4	verb
soggy	4	adjective
spatter	4	verb
splatter	4	verb
spurt	4	verb
submerge	4	verb
thaw	4	verb
wade	4	verb
waterproof	4	adjective
cascade	5	verb
dilute	5	verb

Word	Importance	Part of Speech
douse	5	verb
ebb	5	verb
ford	5	verb
souse	5	verb
surge	5	verb
waterlog	5	verb

128. Transportation (Types)

Related Clusters: 93, 97, 120, 159, 234, 318, 331

Word	Importance	Part of Speech
bicycle	2	noun
bike	2	noun
bus	2	noun
car	2	noun
train	2	noun
tricycle	2	noun
truck	2	noun
van	2	noun
wagon	2	noun
ambulance	3	noun
automobile	3	noun
cab	3	noun
locomotive	3	noun
motorcycle	3	noun
scooter	3	noun
stagecoach	3	noun
subway	3	noun
taxi	3	noun
taxicab	3	noun

Word	Importance	Part of Speech
trailer	3	noun
auto	4	noun
buggy	4	noun
caboose	4	noun
carriage	4	noun
cart	4	noun
chariot	4	noun
jeep	4	noun
pickup	4	noun
streetcar	4	noun
unicycle	4	noun
vehicle	4	noun
jalopy	5	noun
sedan	5	noun
trolley	5	noun

129. Clothing-Related Actions
Related Clusters: 47, 62, 125, 145, 178, 212, 224, 263, 354, 435

Word	Importance	Part of Speech
fit	2	verb
fold	2	verb
sew	2	verb
tear	2	verb
wear	2	verb
braid	3	verb
patch	3	verb
rip	3	verb
wrinkle	3	verb

Word	Importance	Part of Speech
zip	3	verb
clad	4	verb
clothe	4	verb
crease	4	verb
embroider	4	verb
furl	4	verb
knit	4	verb
mend	4	verb
pucker	4	verb
stitch	4	verb
tatter	4	verb
weave	4	verb
alter	5	verb
baste	5	verb
crochet	5	verb
don	5	verb
ravel	5	verb
rumple	5	verb

130. Parts
Related Clusters: 13, 15, 18, 19, 28, 33, 73, 327, 373, 374

Word	Importance	Part of Speech
bit	2	noun
dot	2	noun
flake	2	noun
part	2	noun
piece	2	noun
crumb	3	noun

continued →

Word	Importance	Part of Speech
member	3	noun
portion	3	noun
section	3	noun
slice	3	noun
sliver	3	noun
splinter	3	noun
type	3	noun
chunk	4	noun
department	4	noun
element	4	noun
factor	4	noun
fragment	4	noun
gob	4	noun
item	4	noun
module	4	noun
sample	4	noun
scrap	4	noun
segment	4	noun
slab	4	noun
species	4	noun
speck	4	noun
category	5	noun
jot	5	noun
morsel	5	noun
particle	5	noun
version	5	noun

131. Grabbing and Holding
Related Clusters: 149, 197

Word	Importance	Part of Speech
catch	2	verb
hold	2	verb
hug	2	verb
pick	2	verb
clasp	3	verb
cuddle	3	verb
grab	3	verb
pinch	3	verb
snuggle	3	verb
squeeze	3	verb
clench	4	verb
cling	4	verb
clutch	4	verb
embrace	4	verb
grasp	4	verb
grip	4	verb
nab	4	verb
nuzzle	4	verb
secure	4	verb
strum	4	verb
wrap	4	verb
wring	4	verb
clinch	5	verb
nip	5	verb
pluck	5	verb
vise	5	noun

132. Consciousness/ Unconsciousness
Related Clusters: 46, 67, 137, 154, 225, 249, 277, 347, 348, 349, 384

Word	Importance	Part of Speech
asleep	2	noun
awake	2	noun
nap	2	verb
sleep	2	verb
daydream	3	noun
dream	3	verb
pretend	3	verb
wake	3	verb
conscious	4	noun
daze	4	verb
doze	4	verb
drowsy	4	adjective
fantasy	4	noun
hallucination	4	noun
hibernate	4	verb
nightmare	4	noun
slumber	4	verb
snooze	4	verb
unconscious	4	noun
waken	4	verb
weary	4	adjective
conceive	5	verb
hypnosis	5	noun
rouse	5	verb
stupor	5	noun
trance	5	noun

133. Soil
Related Clusters: 237, 259, 337, 402, 438

Word	Importance	Part of Speech
ground	2	noun
land	2	noun
mud	2	noun
soil	2	noun
clay	3	noun
dirt	3	noun
dust	3	noun
earth	3	noun
humus	4	noun
manure	4	noun
sod	4	noun
turf	4	noun
clod	5	noun
dung	5	noun
peat	5	noun

134. Linens
Related Clusters: 91, 113, 123, 217, 284

Word	Importance	Part of Speech
blanket	2	noun
cover	2	noun
pillow	2	noun
towel	2	noun
bedspread	3	noun
cushion	3	noun
napkin	3	noun
pillowcase	3	noun

continued →

Word	Importance	Part of Speech
sheet	3	noun
tablecloth	3	noun
drape	4	noun
pad	4	noun
quilt	4	noun
doily	5	noun

135. Looking and Perceiving
Related Cluster: 195

Word	Importance	Part of Speech
look	2	verb
see	2	verb
stare	2	verb
watch	2	verb
blink	3	verb
peek	3	verb
spy	3	verb
wink	3	verb
aim	4	verb
attend	4	verb
behold	4	verb
detect	4	verb
distinguish	4	verb
focus	4	verb
gape	4	verb
gaze	4	verb
glance	4	verb
glare	4	verb
glimpse	4	verb

Word	Importance	Part of Speech
identify	4	verb
ignore	4	verb
loom	4	verb
monitor	4	verb
notice	4	verb
observe	4	verb
peer	4	verb
perceive	4	verb
recognize	4	verb
scout	4	verb
sense	4	verb
shun	4	verb
snoop	4	verb
snub	4	verb
squint	4	verb
verify	4	verb
glower	5	verb
vigil	5	noun

136. Meats
Related Clusters: 48, 51, 74, 86, 124, 153, 162, 174, 176, 208, 222, 232, 246

Word	Importance	Part of Speech
bacon	2	noun
beef	2	noun
ham	2	noun
hotdog	2	noun
sausage	2	noun
bologna	3	noun

Word	Importance	Part of Speech
pork	3	noun
steak	3	noun
poultry	4	noun
lard	5	noun
mutton	5	noun
pemmican	5	noun

137. Intelligence
Related Clusters: 46, 67, 132, 154, 225, 249, 277, 347, 348, 349, 384

Word	Importance	Part of Speech
able	2	adjective
smart	2	adjective
stupid	2	adjective
alert	3	adjective
brilliant	3	adjective
wise	3	adjective
aware	4	adjective
capable	4	adjective
clever	4	adjective
competent	4	adjective
creative	4	adjective
curious	4	adjective
ignorant	4	adjective
intelligence	4	noun
intelligent	4	adjective
practical	4	adjective
proficient	4	adjective
skillful	4	adjective

Word	Importance	Part of Speech
wisdom	4	noun
wit	4	noun
adept	5	adjective
crude	5	adjective
deft	5	adjective
imaginative	5	adjective
logical	5	adjective
naïve	5	adjective
rational	5	adjective
versatile	5	adjective
vulgar	5	adjective

138. Literature (Types)
Related Clusters: 53, 71, 112, 248, 256, 279, 319, 320

Word	Importance	Part of Speech
myth	2	noun
story	2	noun
fiction	3	noun
legend	3	noun
literature	3	noun
mystery	3	noun
poetry	3	noun
riddle	3	noun
tale	3	noun
writing	3	noun
comedy	4	noun
fable	4	noun
parable	4	noun

continued →

Word	Importance	Part of Speech
proverb	4	noun
suspense	4	noun
verse	4	noun
prose	5	noun

139. Parks and Yards

Related Clusters: 50, 114, 168, 267, 362, 363, 398

Word	Importance	Part of Speech
garden	2	noun
park	2	noun
yard	2	noun
patio	3	noun
playground	3	noun
schoolyard	3	noun
barnyard	4	noun
cemetery	4	noun
courtyard	4	noun
plaza	4	noun

140. Ears, Eyes, and Nose

Related Clusters: 75, 76, 80, 115, 157, 160, 191, 213, 336, 437

Word	Importance	Part of Speech
ear	2	noun
eye	2	noun
nose	2	noun
eyebrow	3	noun
eyelash	3	noun

Word	Importance	Part of Speech
nostril	3	noun
brow	4	noun
eardrum	4	noun
lobe	4	noun
retina	4	noun

141. Descending Motion (General)

Related Clusters: 38, 39, 40, 44, 66, 147, 169, 170, 182, 199, 215, 216, 247, 280, 281, 282, 283, 300, 301, 302, 322, 338, 403

Word	Importance	Part of Speech
drop	2	verb
fall	2	verb
lay	2	verb
dump	3	verb
slump	3	verb
tumble	3	verb
collapse	4	verb
descend	4	verb
dip	4	verb
droop	4	verb
landslide	4	noun
plunge	4	verb
sag	4	verb
swoop	4	verb
tilt	4	verb
dunk	5	verb
slouch	5	verb
topple	5	verb

142. Rectangular/Square Shapes
Related Clusters: 69, 99, 193, 218, 270, 303, 326

Word	Importance	Part of Speech
block	2	noun
rectangle	2	noun
square	2	noun
triangle	2	noun
cube	3	noun
pyramid	3	noun
triangular	3	adjective
cubic	4	adjective
equilateral	4	adjective
hexagon	4	noun
octagon	4	noun
parallelogram	4	noun
pentagon	4	noun
polygon	4	noun
prism	4	noun
quadrilateral	4	noun
trapezoid	4	noun
foursquare	5	noun

143. Board/Other Games
Related Clusters: 158, 183, 209, 304, 370

Word	Importance	Part of Speech
doll	2	noun
toy	2	noun
toys	2	noun
puppet	3	noun

Word	Importance	Part of Speech
puzzle	3	noun
cards	4	noun
checkers	4	noun
checkmate	4	noun
chess	4	noun
crossword	4	noun
dice	4	noun
hopscotch	4	noun
lottery	4	noun
pinball	4	noun
poker	4	noun
tiddlywinks	4	noun
marionette	5	noun
raffle	5	noun

144. Time Measurement Devices
Related Clusters: 2, 16, 24, 29, 52, 59, 79, 83, 126, 233

Word	Importance	Part of Speech
calendar	2	noun
clock	2	noun
watch	2	noun
date	3	noun
o'clock	3	adverb
hourglass	4	noun
stopwatch	4	noun
sundial	4	noun
wristwatch	4	noun

145. Coats

Related Clusters: 47, 62, 125, 129, 178, 212, 224, 263, 354, 435

Word	Importance	Part of Speech
coat	2	noun
jacket	2	noun
cape	3	noun
raincoat	3	noun
cloak	4	noun
mantle	4	noun
overcoat	4	noun
parka	4	noun
poncho	4	noun
shawl	4	noun
topcoat	5	noun

146. Actions Related to Work

Related Clusters: 68, 88, 167, 173, 229, 236, 257, 264, 265, 266, 297, 333, 334, 355, 356, 357, 358, 359, 360, 361, 392, 393, 394, 395, 396, 397, 436

Word	Importance	Part of Speech
quit	2	verb
work	2	verb
hire	3	verb
labor	3	verb
effort	4	noun
employ	4	verb
retire	4	verb
toil	4	verb
drudge	5	verb

Word	Importance	Part of Speech
engage	5	verb
strive	5	verb
travail	5	verb

147. Beginning Motion

Related Clusters: 38, 39, 40, 44, 66, 141, 169, 170, 182, 199, 215, 216, 247, 280, 281, 282, 283, 300, 301, 302, 322, 338, 403

Word	Importance	Part of Speech
begin	2	verb
start	2	verb
try	2	verb
beginning	3	noun
origin	3	noun
introduce	4	verb
introduction	4	noun
source	4	noun
embark	5	verb
genesis	5	noun
preface	5	verb

148. Receiving/Taking Actions

Related Clusters: 41, 89, 171, 184, 426

Word	Importance	Part of Speech
get	2	verb
steal	2	verb
accept	3	verb
attract	3	verb

Word	Importance	Part of Speech
capture	3	verb
achieve	4	verb
acquire	4	verb
adopt	4	verb
arrest	4	verb
attain	4	verb
deprive	4	verb
kidnap	4	verb
loot	4	noun
obtain	4	verb
plunder	4	verb
reach	4	verb
reap	4	verb
receive	4	verb
regain	4	verb
rob	4	verb
seize	4	verb
theft	4	noun
trespass	4	verb
abduct	5	verb
extract	5	verb
hijack	5	verb
inherit	5	verb
ransack	5	verb

149. Specific Actions Done With the Hands
Related Clusters: 131, 197

Word	Importance	Part of Speech
point	2	verb
wave	2	verb
clap	3	verb
handshake	3	noun
salute	3	verb
shrug	4	verb
fumble	5	verb
handiwork	5	noun
wield	5	verb

150. Contractions (Have)
Related Clusters: 42, 81, 85, 235, 274

Word	Importance	Part of Speech
I've	2	contraction
they've	2	contraction
we've	3	contraction
you've	3	contraction

151. Facial Expressions
Related Clusters: 152, 196, 241

Word	Importance	Part of Speech
grin	2	noun
smile	2	noun
frown	3	noun
nod	3	noun

continued →

Word	Importance	Part of Speech
blush	4	noun
scowl	4	noun
smirk	4	noun
sneer	4	noun

152. Actions Associated With the Mouth

Related Clusters: 151, 196, 241

Word	Importance	Part of Speech
kiss	2	verb
suck	2	verb
lick	3	verb
spit	3	verb
spew	5	verb

153. Candy and Sweets

Related Clusters: 48, 51, 74, 86, 124, 136, 162, 174, 176, 208, 222, 232, 246

Word	Importance	Part of Speech
cake	2	noun
candy	2	noun
cookie	2	noun
cupcake	2	noun
doughnut	2	noun
gum	2	noun
honey	2	noun
jam	2	noun
pie	2	noun
pudding	2	noun

Word	Importance	Part of Speech
syrup	2	noun
brownie	3	noun
butterscotch	3	noun
caramel	3	noun
chocolate	3	noun
cocoa	3	noun
fudge	3	noun
licorice	3	noun
lollipop	3	noun
marshmallow	3	noun
sherbet	3	noun
sundae	3	noun
vanilla	3	noun
lozenge	4	noun
marmalade	4	noun
molasses	4	noun
pastry	4	noun
patty	4	noun
peppermint	4	noun
popover	4	noun
spearmint	4	noun
taffy	4	noun
tart	4	noun
toffee	4	noun
bonbon	5	noun
shortcake	5	noun
wafer	5	noun

154. Learning and Teaching
Related Clusters: 46, 67, 132, 137, 225, 249, 277, 347, 348, 349, 384

Word	Importance	Part of Speech
coach	2	verb
direction	2	noun
know	2	verb
learn	2	verb
teach	2	verb
understand	2	verb
advice	3	noun
comprehend	3	verb
confuse	3	verb
discover	3	verb
information	3	noun
instruct	3	verb
outsmart	3	verb
study	3	verb
suggest	3	verb
trick	3	verb
complicate	4	verb
decoy	4	noun
educate	4	verb
fake	4	verb
input	4	verb
realize	4	verb
suggestion	4	noun
breakthrough	5	noun
confound	5	verb
glean	5	verb

Word	Importance	Part of Speech
lore	5	noun
mystify	5	verb
outwit	5	verb

155. Parts of Animals
Related Clusters: 32, 35, 64, 65, 70, 82, 95, 117, 188, 189, 194, 309, 310, 341

Word	Importance	Part of Speech
feather	2	noun
fur	2	noun
hide	2	noun
paw	2	noun
tail	2	noun
whisker	2	noun
beak	3	noun
bill	3	noun
claw	3	noun
fin	3	noun
flipper	3	noun
hoof	3	noun
snout	3	noun
antenna	4	noun
antler	4	noun
bristle	4	noun
gill	4	noun
pelt	4	noun
plume	4	noun
pouch	4	noun

continued →

Word	Importance	Part of Speech
quill	4	noun
cud	5	noun
fleece	5	noun
ivory	5	noun
mane	5	noun
rawhide	5	noun
talon	5	noun
tusk	5	noun

156. Noises That People Make
Related Clusters: 84, 103, 165, 175

Word	Importance	Part of Speech
cheer	2	verb
cry	2	verb
laugh	2	verb
roar	2	verb
shout	2	verb
sing	2	verb
whisper	2	verb
yell	2	verb
applause	3	noun
chuckle	3	verb
cough	3	verb
giggle	3	verb
holler	3	verb
laughter	3	noun
scream	3	verb
snore	3	verb
whistle	3	verb

Word	Importance	Part of Speech
yawn	3	verb
applaud	4	verb
babble	4	verb
bawl	4	verb
belch	4	verb
burp	4	verb
burr	4	verb
chant	4	verb
gasp	4	verb
groan	4	verb
gulp	4	verb
hiccup	4	verb
hum	4	verb
moan	4	verb
mumble	4	verb
murmur	4	verb
mutter	4	verb
ruckus	4	noun
rumpus	4	noun
screech	4	verb
shriek	4	verb
sigh	4	verb
snicker	4	verb
sob	4	verb
squeal	4	verb
stammer	4	verb
stutter	4	verb
uproar	4	noun
wail	4	verb
weep	4	verb

Word	Importance	Part of Speech
wheeze	4	verb
whimper	4	verb
whine	4	verb
whoop	4	verb
yodel	4	verb
bellow	5	verb
blurt	5	verb
fracas	5	noun
ovation	5	noun
rant	5	verb
rave	5	verb
titter	5	verb

157. Body Coverings and Marks
Related Clusters: 75, 76, 80, 115, 140, 160, 191, 213, 336, 437

Word	Importance	Part of Speech
bump	2	noun
hair	2	noun
rash	2	noun
skin	2	noun
bald	3	adjective
beard	3	noun
bruise	3	noun
freckle	3	noun
pigtail	3	noun
scar	3	noun
birthmark	4	noun
blubber	4	noun

Word	Importance	Part of Speech
complexion	4	noun
dandruff	4	noun
flesh	4	noun
hairline	4	noun
hump	4	noun
lump	4	noun
mustache	4	noun
pimple	4	noun
pore	4	noun
ruddy	4	adjective
scalp	4	noun
sideburns	4	noun
suntan	4	noun
tissue	4	noun
tumor	4	noun
wart	4	noun
wig	4	noun
blackhead	5	noun
blemish	5	noun
cowlick	5	noun
dermis	5	noun
membrane	5	noun
pock	5	noun
tuft	5	noun

158. Recreation/Sports Equipment
Related Clusters: 143, 183, 209, 304, 370

Word	Importance	Part of Speech
ball	2	noun
bat	2	noun
glove	2	noun
swing	2	verb
base	3	noun
goal	3	noun
net	3	noun
softball	3	noun
touchdown	3	noun
arcade	4	noun
carousel	4	noun
defense	4	noun
dumbbell	4	noun
inning	4	noun
knockout	4	noun
maypole	4	noun
offense	4	noun
out	4	noun
puck	4	noun
putter	4	verb
racket	4	noun
ski	4	verb
tackle	4	verb
target	4	noun
tee	4	noun
trampoline	4	noun
trapeze	4	noun

Word	Importance	Part of Speech
volley	4	noun
bunt	5	verb
homer	5	noun
hurdle	5	noun
javelin	5	noun
reel	5	noun

159. Vehicles (Sea Transportation)
Related Clusters: 93, 97, 120, 128, 234, 318, 331

Word	Importance	Part of Speech
boat	2	noun
canoe	2	noun
ship	2	noun
raft	3	noun
submarine	3	noun
tugboat	3	noun
yacht	3	noun
ark	4	noun
battleship	4	noun
carrier	4	noun
ferry	4	noun
kayak	4	noun
lifeboat	4	noun
liner	4	noun
motorboat	4	noun
shipwreck	4	noun
tug	4	noun

Word	Importance	Part of Speech
vessel	4	noun
barge	5	noun
cutter	5	noun
dinghy	5	noun
flagship	5	noun
schooner	5	noun

160. The Body (General)
Related Clusters: 75, 76, 80, 115, 140, 157, 191, 213, 336, 437

Word	Importance	Part of Speech
body	2	noun
lap	2	noun
neck	2	noun
belly	3	noun
chest	3	noun
hip	3	noun
waist	3	noun
breast	4	noun
limbs	4	noun
mental	4	adjective
physical	4	adjective
rump	4	noun
thorax	4	noun
trunk	4	noun
udder	4	noun
vertebrate	4	adjective
bosom	5	noun
nape	5	noun

Word	Importance	Part of Speech
organ	5	noun
scruff	5	noun

161. Actions Harmful to Humans
Related Clusters: 110, 250, 260

Word	Importance	Part of Speech
hurt	2	verb
kill	2	verb
punish	2	verb
harm	3	verb
injure	3	verb
murder	3	verb
shoot	3	verb
abuse	4	verb
ambush	4	verb
attack	4	verb
deadly	4	adverb
discipline	4	verb
fatal	4	adjective
offend	4	verb
overwhelm	4	verb
painful	4	adjective
paralyze	4	verb
penalty	4	noun
poisonous	4	adjective
scourge	4	verb
slaughter	4	verb
slay	4	verb

continued →

Word	Importance	Part of Speech
stun	4	verb
suicide	4	noun
toxic	4	adjective
vengeance	4	noun
afflict	5	verb
assault	5	noun
beset	5	verb
cripple	5	verb
execute	5	verb
massacre	5	verb
molest	5	verb
persecute	5	verb
prosecute	5	verb
rape	5	verb
torment	5	verb
torture	5	verb
violate	5	verb

162. Food-Related Actions

Related Clusters: 48, 51, 74, 86, 124, 136, 153, 174, 176, 208, 222, 232, 246

Word	Importance	Part of Speech
bake	2	verb
boil	2	verb
cook	2	verb
barbecue	3	verb
broil	3	verb
fry	3	verb
grill	3	verb

Word	Importance	Part of Speech
roast	3	verb
serve	3	verb
brew	4	verb
churn	4	verb
cookout	4	noun
decay	4	verb
knead	4	verb
poach	4	verb
rot	4	verb
sift	4	verb
spoil	4	verb
deteriorate	5	verb
scald	5	verb
simmer	5	verb
taint	5	verb

163. Cutting Tools

Related Clusters: 92, 96, 118, 119, 242, 254, 275, 276, 314, 315, 316, 419, 420

Word	Importance	Part of Speech
ax	2	noun
knife	2	noun
scissors	2	noun
axe	3	noun
blade	3	noun
lawnmower	3	noun
pocketknife	3	noun
clipper	4	noun
hatchet	4	noun

Word	Importance	Part of Speech
jackknife	4	noun
razor	4	noun
straightedge	4	noun
barb	5	noun
scythe	5	noun
sickle	5	noun

164. Containers
Related Clusters: 107, 181, 251, 268, 325, 367

Word	Importance	Part of Speech
bag	2	noun
basket	2	noun
bath	2	noun
bathtub	2	noun
bottle	2	noun
box	2	noun
bucket	2	noun
jar	2	noun
barrel	3	noun
coffeepot	3	noun
container	3	noun
crate	3	noun
folder	3	noun
hamper	3	noun
jug	3	noun
package	3	noun
pail	3	noun
pitcher	3	noun

Word	Importance	Part of Speech
sack	3	noun
suitcase	3	noun
tub	3	noun
baggage	4	noun
basin	4	noun
canteen	4	noun
capsule	4	noun
cargo	4	noun
carton	4	noun
cartridge	4	noun
case	4	noun
cask	4	noun
coffin	4	noun
compartment	4	noun
cubbyhole	4	noun
envelope	4	noun
flask	4	noun
freight	4	noun
holder	4	noun
hopper	4	noun
keg	4	noun
luggage	4	noun
packet	4	noun
parcel	4	noun
shipment	4	noun
tank	4	noun
tinderbox	4	noun
trough	4	noun
vat	4	noun

continued →

Word	Importance	Part of Speech
water bottle	4	noun
bin	5	noun
cistern	5	noun
gourd	5	noun
knapsack	5	noun
rack	5	noun
socket	5	noun
valise	5	noun
washtub	5	noun

165. Noises That Objects Make
Related Clusters: 84, 103, 156, 175

Word	Importance	Part of Speech
bang	2	noun
beep	2	noun
boom	2	noun
ring	2	noun
tick	2	noun
click	3	noun
creak	3	noun
plop	3	noun
rattle	3	noun
slam	3	noun
squeak	3	noun
toot	3	noun
zoom	3	noun
chug	4	noun
clang	4	noun
clank	4	noun

Word	Importance	Part of Speech
clink	4	noun
clop	4	noun
crunch	4	noun
fizz	4	noun
gurgle	4	noun
jingle	4	noun
ping	4	noun
plunk	4	noun
rustle	4	noun
swish	4	noun
thud	4	noun
thump	4	noun
ting	4	noun
tinkle	4	noun
twang	4	noun
wail	4	noun
whir	4	noun
whoosh	4	noun
jangle	5	noun

166. Mathematical Operations
Related Clusters: 340, 410, 423

Word	Importance	Part of Speech
add	2	verb
count	2	verb
minus	2	preposition
plus	2	preposition
subtract	2	verb

Word	Importance	Part of Speech
addition	3	noun
cube	3	verb
divide	3	verb
division	3	noun
multiplication	3	noun
multiply	3	verb
subtraction	3	noun
divisible	4	noun
per	4	preposition
times	4	noun
tally	5	verb

167. Performers and Entertainers
Related Clusters: 68, 88, 146, 173, 229, 236, 257, 264, 265, 266, 297, 333, 334, 355, 356, 357, 358, 359, 360, 361, 392, 393, 394, 395, 396, 397, 436

Word	Importance	Part of Speech
clown	2	noun
dancer	2	noun
actor	3	noun
actress	3	noun
magician	3	noun
model	3	noun
comic	4	noun
performer	4	noun
ventriloquist	4	noun

168. Hills and Mountains
Related Clusters: 50, 114, 139, 267, 362, 363, 398

Word	Importance	Part of Speech
hill	2	noun
mountain	2	noun
cliff	3	noun
hillside	3	noun
mound	3	noun
bluff	4	noun
butte	4	noun
crag	4	noun
dune	4	noun
foothill	4	noun
hilltop	4	noun
mountainside	4	noun
mountaintop	4	noun
plateau	4	noun
range	4	noun
ridge	4	noun
sierra	4	noun
slope	4	noun
volcano	4	noun
crest	5	noun
embankment	5	noun
knoll	5	noun
mesa	5	noun
watershed	5	noun

169. Lack of Motion

Related Clusters: 38, 39, 40, 44, 66, 141, 147, 170, 182, 199, 215, 216, 247, 280, 281, 282, 283, 300, 301, 302, 322, 338, 403

Word	Importance	Part of Speech
rest	2	verb
stay	2	verb
delay	3	verb
pause	3	verb
relax	3	verb
remain	3	verb
wait	3	verb
await	4	verb
dangle	4	verb
deadlock	4	noun
hang	4	verb
hesitate	4	verb
interrupt	4	verb
intervene	4	verb
lag	4	verb
linger	4	verb
lounge	4	verb
motionless	4	adjective
postpone	4	verb
procrastinate	4	verb
putter	4	verb
settle	4	verb
standstill	4	noun
static	4	adjective
suspension	4	noun
waylay	4	verb

Word	Importance	Part of Speech
detain	5	verb
falter	5	verb
hinder	5	verb
hover	5	verb
inert	5	adjective
probation	5	noun
stationary	5	adjective
suspend	5	verb

170. Descending Motion

Related Clusters: 38, 39, 40, 44, 66, 141, 147, 169, 182, 199, 215, 216, 247, 280, 281, 282, 283, 300, 301, 302, 322, 338, 403

Word	Importance	Part of Speech
lie	2	verb
sit	2	verb
crouch	3	verb
kneel	3	verb
squat	3	verb
flop	4	verb
sprawl	4	verb
stoop	4	verb

171. Finding/Keeping

Related Clusters: 41, 89, 148, 184, 426

Word	Importance	Part of Speech
find	2	verb
keep	2	verb
bury	3	verb

Word	Importance	Part of Speech
hide	3	verb
spot	3	verb
conceal	4	verb
conserve	4	verb
disguise	4	verb
distinguish	4	verb
locate	4	verb
masquerade	4	verb
reserve	4	verb
tuck	4	verb
withhold	4	verb
camouflage	5	noun
hoard	5	verb
pinpoint	5	verb
restrict	5	verb
retain	5	verb

172. Locations Where People Might Live
Related Cluster: 180

Word	Importance	Part of Speech
city	2	noun
neighborhood	2	noun
state	2	noun
town	2	noun
village	2	noun
camp	3	noun
county	3	noun
downtown	3	noun

Word	Importance	Part of Speech
ghetto	3	noun
heaven	3	noun
slum	3	noun
suburb	3	noun
birthplace	4	noun
capital	4	noun
colony	4	noun
empire	4	noun
hell	4	noun
homeland	4	noun
kingdom	4	noun
outskirts	4	noun
province	4	noun
resort	4	noun
spa	4	noun
underworld	4	noun
district	5	noun
metropolis	5	noun
paradise	5	noun
wonderland	5	noun

173. Royalty and Statesmen
Related Clusters: 68, 88, 146, 167, 229, 236, 257, 264, 265, 266, 297, 333, 334, 355, 356, 357, 358, 359, 360, 361, 392, 393, 394, 395, 396, 397, 436

Word	Importance	Part of Speech
king	2	noun
mayor	2	noun
president	2	noun

continued →

Word	Importance	Part of Speech
candidate	3	noun
knight	3	noun
official	3	noun
prince	3	noun
princess	3	noun
queen	3	noun
ambassador	4	noun
chief	4	noun
dictator	4	noun
duchess	4	noun
duke	4	noun
earl	4	noun
lord	4	noun
monarch	4	noun
politician	4	noun
senator	4	noun
sire	4	noun
sultan	4	noun
vice president	4	noun
baron	5	noun
congressman	5	noun
congresswoman	5	noun
councilman	5	noun
councilwoman	5	noun
czar	5	noun
delegate	5	noun
diplomat	5	noun
figurehead	5	noun
nobleman	5	noun
prefect	5	noun

Word	Importance	Part of Speech
squire	5	noun
statesman	5	noun
tribune	5	noun

174. Fruits
Related Clusters: 48, 51, 74, 86, 124, 136, 153, 162, 176, 208, 222, 232, 246

Word	Importance	Part of Speech
apple	2	noun
banana	2	noun
cherry	2	noun
grape	2	noun
orange	2	noun
peach	2	noun
pear	2	noun
strawberry	2	noun
avocado	3	noun
berry	3	noun
blueberry	3	noun
coconut	3	noun
cranberry	3	noun
grapefruit	3	noun
lemon	3	noun
melon	3	noun
pineapple	3	noun
plum	3	noun
prune	3	noun
raisin	3	noun
raspberry	3	noun

Word	Importance	Part of Speech
applesauce	4	noun
apricot	4	noun
fig	4	noun
honeydew	4	noun
lime	4	noun
tangerine	4	noun
watermelon	4	noun

175. Noises That Animals Make
Related Clusters: 84, 103, 156, 165

Word	Importance	Part of Speech
bark	2	noun
buzz	2	noun
meow	2	noun
moo	2	noun
baa	3	noun
cluck	3	noun
gobble	3	noun
growl	3	noun
peep	3	noun
purr	3	noun
quack	3	noun
bleat	4	noun
cackle	4	noun
caw	4	noun
cheep	4	noun
chirp	4	noun
croak	4	noun

Word	Importance	Part of Speech
grunt	4	noun
hiss	4	noun
honk	4	noun
hoot	4	noun
howl	4	noun
snarl	4	noun
snort	4	noun
squawk	4	noun
whinny	4	noun
yap	4	noun
yelp	4	noun
yip	4	noun
yowl	4	noun
bray	5	noun
neigh	5	noun
warble	5	noun

176. Drinks
Related Clusters: 48, 51, 74, 86, 124, 136, 153, 162, 174, 208, 222, 232, 246

Word	Importance	Part of Speech
juice	2	noun
milk	2	noun
pop	2	noun
soup	2	noun
beer	3	noun
chili	3	noun
coffee	3	noun
soda	3	noun

continued →

Word	Importance	Part of Speech
stew	3	noun
tea	3	noun
wine	3	noun
alcohol	4	noun
broth	4	noun
chowder	4	noun
cider	4	noun
nectar	4	noun
beverage	5	noun
champagne	5	noun
gin	5	noun
liquor	5	noun
moonshine	5	noun
whiskey	5	noun

177. Questioning
Related Clusters: 14, 61, 100, 105, 198, 207, 255, 345, 346, 383

Word	Importance	Part of Speech
answer	2	verb
ask	2	verb
call	2	verb
offer	3	verb
question	3	verb
reply	3	verb
request	3	verb
respond	3	verb
test	3	verb
bid	4	verb

Word	Importance	Part of Speech
consult	4	verb
inquire	4	verb
interview	4	verb
invite	4	verb
poll	4	verb
quiz	4	verb
beckon	5	verb
confer	5	verb
propose	5	verb

178. Fabrics
Related Clusters: 47, 62, 125, 129, 145, 212, 224, 263, 354, 435

Word	Importance	Part of Speech
cloth	2	noun
rag	2	noun
thread	2	noun
cotton	3	noun
lace	3	noun
leather	3	noun
nylon	3	noun
silk	3	noun
wool	3	noun
calico	4	noun
denim	4	noun
fabric	4	noun
fiber	4	noun
flannel	4	noun
linen	4	noun

Word	Importance	Part of Speech
satin	4	noun
skein	4	noun
suede	4	noun
terry	4	noun
textile	4	noun
texture	4	noun
tint	4	noun
velvet	4	noun
yarn	4	noun
buckskin	5	noun
dry goods	5	noun
felt	5	noun
gauze	5	noun
homespun	5	noun
khaki	5	noun

179. Recreational Events and Festivals

Related Clusters: 412, 413

Word	Importance	Part of Speech
birthday	2	noun
party	2	noun
recess	2	noun
circus	3	noun
date	3	noun
fair	3	noun
holiday	3	noun
parade	3	noun
vacation	3	noun

Word	Importance	Part of Speech
amusement	4	noun
anniversary	4	noun
caravan	4	noun
carnival	4	noun
ceremony	4	noun
festival	4	noun
honeymoon	4	noun
masquerade	4	noun
pageant	4	noun
pastime	4	noun
procession	4	noun
prom	4	noun
rodeo	4	noun
bazaar	5	noun
debut	5	noun
leisure	5	noun

180. Countries and Continents

Related Cluster: 172

Word	Importance	Part of Speech
country	2	noun
nation	2	noun
continent	3	noun
equator	3	noun
hemisphere	3	noun
nationwide	4	adjective
sovereign	4	noun

181. Wooden Building Materials
Related Clusters: 107, 164, 251, 268, 325, 367

Word	Importance	Part of Speech
stick	2	noun
wood	2	noun
board	3	noun
log	3	noun
post	3	noun
timber	3	noun
lumber	4	noun
panel	4	noun
pillar	4	noun
plywood	4	noun
shingle	4	noun
slat	4	noun
basswood	5	noun
palette	5	noun
veneer	5	noun

182. Pulling and Pushing
Related Clusters: 38, 39, 40, 44, 66, 141, 147, 169, 170, 199, 215, 216, 247, 280, 281, 282, 283, 300, 301, 302, 322, 338, 403

Word	Importance	Part of Speech
pull	2	verb
push	2	verb
drag	3	verb

Word	Importance	Part of Speech
haul	3	verb
shove	3	verb
yank	3	verb
gravity	4	noun
insert	4	verb
propel	4	verb
tow	4	verb
inject	5	verb
lug	5	verb

183. Recreation and Sports
Related Clusters: 143, 158, 209, 304, 370

Word	Importance	Part of Speech
game	2	noun
recess	2	noun
contest	3	noun
race	3	noun
recreation	3	noun
sport	3	noun
compete	4	verb
competition	4	noun
hobby	4	noun
match	4	noun
derby	5	noun
marathon	5	noun
tournament	5	noun

184. Giving Up/Losing
Related Clusters: 41, 89, 148, 171, 426

Word	Importance	Part of Speech
show	2	verb
trade	2	verb
borrow	3	verb
lose	3	verb
loser	3	noun
share	3	verb
abandon	4	verb
dismiss	4	verb
displace	4	verb
dispose	4	verb
exchange	4	verb
lease	4	verb
lend	4	verb
loan	4	verb
swap	4	verb
alternate	5	verb
barter	5	verb
discard	5	verb
eject	5	verb

185. Cleanliness/Hygiene
Related Clusters: 223, 288

Word	Importance	Part of Speech
clean	2	verb
wipe	2	verb
rinse	3	verb
scrub	3	verb

Word	Importance	Part of Speech
sweep	3	verb
wash	3	verb
bathe	4	verb
buff	4	verb
cleanliness	4	noun
filter	4	verb
haircut	4	noun
manicure	4	noun
pasteurize	4	verb
polish	4	verb
sterile	4	adjective
strain	4	verb
turnout	4	verb
wax	4	verb
hygiene	5	noun
immaculate	5	adjective
preen	5	verb
purge	5	verb
purify	5	verb
scour	5	verb
swab	5	verb

186. Attractiveness
Related Clusters: 187, 253, 407

Word	Importance	Part of Speech
pretty	2	adjective
ugly	2	adjective
beautiful	3	adjective
cute	3	adjective

continued →

Word	Importance	Part of Speech
handsome	3	adjective
lovely	3	adjective
adorable	4	adjective
attractive	4	adjective
breathtaking	4	adjective
elegant	4	adjective
formal	4	adjective
homely	4	adjective
sightly	4	adjective
unattractive	4	adjective
bonny	5	adjective
classic	5	adjective
exquisite	5	adjective
gorgeous	5	adjective
hideous	5	adjective
sleek	5	adjective

187. Physical Trait (Size)
Related Clusters: 186, 253, 407

Word	Importance	Part of Speech
fat	2	adjective
heavy	2	adjective
chubby	3	adjective
lean	3	adjective
skinny	3	adjective
slim	3	adjective
husky	4	adjective
obese	4	adjective
plump	4	adjective

Word	Importance	Part of Speech
pudgy	4	adjective
slender	4	adjective
slight	4	adjective
burly	5	adjective
dainty	5	adjective
scrag	5	noun
stout	5	adjective

188. Rodents
Related Clusters: 32, 35, 64, 65, 70, 82, 95, 117, 155, 189, 194, 309, 310, 341

Word	Importance	Part of Speech
mouse	2	noun
squirrel	2	noun
beaver	3	noun
groundhog	3	noun
hamster	3	noun
rat	3	noun
chipmunk	4	noun
muskrat	4	noun
otter	4	noun
porcupine	4	noun
woodchuck	4	noun
rodent	5	noun

189. Dwellings for Animals
Related Clusters: 32, 35, 64, 65, 70, 82, 95, 117, 155, 188, 194, 309, 310, 341

Word	Importance	Part of Speech
nest	2	noun
zoo	2	noun
aquarium	3	noun
beehive	3	noun
birdhouse	3	noun
cocoon	3	noun
hive	3	noun
coop	4	noun
corral	4	noun
kennel	4	noun
roost	4	noun
stable	4	noun
stall	4	noun
honeycomb	5	noun
lair	5	noun
perch	5	noun

190. Places Related to Sports/ Entertainment
Related Clusters: 60, 106, 121, 210, 321, 324, 335, 364, 365, 366, 399, 400

Word	Importance	Part of Speech
theater	2	noun
court	3	noun
gym	3	noun
stadium	3	noun

Word	Importance	Part of Speech
arena	4	noun
auditorium	4	noun
coliseum	4	noun
grandstand	4	noun
opera	4	noun
playhouse	4	noun
rink	4	noun

191. Body Fluids
Related Clusters: 75, 76, 80, 115, 140, 157, 160, 213, 336, 437

Word	Importance	Part of Speech
blood	2	noun
bleed	3	verb
sweat	3	verb
artery	4	noun
clot	4	noun
pus	4	noun
saliva	4	noun
sperm	4	noun
vein	4	noun
vessel	4	noun
capillary	5	noun
circulate	5	verb
hemoglobin	5	noun
mucus	5	noun
perspiration	5	noun
ventricle	5	noun

192. Vegetation (Other)
Related Clusters: 36, 108, 269, 421

Word	Importance	Part of Speech
grass	2	noun
lawn	3	noun
root	3	noun
vine	3	noun
bamboo	4	noun
clover	4	noun
cob	4	noun
fern	4	noun
fungus	4	noun
hay	4	noun
husk	4	noun
kelp	4	noun
mildew	4	noun
moss	4	noun
mushroom	4	noun
ragweed	4	noun
reed	4	noun
rind	4	noun
seaweed	4	noun
stalk	4	noun
straw	4	noun
thatch	4	noun
toadstool	4	noun
alfalfa	5	noun
algae	5	noun
cattail	5	noun
lichen	5	noun

193. Inclination
Related Clusters: 69, 99, 142, 218, 270, 303, 326

Word	Importance	Part of Speech
flat	2	adjective
even	3	adjective
lean	3	verb
level	3	adjective
steep	3	adjective
incline	4	noun
plumb	4	adjective
slant	4	verb
tilt	4	verb
erect	5	adjective

194. Animals (General)
Related Clusters: 32, 35, 64, 65, 70, 82, 95, 117, 155, 188, 189, 309, 310, 341

Word	Importance	Part of Speech
animal	2	noun
pet	3	noun
wildlife	3	noun
beast	4	noun
carnivorous	4	adjective
creature	4	noun
fossil	4	noun
mammal	4	noun
mascot	4	noun
amphibian	5	noun
prey	5	noun

195. Visual Perceptions and Images
Related Cluster: 135

Word	Importance	Part of Speech
appearance	3	noun
badge	3	noun
flag	3	noun
image	3	noun
scene	3	noun
sight	3	noun
view	3	noun
demonstration	4	noun
display	4	noun
emblem	4	noun
identify	4	verb
observer	4	noun
panorama	4	noun
reflect	4	verb
reflection	4	noun
represent	4	verb
reveal	4	verb
visible	4	adjective
vision	4	noun
visual	4	noun
witness	4	verb
distract	5	verb
flaunt	5	verb
phenomenon	5	noun
portray	5	verb
prospect	5	noun
scope	5	noun

196. Breathing
Related Clusters: 151, 152, 241

Word	Importance	Part of Speech
blow	2	verb
breath	3	noun
choke	3	verb
exhale	3	verb
pant	4	verb
puff	4	verb
strangle	4	verb
whiff	4	noun
respire	5	verb

197. Feeling and Striking
Related Clusters: 131, 149

Word	Importance	Part of Speech
hit	2	verb
slap	2	verb
spank	2	verb
touch	2	verb
beat	3	verb
feel	3	verb
knock	3	verb
pat	3	verb
pound	3	verb
punch	3	verb
smash	3	verb
tap	3	verb
tickle	3	verb
buffet	4	verb

continued →

Word	Importance	Part of Speech
butt	4	verb
dab	4	verb
grope	4	verb
jab	4	verb
knead	4	verb
lash	4	verb
lob	4	verb
nudge	4	verb
poke	4	verb
pulse	4	noun
rap	4	verb
smack	4	verb
spur	4	verb
strike	4	verb
stroke	4	verb
thrash	4	verb
whack	4	verb
wham	4	verb
whop	4	verb
caress	5	verb
fondle	5	verb
massage	5	verb
prod	5	verb
putt	5	verb
wallop	5	verb

198. Communication (Confrontation/Negative Information)

Related Clusters: 14, 61, 100, 105, 177, 207, 255, 345, 346, 383

Word	Importance	Part of Speech
blame	2	verb
cheat	2	verb
lie	2	verb
accuse	3	verb
argue	3	verb
complain	3	verb
dare	3	verb
disagree	3	verb
disobey	3	verb
quarrel	3	noun
scold	3	verb
tease	3	verb
warn	3	verb
annoy	4	verb
betray	4	verb
caution	4	verb
challenge	4	verb
complaint	4	noun
confront	4	verb
controversy	4	noun
criticism	4	noun
criticize	4	verb
curse	4	verb
deceit	4	noun
deceive	4	verb

Word	Importance	Part of Speech
decline	4	verb
delude	4	verb
detract	4	verb
disgrace	4	verb
dispute	4	verb
embarrass	4	verb
exaggerate	4	verb
fib	4	verb
insult	4	verb
mock	4	verb
nag	4	verb
object	4	verb
objection	4	noun
protest	4	verb
rebel	4	verb
revolt	4	verb
ridicule	4	verb
rumor	4	verb
scoff	4	verb
swear	4	verb
taunt	4	verb
threat	4	noun
threaten	4	verb
trial	4	noun
warning	4	noun
cant	5	noun
con	5	verb
condemn	5	verb
damn	5	verb

Word	Importance	Part of Speech
debate	5	verb
defy	5	verb
denounce	5	verb
distort	5	verb
gripe	5	verb
hyperbole	5	noun
jeer	5	verb
menace	5	verb
prophecy	5	noun
reject	5	verb
retort	5	verb
slur	5	verb
spat	5	noun
squabble	5	verb
sue	5	verb

199. Angular and Circular Motions

Related Clusters: 38, 39, 40, 44, 66, 141, 147, 169, 170, 182, 215, 216, 247, 280, 281, 282, 283, 300, 301, 302, 322, 338, 403

Word	Importance	Part of Speech
around	2	preposition
roll	2	verb
turn	2	verb
clockwise	3	adverb
counterclockwise	3	adverb
rotate	3	verb

continued →

Word	Importance	Part of Speech
spin	3	verb
surround	3	verb
swing	3	verb
twirl	3	verb
twist	3	verb
circulation	4	noun
invert	4	verb
orbit	4	noun
pinwheel	4	noun
recoil	4	verb
reverse	4	verb
swirl	4	verb
whirl	4	verb
reciprocal	5	adjective
revolve	5	verb
swerve	5	verb
swivel	5	verb

200. Social and Political Groups
Related Clusters: 98, 258, 298, 401

Word	Importance	Part of Speech
country	2	noun
family	2	noun
community	3	noun
democracy	3	noun
nation	3	noun
race	3	noun
society	3	noun

Word	Importance	Part of Speech
tribe	3	noun
civilization	4	noun
clan	4	noun
congress	4	noun
culture	4	noun
federal	4	adjective
international	4	adjective
jury	4	noun
minority	4	noun
national	4	adjective
parliament	4	noun
republic	4	noun
senate	4	noun
cabinet	5	noun
caste	5	noun
civic	5	adjective
cult	5	noun
regime	5	noun
sect	5	noun

201. Money/Goods (Received)
Related Clusters: 104, 109, 116, 122, 214

Word	Importance	Part of Speech
gift	2	noun
prize	2	noun
award	3	noun
medal	3	noun
reward	3	noun

Word	Importance	Part of Speech
savings	3	noun
treasure	3	noun
allowance	4	noun
bonus	4	noun
contribution	4	noun
credit	4	noun
fortune	4	noun
gain	4	noun
income	4	noun
insurance	4	noun
premium	4	noun
profit	4	noun
salary	4	noun
scholarship	4	noun
trophy	4	noun
wage	4	noun
bounty	5	noun
grant	5	noun
legacy	5	noun
patent	5	noun
refund	5	noun
windfall	5	noun

202. Texture
Related Clusters: 323, 441

Word	Importance	Part of Speech
hard	2	adjective
soft	2	adjective
bumpy	3	adjective

Word	Importance	Part of Speech
firm	3	adjective
rough	3	adjective
smooth	3	adjective
tight	3	adjective
coarse	4	adjective
crisp	4	adjective
rigid	4	adjective
solid	4	adjective
stiff	4	adjective
texture	4	noun
tough	4	adjective
tangible	5	adjective
taut	5	adjective

203. Males
Related Clusters: 56, 94, 111, 204, 205, 206, 227, 317, 330, 343, 344, 382, 432, 444

Word	Importance	Part of Speech
boy	2	noun
man	2	noun
guy	3	noun
hero	3	noun
male	3	noun
schoolboy	3	noun
sir	3	noun
dude	4	noun
fellow	4	noun
host	4	noun
junior	4	noun

continued →

Word	Importance	Part of Speech
lad	4	noun
masculine	4	noun
master	4	noun
mister	4	noun
bachelor	5	noun
señor	5	noun

204. Names That Indicate Age

Related Clusters: 56, 94, 111, 203, 205, 206, 227, 317, 330, 343, 344, 382, 432, 444

Word	Importance	Part of Speech
baby	2	noun
child	2	noun
adult	3	noun
grown-up	3	noun
kid	3	noun
teenager	3	noun
toddler	3	noun
babe	4	noun
elder	4	noun
infant	4	noun
juvenile	4	noun
minor	4	noun
newborn	4	noun
orphan	4	noun
papoose	4	noun
senior	4	noun
tot	4	noun
youngster	4	noun
embryo	5	noun

205. Names That Indicate Camaraderie/Friendship

Related Clusters: 56, 94, 111, 203, 204, 206, 227, 317, 330, 343, 344, 382, 432, 444

Word	Importance	Part of Speech
friend	2	noun
neighbor	2	noun
boyfriend	3	noun
classmate	3	noun
pal	3	noun
partner	3	noun
playmate	3	noun
acquaintance	4	noun
buddy	4	noun
chum	4	noun
companion	4	noun
darling	4	noun
lover	4	noun
mate	4	noun
peer	4	noun
schoolmate	4	noun
sweetheart	4	noun
teammate	4	noun
ally	5	noun
fiancé	5	noun
suitor	5	noun

206. Names That Indicate Negative Characteristics About People

Related Clusters: 56, 94, 111, 203, 204, 205, 227, 317, 330, 343, 344, 382, 432, 444

Word	Importance	Part of Speech
bandit	2	noun
villain	2	noun
bully	3	noun
criminal	3	noun
enemy	3	noun
killer	3	noun
liar	3	noun
pirate	3	noun
thief	3	noun
blockhead	4	noun
brute	4	noun
burglar	4	noun
cad	4	noun
cannibal	4	noun
convict	4	noun
coward	4	noun
crook	4	noun
culprit	4	noun
dope	4	noun
dunce	4	noun
foe	4	noun
fool	4	noun
gossip	4	noun
jailbird	4	noun
opponent	4	noun

Word	Importance	Part of Speech
outlaw	4	noun
pest	4	noun
prey	4	noun
rascal	4	noun
rival	4	noun
rustler	4	noun
scamp	4	noun
slowpoke	4	noun
snob	4	noun
storyteller	4	noun
suspect	4	noun
telltale	4	noun
vandal	4	noun
victim	4	noun
wallflower	4	noun
captive	5	noun
delinquent	5	noun
dolt	5	noun
hostage	5	noun
moron	5	noun
nuisance	5	noun
pickpocket	5	noun
ruffian	5	noun
scoundrel	5	noun
tyrant	5	noun

207. Communication (Supervision/Commands)

Related Clusters: 14, 61, 100, 105, 177, 198, 255, 345, 346, 383

Word	Importance	Part of Speech
correct	2	verb
let	2	verb
obey	2	verb
advice	3	noun
allow	3	verb
command	3	verb
control	3	verb
demand	3	verb
direct	3	verb
direction	3	noun
excuse	3	verb
forbid	3	verb
force	3	verb
permit	3	verb
refuse	3	verb
remind	3	verb
require	3	verb
administer	4	verb
authority	4	noun
ban	4	verb
compel	4	verb
compromise	4	verb
consent	4	verb
counsel	4	verb
deny	4	verb

Word	Importance	Part of Speech
govern	4	verb
input	4	noun
insist	4	verb
instruction	4	noun
leadership	4	noun
license	4	noun
manage	4	verb
reign	4	verb
revoke	4	verb
suggestion	4	noun
taboo	4	noun
veto	4	verb
yield	4	verb
commission	5	verb
conform	5	verb
decree	5	verb
demote	5	verb
enforce	5	verb
manipulate	5	verb
preside	5	verb
regulate	5	verb
reinstate	5	verb
repeal	5	verb
reprimand	5	verb
submit	5	verb
summon	5	verb
supervise	5	verb
suppress	5	verb

208. Vegetables, Grains, and Nuts
Related Clusters: 48, 51, 74, 86, 124, 136, 153, 162, 174, 176, 222, 232, 246

Word	Importance	Part of Speech
carrot	2	noun
corn	2	noun
nut	2	noun
peanut	2	noun
popcorn	2	noun
seed	2	noun
almond	3	noun
bean	3	noun
cashew	3	noun
celery	3	noun
cucumber	3	noun
lettuce	3	noun
olive	3	noun
onion	3	noun
peas	3	noun
pickle	3	noun
potato	3	noun
pumpkin	3	noun
rice	3	noun
spinach	3	noun
squash	3	noun
tomato	3	noun
walnut	3	noun
wheat	3	noun
acorn	4	noun
asparagus	4	noun

Word	Importance	Part of Speech
beet	4	noun
cabbage	4	noun
cauliflower	4	noun
chestnut	4	noun
grain	4	noun
kernel	4	noun
maize	4	noun
malt	4	noun
oats	4	noun
pecan	4	noun
radish	4	noun
soybean	4	noun
turnip	4	noun
barley	5	noun
bran	5	noun
eggplant	5	noun
gourd	5	noun
rye	5	noun
yam	5	noun

209. Sports (Specific Types)
Related Clusters: 143, 158, 183, 304, 370

Word	Importance	Part of Speech
baseball	2	noun
soccer	2	noun
softball	2	noun
swim	2	verb
swimming	2	noun
basketball	3	noun

continued →

Word	Importance	Part of Speech
bicycle	3	noun
bowling	3	noun
boxing	3	noun
football	3	noun
golf	3	noun
hockey	3	noun
racing	3	noun
skating	3	verb
skating	3	noun
skiing	3	noun
skiing	3	verb
tennis	3	noun
volleyball	3	noun
wrestling	3	noun
archery	4	noun
badminton	4	noun
handball	4	noun
lacrosse	4	noun
polo	4	noun
backhand	5	noun
croquet	5	noun
fencing	5	verb
steeplechase	5	noun

210. Places Where Goods Can Be Bought/Sold
Related Clusters: 60, 106, 121, 190, 321, 324, 335, 364, 365, 366, 399, 400

Word	Importance	Part of Speech
grocery	2	noun
store	2	noun
bakery	3	noun
bookstore	3	noun
cafeteria	3	noun
drugstore	3	noun
lunchroom	3	noun
restaurant	3	noun
booth	4	noun
café	4	noun
casino	4	noun
market	4	noun
pharmacy	4	noun
salon	4	noun
saloon	4	noun
supermarket	4	noun
tavern	5	noun

211. Courage and Loyalty
Related Clusters: 228, 278, 294, 295, 332, 350, 351, 385, 386, 387, 388, 389, 429, 433, 434

Word	Importance	Part of Speech
brave	2	adjective
courage	3	noun
heroic	3	adjective

Word	Importance	Part of Speech
honest	3	adjective
loyal	3	adjective
adventurous	4	adjective
allegiance	4	noun
bold	4	adjective
bravery	4	noun
chivalry	4	noun
courageous	4	adjective
devotion	4	noun
gallant	4	adjective
obedience	4	noun
grit	5	noun
valor	5	noun

212. Clothing Parts
Related Clusters: 47, 62, 125, 129, 145, 178, 224, 263, 354, 435

Word	Importance	Part of Speech
button	2	noun
collar	3	noun
sleeve	3	noun
zipper	3	noun
bib	4	noun
cuff	4	noun
frill	4	noun
fringe	4	noun
hem	4	noun
pompom	4	noun
ruff	4	noun

Word	Importance	Part of Speech
ruffle	4	noun
seam	4	noun
tassel	4	noun

213. Muscles, Bones, and Nerves
Related Clusters: 75, 76, 80, 115, 140, 157, 160, 191, 336, 437

Word	Importance	Part of Speech
bone	2	noun
joint	3	noun
muscle	3	noun
skeleton	3	noun
backbone	4	noun
cartilage	4	noun
rib	4	noun
spine	4	noun
ligament	5	noun
nerve	5	noun
sinew	5	noun
tendon	5	noun

214. Money/Goods (Paid Out)
Related Clusters: 104, 109, 116, 122, 201

Word	Importance	Part of Speech
price	2	noun
cost	3	noun
payment	3	noun

continued →

Word	Importance	Part of Speech
rent	3	noun
bail	4	noun
debt	4	noun
fare	4	noun
fee	4	noun
loss	4	noun
product	4	noun
tab	4	noun
tax	4	noun
taxation	4	noun
toll	4	noun
tuition	4	noun
interest	5	noun
levy	5	noun
mortgage	5	noun
tariff	5	noun

215. Completion

Related Clusters: 38, 39, 40, 44, 66, 141, 147, 169, 170, 182, 199, 216, 247, 280, 281, 282, 283, 300, 301, 302, 322, 338, 403

Word	Importance	Part of Speech
end	2	verb
complete	3	verb
finish	3	verb
last	3	adjective
accomplish	4	verb
completion	4	noun
deadline	4	noun

Word	Importance	Part of Speech
deed	4	noun
final	4	adjective
graduate	4	verb
fulfill	5	verb

216. Shifting Motion

Related Clusters: 38, 39, 40, 44, 66, 141, 147, 169, 170, 182, 199, 215, 247, 280, 281, 282, 283, 300, 301, 302, 322, 338, 403

Word	Importance	Part of Speech
slip	2	verb
rock	3	verb
skid	3	verb
slide	3	verb
shift	4	verb
sway	4	verb

217. Fences and Ledges

Related Clusters: 91, 113, 123, 134, 284

Word	Importance	Part of Speech
gate	2	noun
fence	3	noun
mailbox	3	noun
shelf	3	noun
curb	4	noun
gutter	4	noun
hedge	4	noun
ledge	4	noun

Word	Importance	Part of Speech
screen	4	noun
trellis	5	noun

218. Crookedness/ Straightness
Related Clusters: 69, 99, 142, 193, 270, 303, 326

Word	Importance	Part of Speech
line	2	noun
bent	3	adjective
crooked	3	adjective
cross	3	noun
straight	3	adjective
stripe	3	noun
strip	4	noun
zigzag	4	noun
beeline	5	noun
crisscross	5	noun

219. Alphabet and Letters
Related Clusters: 238, 286

Word	Importance	Part of Speech
alphabet	2	noun
consonant	3	noun
letter	3	noun
symbol	3	noun
vowel	3	noun
alphabetically	4	adverb
Braille	4	noun

Word	Importance	Part of Speech
code	4	noun
alpha	5	noun
beta	5	noun
cuneiform	5	noun
italics	5	noun

220. Fire
Related Clusters: 78, 376, 414, 442

Word	Importance	Part of Speech
fire	2	noun
burn	3	verb
campfire	3	noun
flame	3	noun
spark	3	noun
blaze	4	noun
bonfire	4	noun
ignite	4	verb
scorch	4	verb
singe	4	verb
stoke	4	verb
torch	4	noun
wildfire	4	noun
arson	5	noun
backfire	5	noun
combustion	5	noun
inferno	5	noun
kindle	5	verb
sizzle	5	verb
smolder	5	verb

221. Ease and Difficulty
Related Clusters: 240

Word	Importance	Part of Speech
easy	2	adjective
difficult	3	adjective
impossible	3	adjective
problem	3	noun
cinch	4	noun
comfortable	4	adjective
convenient	4	adjective
difficulty	4	noun
ease	4	noun
simplify	4	verb
tiresome	4	adjective
troublesome	4	adjective
unbearable	4	adjective
uneasy	4	adjective
fluent	5	adjective
grueling	5	adjective
hardship	5	adjective
predicament	5	noun

222. Tastes Related to Food
Related Clusters: 48, 51, 74, 86, 124, 136, 153, 162, 174, 176, 208, 232, 246

Word	Importance	Part of Speech
taste	2	noun
flavor	3	noun
juicy	3	adjective
ripe	3	adjective
sour	3	adjective
sweet	3	adjective
tasty	3	adjective
bitter	4	adjective
delicious	4	adjective
edible	4	adjective
stale	4	adjective
savor	5	verb
succulent	5	adjective
tangy	5	adjective

223. Cleaning Tools
Related Clusters: 185, 288

Word	Importance	Part of Speech
brush	2	noun
soap	2	noun
broomstick	3	noun
floss	3	noun
mop	3	noun
shampoo	3	noun
sponge	3	noun
suds	3	noun
toothbrush	3	noun
toothpaste	3	noun
broom	4	noun
cleaner	4	noun
detergent	4	noun
lather	4	noun

Word	Importance	Part of Speech
lotion	4	noun
toothpick	4	noun
vacuum	4	noun
bleach	5	noun
lye	5	noun

224. Clothing and Grooming Accessories
Related Clusters: 47, 62, 125, 129, 145, 178, 212, 263, 354, 435

Word	Importance	Part of Speech
brush	2	noun
comb	2	noun
handkerchief	2	noun
buckle	3	noun
fan	3	noun
jewelry	3	noun
kerchief	3	noun
necklace	3	noun
perfume	3	noun
pin	3	noun
ribbon	3	noun
ring	3	noun
scarf	3	noun
tie	3	noun
umbrella	3	noun
bead	4	noun
bracelet	4	noun
cane	4	noun

Word	Importance	Part of Speech
cologne	4	noun
garland	4	noun
lipstick	4	noun
locket	4	noun
makeup	4	noun
muffler	4	noun
necktie	4	noun
parasol	4	noun
razor	4	noun
sash	4	noun
suspender	4	noun
trinket	4	noun
bandanna	5	noun
corsage	5	noun
cosmetics	5	noun
pendant	5	noun
scepter	5	noun
sequin	5	noun

225. Mental Exploration
Related Clusters: 46, 67, 132, 137, 154, 249, 277, 347, 348, 349, 384

Word	Importance	Part of Speech
news	2	noun
search	2	verb
analyze	3	verb
exam	3	noun
experiment	3	noun
explore	3	verb

continued →

Word	Importance	Part of Speech
homework	3	noun
investigate	3	verb
lesson	3	noun
schoolwork	3	noun
inspect	4	verb
inspection	4	noun
probe	4	verb
research	4	noun
review	4	verb
survey	4	noun
hypothesis	5	noun
imprint	5	verb
rummage	5	verb

226. Wind and Storms
Related Clusters: 90, 307, 375, 406

Word	Importance	Part of Speech
storm	2	noun
thunder	2	noun
blizzard	3	noun
downpour	3	noun
draft	3	noun
hurricane	3	noun
lightning	3	noun
thunderstorm	3	noun
tornado	3	noun
wind	3	noun
breeze	4	noun

Word	Importance	Part of Speech
cyclone	4	noun
gale	4	noun
gust	4	noun
monsoon	4	noun
rainstorm	4	noun
snowstorm	4	noun
squall	4	noun
tempest	4	noun
thunderbolt	4	noun
twister	4	noun
windstorm	4	noun
Chinook	5	noun
torrent	5	noun
typhoon	5	noun

227. Names for Spiritual/ Mythological Characters
Related Clusters: 56, 94, 111, 203, 204, 205, 206, 317, 330, 343, 344, 382, 432, 444

Word	Importance	Part of Speech
angel	2	noun
god	2	noun
cupid	3	noun
devil	3	noun
elf	3	noun
fairy	3	noun
ghost	3	noun
monster	3	noun

Word	Importance	Part of Speech
witch	3	noun
wizard	3	noun
deity	4	noun
demon	4	noun
genie	4	noun
goblin	4	noun
imp	4	noun
phantom	4	noun
pixie	4	noun
saint	4	noun
spook	4	noun
vampire	4	noun
werewolf	4	noun
ghoul	5	noun
hag	5	noun
soul	5	noun

228. Goodness and Kindness

Related Clusters: 211, 278, 294, 295, 332, 350, 351, 385, 386, 387, 388, 389, 429, 433, 434

Word	Importance	Part of Speech
thankful	2	adjective
considerate	3	adjective
courteous	3	adjective
gentle	3	adjective
grateful	3	adjective
kind	3	adjective
nice	3	adjective

Word	Importance	Part of Speech
polite	3	adjective
respectful	3	adjective
affectionate	4	adjective
charity	4	noun
civil	4	adjective
consideration	4	noun
generous	4	adjective
grace	4	noun
kindness	4	noun
mercy	4	noun
noble	4	adjective
pleasant	4	adjective
sensitive	4	adjective
social	4	adjective
tender	4	adjective
thoughtful	4	adjective
unselfish	4	adjective
willing	4	adjective
amiable	5	adjective
hospitality	5	noun
liberal	5	adjective
sympathetic	5	adjective
tactful	5	adjective

229. Names of People in Sports

Related Clusters: 68, 88, 146, 167, 173, 236, 257, 264, 265, 266, 297, 333, 334, 355, 356, 357, 358, 359, 360, 361, 392, 393, 394, 395, 396, 397, 436

Word	Importance	Part of Speech
athlete	2	noun
batter	3	noun
boxer	3	noun
catcher	3	noun
coach	3	noun
loser	3	noun
runner	3	noun
winner	3	noun
acrobat	4	noun
ballplayer	4	noun
lifeguard	4	noun
player	4	noun
quarterback	4	noun
shortstop	4	noun
skier	4	noun
swimmer	4	noun
trainer	4	noun
umpire	4	noun
underdog	4	noun
wrestler	4	noun
daredevil	5	noun
fullback	5	noun
halfback	5	noun
horseman	5	noun
horsewoman	5	noun

Word	Importance	Part of Speech
jockey	5	noun
marksman	5	noun
referee	5	noun
timekeeper	5	noun

230. Disease

Related Clusters: 231, 287, 305, 371, 404

Word	Importance	Part of Speech
sick	2	adjective
disease	3	noun
health	3	noun
ill	3	adjective
injury	3	noun
well	3	adjective
ailment	4	noun
condition	4	noun
contagious	4	adjective
epidemic	4	noun
famine	4	noun
infection	4	noun
plague	4	noun
sickness	4	noun
symptom	4	noun
hale	5	adjective
robust	5	adjective
sane	5	adjective
wholesome	5	adjective

231. Medicine
Related Clusters: 230, 287, 305, 371, 404

Word	Importance	Part of Speech
pill	2	noun
aspirin	3	noun
bandage	3	noun
crutch	3	noun
medicine	3	noun
vitamin	3	noun
antibiotics	4	noun
Band-Aid	4	noun
cast	4	noun
diagnose	4	verb
drug	4	noun
ointment	4	noun
operate	4	verb
operation	4	noun
penicillin	4	noun
potion	4	noun
sling	4	noun
surgery	4	noun
transplant	4	verb
treatment	4	noun
vaccination	4	noun
vaccine	4	noun
antidote	5	noun
dissect	5	verb
dose	5	noun
inoculate	5	verb
iodine	5	noun
narcotic	5	noun

Word	Importance	Part of Speech
remedy	5	noun
serum	5	noun
splint	5	noun
therapy	5	noun
tonic	5	noun
transfusion	5	noun

232. Hunger and Thirst
Related Clusters: 48, 51, 74, 86, 124, 136, 153, 162, 174, 176, 208, 222, 246

Word	Importance	Part of Speech
hungry	2	adjective
hunger	3	noun
starve	3	verb
thirst	3	noun
thirsty	3	adjective
appetite	4	noun

233. Time (General)
Related Clusters: 2, 16, 24, 29, 52, 59, 79, 83, 126, 144

Word	Importance	Part of Speech
time	2	noun
bedtime	3	noun
daytime	3	noun
dinnertime	3	noun
lunchtime	3	noun
lifetime	4	noun
mealtime	4	noun

continued →

Word	Importance	Part of Speech
springtime	4	noun
summertime	4	noun
suppertime	4	noun
wartime	4	noun
wintertime	4	noun

234. Parts of Vehicles
Related Clusters: 93, 97, 120, 128, 159, 318, 331

Word	Importance	Part of Speech
paddle	2	noun
wheel	2	noun
anchor	3	noun
fender	3	noun
mirror	3	noun
oar	3	noun
parachute	3	noun
seatbelt	3	noun
tail	3	noun
tire	3	noun
trunk	3	noun
wing	3	noun
axle	4	noun
buoy	4	noun
cockpit	4	noun
deck	4	noun
gangplank	4	noun
mast	4	noun
propeller	4	noun

Word	Importance	Part of Speech
rudder	4	noun
windshield	4	noun
dashboard	5	noun
helm	5	noun
hub	5	noun
mainstay	5	noun
outboard	5	noun
prow	5	noun
rotor	5	noun

235. Contractions (Not)
Related Clusters: 42, 81, 85, 150, 274

Word	Importance	Part of Speech
don't	2	contraction
isn't	2	contraction
ain't	3	contraction
aren't	3	contraction
can't	3	contraction
couldn't	3	contraction
doesn't	3	contraction
hasn't	3	contraction
haven't	3	contraction
shouldn't	3	contraction
weren't	3	contraction
won't	3	contraction
wouldn't	3	contraction
hadn't	4	contraction
mustn't	4	contraction
wasn't	4	contraction

236. Occupations (General)

Related Clusters: 68, 88, 146, 167, 173, 229, 257, 264, 265, 266, 297, 333, 334, 355, 356, 357, 358, 359, 360, 361, 392, 393, 394, 395, 396, 397, 436

Word	Importance	Part of Speech
job	2	noun
career	3	noun
chore	3	noun
housework	3	noun
profession	3	noun
task	3	noun
worker	3	noun
craft	4	noun
errand	4	noun
homemaker	4	noun
livelihood	4	noun
occupation	4	noun
production	4	noun
profession	4	noun
role	4	noun
workman	4	noun
breadwinner	5	noun
sideline	5	noun
vocation	5	noun

237. Rocks and Jewels

Related Clusters: 133, 259, 337, 402, 438

Word	Importance	Part of Speech
rock	2	noun
boulder	3	noun
diamond	3	noun
jewel	3	noun
marble	3	noun
stone	3	noun
bedrock	4	noun
charcoal	4	noun
coal	4	noun
cobblestone	4	noun
coke	4	noun
crystal	4	noun
emerald	4	noun
gem	4	noun
granite	4	noun
gravel	4	noun
limestone	4	noun
nugget	4	noun
opal	4	noun
pearl	4	noun
rubble	4	noun
ruby	4	noun
shale	4	noun
slate	4	noun
turquoise	4	noun
aggregate	5	noun
amethyst	5	noun

continued →

Word	Importance	Part of Speech
anthracite	5	noun
asphalt	5	noun
conglomerate	5	noun
jade	5	noun
topaz	5	noun

238. Words, Phrases, and Sentences
Related Clusters: 219, 286

Word	Importance	Part of Speech
word	2	noun
adjective	3	noun
adverb	3	noun
noun	3	noun
sentence	3	noun
verb	3	noun
affix	4	noun
antonym	4	noun
clause	4	noun
conjunction	4	noun
object	4	noun
participle	4	noun
phrase	4	noun
predicate	4	noun
prefix	4	noun
preposition	4	noun
pronoun	4	noun
pun	4	noun

Word	Importance	Part of Speech
subject	4	noun
suffix	4	noun
superlative	4	noun
syllable	4	noun
synonym	4	noun
homograph	5	noun
homonym	5	noun
homophone	5	noun

239. Art
Related Clusters: 54, 77, 244

Word	Importance	Part of Speech
art	2	noun
painting	3	noun
photo	3	noun
photograph	3	noun
picture	3	noun
statue	3	noun
album	4	noun
mural	4	noun
portfolio	4	noun
portrait	4	noun
snapshot	4	noun
space	4	noun
tattoo	4	noun
mosaic	5	noun

240. Safety and Danger
Related Cluster: 221

Word	Importance	Part of Speech
safe	2	adjective
danger	3	noun
dangerous	3	adjective
risk	3	noun
trouble	3	noun
unsafe	3	adjective
harmful	4	adjective
harmless	4	adjective
hazard	4	noun
immune	4	adjective
protective	4	adjective
secure	4	adjective
jeopardy	5	noun
peril	5	noun
pitfall	5	noun
treacherous	5	adjective

241. Actions Associated With the Nose
Related Clusters: 151, 152, 196

Word	Importance	Part of Speech
smell	2	verb
sneeze	3	verb
sniff	3	verb
snore	3	verb
snort	3	verb

Word	Importance	Part of Speech
stink	3	noun
aroma	4	noun
fragrant	4	adjective
fume	4	noun
incense	4	noun
inhale	4	verb
odor	4	noun
perfume	4	noun
scent	4	noun
reek	5	noun
stench	5	noun

242. Abrasive/Cutting Actions
Related Clusters: 92, 96, 118, 119, 163, 254, 275, 276, 314, 315, 316, 419, 420

Word	Importance	Part of Speech
cut	2	verb
rub	2	verb
carve	3	verb
chop	3	verb
clip	3	verb
dig	3	verb
mow	3	verb
peel	3	verb
scoop	3	verb
scratch	3	verb
shave	3	verb
slice	3	verb
snip	3	verb

continued →

Word	Importance	Part of Speech
stab	3	verb
bulldoze	4	verb
burrow	4	verb
chafe	4	verb
crop	4	verb
grate	4	verb
grind	4	verb
peck	4	verb
pierce	4	verb
prick	4	verb
scrape	4	verb
shear	4	verb
shred	4	verb
slash	4	verb
slit	4	verb
whittle	4	verb
dredge	5	verb
excavate	5	verb
gnash	5	verb
hack	5	verb
mince	5	verb
pare	5	verb

243. Lack of Value
Related Clusters: 58, 72, 368

Word	Importance	Part of Speech
bad	2	adjective
awful	3	adjective
evil	3	adjective

Word	Importance	Part of Speech
terrible	3	adjective
wicked	3	adjective
worse	3	adjective
worst	3	adjective
absurd	4	adjective
foul	4	adjective
grim	4	adjective
horrible	4	adjective
inferior	4	adjective
negative	4	adjective
ridiculous	4	adjective
unimportant	4	adjective
useless	4	adjective
worthless	4	adjective
corrupt	5	adjective
dire	5	adjective
ghastly	5	adjective
petty	5	adjective
shabby	5	adjective
shoddy	5	adjective
sinister	5	adjective

244. Musical Instruments
Related Clusters: 54, 77, 239

Word	Importance	Part of Speech
instrument	2	noun
banjo	3	noun
drum	3	noun
guitar	3	noun

Word	Importance	Part of Speech
piano	3	noun
triangle	3	noun
violin	3	noun
accordion	4	noun
alto	4	noun
bagpipe	4	noun
bass	4	noun
bugle	4	noun
cello	4	noun
clarinet	4	noun
cornet	4	noun
fiddle	4	noun
flute	4	noun
harmonica	4	noun
harp	4	noun
keyboard	4	noun
organ	4	noun
percussion	4	noun
piccolo	4	noun
recorder	4	noun
saxophone	4	noun
tambourine	4	noun
trombone	4	noun
trumpet	4	noun
tuba	4	noun
xylophone	4	noun
cymbal	5	noun
fife	5	noun
glockenspiel	5	noun

Word	Importance	Part of Speech
harpsichord	5	noun
lute	5	noun
lyre	5	noun
mandolin	5	noun
oboe	5	noun
spinet	5	noun
tom-tom	5	noun
ukulele	5	noun
viola	5	noun
woodwind	5	noun

245. Birth, Life, and Death
Related Cluster: 329

Word	Importance	Part of Speech
dead	2	adjective
alive	3	adjective
born	3	verb
die	3	verb
egg	3	noun
hatch	3	verb
life	3	noun
live	3	verb
wake	3	verb
birth	4	noun
breed	4	verb
burial	4	noun
death	4	noun
exist	4	verb

continued →

Word	Importance	Part of Speech
extinct	4	adjective
fertile	4	adjective
inhabit	4	verb
mortal	4	adjective
mummy	4	noun
perish	4	verb
pregnant	4	adjective
reproduction	4	noun
sex	4	noun
sperm	4	noun
subsist	4	verb
animate	5	verb
carcass	5	noun
conceive	5	verb
corpse	5	noun
dwell	5	verb
entity	5	noun
funeral	5	noun
gene	5	noun
genetic	5	adjective
germinate	5	verb
incubate	5	verb
natal	5	adjective
populate	5	verb
reside	5	verb
spawn	5	verb
suffocate	5	verb

246. Types of Food
Related Clusters: 48, 51, 74, 86, 124, 136, 153, 162, 174, 176, 208, 222, 232

Word	Importance	Part of Speech
food	2	noun
crop	3	noun
fruit	3	noun
meat	3	noun
seafood	3	noun
sweets	3	noun
vegetables	3	noun
calorie	4	noun
carbohydrate	4	noun
diet	4	noun
nutrition	4	noun
protein	4	noun
relish	4	noun
supplies	4	noun
cellulose	5	noun
garnish	5	noun
glucose	5	noun
hash	5	noun
legume	5	noun
nourishment	5	noun
nutrient	5	noun
provisions	5	noun
pulp	5	noun

247. Joining
Related Clusters: 38, 39, 40, 44, 66, 141, 147, 169, 170, 182, 199, 215, 216, 280, 281, 282, 283, 300, 301, 302, 322, 338, 403

Word	Importance	Part of Speech
meet	2	verb
attach	3	verb
combine	3	verb
connect	3	verb
fasten	3	verb
include	3	verb
join	3	verb
marriage	3	noun
marry	3	verb
stick	3	verb
wedding	3	noun
accompany	4	verb
connection	4	noun
consist	4	verb
constitute	4	verb
contain	4	verb
hitch	4	verb
intersect	4	verb
involve	4	verb
junction	4	noun
link	4	verb
matrimony	4	noun
seam	4	noun
splice	4	verb
synthesis	4	noun

Word	Importance	Part of Speech
tether	4	verb
union	4	noun
unite	4	verb
wed	4	verb
affix	5	verb
associate	5	verb
bond	5	verb
collide	5	verb
comprise	5	verb
engage	5	verb
fuse	5	verb
graft	5	verb
merge	5	verb
shackle	5	verb

248. Publication Types
Related Clusters: 53, 71, 112, 138, 256, 279, 319, 320

Word	Importance	Part of Speech
book	2	noun
bible	3	noun
booklet	3	noun
chapter	3	noun
cookbook	3	noun
diary	3	noun
dictionary	3	noun
essay	3	noun
journal	3	noun
magazine	3	noun

continued →

Word	Importance	Part of Speech
newspaper	3	noun
novel	3	noun
outline	3	noun
storybook	3	noun
summary	3	noun
text	3	noun
textbook	3	noun
album	4	noun
almanac	4	noun
appendix	4	noun
article	4	noun
atlas	4	noun
autobiography	4	noun
bibliography	4	noun
biography	4	noun
catalogue	4	noun
column	4	noun
document	4	noun
encyclopedia	4	noun
episode	4	noun
foreword	4	noun
glossary	4	noun
headline	4	noun
index	4	noun
issue	4	noun
manual	4	noun
pamphlet	4	noun
paperback	4	noun
paragraph	4	noun

Word	Importance	Part of Speech
passage	4	noun
preface	4	noun
primer	4	noun
publication	4	noun
report	4	noun
schoolbook	4	noun
script	4	noun
scripture	4	noun
testament	4	noun
thesaurus	4	noun
thesis	4	noun
volume	4	noun
excerpt	5	noun
format	5	noun
log	5	noun
manuscript	5	noun
media	5	noun

249. Conclusions

Related Clusters: 46, 67, 132, 137, 154, 225, 277, 347, 348, 349, 384

Word	Importance	Part of Speech
guess	2	verb
calculate	3	verb
clue	3	noun
compose	3	verb
conclude	3	verb
create	3	verb
design	3	verb

Word	Importance	Part of Speech
estimate	3	verb
fact	3	noun
information	3	noun
invent	3	verb
invention	3	noun
mystery	3	noun
prediction	3	noun
prove	3	verb
solve	3	verb
suppose	3	verb
assume	4	verb
calculation	4	noun
compute	4	verb
confirm	4	verb
determine	4	verb
discovery	4	noun
evaluate	4	verb
evidence	4	noun
forecast	4	verb
hunch	4	noun
infer	4	verb
principle	4	noun
proof	4	noun
revise	4	verb
solution	4	noun
suspect	4	verb
theory	4	noun
abstract	5	noun
basis	5	noun

Word	Importance	Part of Speech
criteria	5	noun
devise	5	verb
enigma	5	noun
foresee	5	verb
improvise	5	verb
predict	5	verb
resolve	5	verb
speculate	5	verb
suspicion	5	noun

250. Destructive Actions
Related Clusters: 110, 161, 260

Word	Importance	Part of Speech
accident	3	noun
break	3	verb
crash	3	verb
crush	3	verb
damage	3	verb
dent	3	verb
destroy	3	verb
mark	3	verb
ruin	3	verb
scratch	3	verb
waste	3	verb
wreck	3	verb
chip	4	verb
demolish	4	verb
destruction	4	noun
erase	4	verb

continued →

Word	Importance	Part of Speech
extinguish	4	verb
mar	4	verb
mash	4	verb
puncture	4	verb
shatter	4	verb
squelch	4	verb
wreckage	4	noun
devastate	5	verb
erode	5	verb
fracture	5	verb
mangle	5	verb
mishap	5	noun
nick	5	verb
rupture	5	verb
snuff	5	verb

251. Building Materials (General)
Related Clusters: 107, 164, 181, 268, 325, 367

Word	Importance	Part of Speech
bar	3	noun
brick	3	noun
cardboard	3	noun
paste	3	noun
pipe	3	noun
plastic	3	noun
sewer	3	noun
tube	3	noun
wire	3	noun

Word	Importance	Part of Speech
adobe	4	noun
asbestos	4	noun
brace	4	noun
cement	4	noun
ceramic	4	noun
concrete	4	noun
culvert	4	noun
drainpipe	4	noun
duct	4	noun
hoop	4	noun
pavement	4	noun
plaster	4	noun
pole	4	noun
porcelain	4	noun
prop	4	noun
putty	4	noun
rod	4	noun
rung	4	noun
stilt	4	noun
support	4	noun
tar	4	noun
tile	4	noun
tin	4	noun
adhesive	5	noun
bracket	5	noun
clapboard	5	noun
cornerstone	5	noun
fixture	5	noun
grout	5	noun

Word	Importance	Part of Speech
mainstay	5	noun
mortar	5	noun
pedestal	5	noun
stucco	5	noun

252. Similarity
Related Clusters: 5, 27, 299

Word	Importance	Part of Speech
alike	3	adjective
copy	3	noun
equal	3	adjective
even	3	adjective
example	3	noun
like	3	adjective
same	3	adjective
similar	3	adjective
twin	3	noun
agreement	4	noun
approximate	4	adjective
artificial	4	adjective
comparison	4	noun
consistent	4	adjective
counterfeit	4	adjective
echo	4	noun
exact	4	adjective
harmony	4	noun
imitate	4	verb
imitation	4	noun

Word	Importance	Part of Speech
likeness	4	noun
match	4	noun
mimic	4	verb
parallel	4	adjective
related	4	adjective
resemblance	4	noun
resemble	4	verb
similarity	4	noun
unanimous	4	adjective
accord	5	noun
alternate	5	noun
analogy	5	noun
compatible	5	adjective
conform	5	verb
congruent	5	adjective
ditto	5	noun
duplicate	5	noun
identical	5	adjective
metaphor	5	noun
mimeograph	5	noun
monotony	5	noun
simile	5	noun
substitute	5	noun
synthetic	5	adjective

253. Physical Characteristics
Related Clusters: 186, 187, 407

Word	Importance	Part of Speech
athletic	3	adjective
beauty	3	noun
clumsy	3	adjective
health	3	noun
might	3	noun
power	3	noun
strength	3	noun
strong	3	adjective
weak	3	adjective
weakness	3	noun
agile	4	adjective
awkward	4	adjective
frail	4	adjective
handicap	4	noun
muscular	4	adjective
nimble	4	adjective
powerful	4	adjective
puny	4	adjective
rickety	4	adjective
rugged	4	adjective
scrawny	4	adjective
vigor	4	noun
agility	5	noun
brawn	5	noun
dexterity	5	noun
feeble	5	adjective
gaunt	5	adjective

Word	Importance	Part of Speech
gawky	5	adjective
potent	5	adjective
spry	5	adjective

254. Weapons and Explosives
Related Clusters: 92, 96, 118, 119, 163, 242, 275, 276, 314, 315, 316, 419, 420

Word	Importance	Part of Speech
arrow	3	noun
bomb	3	noun
bullet	3	noun
firecracker	3	noun
fireworks	3	noun
gun	3	noun
sword	3	noun
ammunition	4	noun
arms	4	noun
boomerang	4	noun
bow	4	noun
cannon	4	noun
dagger	4	noun
dart	4	noun
dynamite	4	noun
firearms	4	noun
grenade	4	noun
harpoon	4	noun
holster	4	noun
missile	4	noun
pellet	4	noun

Word	Importance	Part of Speech
pistol	4	noun
revolver	4	noun
rifle	4	noun
shotgun	4	noun
sling	4	noun
slingshot	4	noun
spear	4	noun
tomahawk	4	noun
torpedo	4	noun
weapon	4	noun
whip	4	noun
cutlass	5	noun
guillotine	5	noun
javelin	5	noun
lance	5	noun
musket	5	noun
noose	5	noun

Word	Importance	Part of Speech
suggest	3	verb
coax	4	verb
hint	4	verb
influence	4	verb
petition	4	verb
plead	4	verb
sway	4	verb
tempt	4	verb
urge	4	verb
bait	5	verb
bias	5	noun
bribe	5	verb
canvass	5	noun
corrupt	5	verb
induce	5	verb
lure	5	verb
petition	5	verb

255. Persuasion/Advice
Related Clusters: 14, 61, 100, 105, 177, 198, 207, 345, 346, 383

Word	Importance	Part of Speech
advise	3	verb
appeal	3	verb
beg	3	verb
convince	3	verb
cue	3	verb
persuade	3	verb
recommend	3	verb

256. Messages
Related Clusters: 53, 71, 112, 138, 248, 279, 319, 320

Word	Importance	Part of Speech
letter	3	noun
message	3	noun
note	3	noun
postcard	3	noun
poster	3	noun
signal	3	noun
valentine	3	noun

continued →

Word	Importance	Part of Speech
advertisement	4	noun
bulletin	4	noun
commercial	4	noun
motto	4	noun
signpost	4	noun
slogan	4	noun
telegram	4	noun
tidings	4	noun
billboard	5	noun
memo	5	noun

257. Domains of Work
Related Clusters: 68, 88, 146, 167, 173, 229, 236, 264, 265, 266, 297, 333, 334, 355, 356, 357, 358, 359, 360, 361, 392, 393, 394, 395, 396, 397, 436

Word	Importance	Part of Speech
business	3	noun
law	3	noun
medicine	3	noun
military	3	noun
religion	3	noun
science	3	noun
technology	3	noun
agriculture	4	noun
industry	4	noun
politics	4	noun

258. Groups of Animals and People
Related Clusters: 98, 200, 298, 401

Word	Importance	Part of Speech
band	3	noun
class	3	noun
club	3	noun
crowd	3	noun
herd	3	noun
team	3	noun
cast	4	noun
chorus	4	noun
crew	4	noun
flock	4	noun
gang	4	noun
horde	4	noun
huddle	4	noun
mob	4	noun
multitude	4	noun
posse	4	noun
quartet	4	noun
species	4	noun
throng	4	noun
trio	4	noun
bevy	5	noun
brood	5	noun
covey	5	noun
denomination	5	noun
ensemble	5	noun
fraternity	5	noun

Word	Importance	Part of Speech
gaggle	5	noun
mass	5	noun
phylum	5	noun
pod	5	noun
quintet	5	noun

259. Metals
Related Clusters: 133, 237, 337, 402, 438

Word	Importance	Part of Speech
gold	3	noun
iron	3	noun
magnet	3	noun
metal	3	noun
silver	3	noun
steel	3	noun
aluminum	4	noun
brass	4	noun
bronze	4	noun
calcium	4	noun
carbon	4	noun
chrome	4	noun
copper	4	noun
flint	4	noun
lava	4	noun
lead	4	noun
ore	4	noun
uranium	4	noun
zinc	4	noun
alloy	5	noun

Word	Importance	Part of Speech
bauxite	5	noun
beryllium	5	noun
cobalt	5	noun
feldspar	5	noun
gneiss	5	noun
graphite	5	noun
lodestone	5	noun
magma	5	noun
magnesium	5	noun
manganese	5	noun
mica	5	noun
obsidian	5	noun
phosphorus	5	noun
potassium	5	noun
pumice	5	noun
quartz	5	noun
radium	5	noun
silicon	5	noun
solder	5	noun
talc	5	noun
tungsten	5	noun

260. War and Fighting
Related Clusters: 110, 161, 250

Word	Importance	Part of Speech
battle	3	noun
fight	3	verb
peace	3	noun
revolution	3	noun

continued →

Word	Importance	Part of Speech
war	3	noun
wrestle	3	verb
brawl	4	noun
challenge	4	verb
clash	4	verb
combat	4	verb
conflict	4	noun
duel	4	verb
friction	4	noun
invade	4	verb
invasion	4	noun
raid	4	noun
repel	4	verb
revolution	4	noun
riot	4	noun
rumble	4	verb
scuffle	4	verb
showdown	4	noun
skirmish	4	noun
strife	4	noun
struggle	4	verb
fray	5	verb
onslaught	5	noun
siege	5	noun
warfare	5	noun

261. Likelihood and Certainty
Related Clusters: 289, 328

Word	Importance	Part of Speech
bet	3	noun
certain	3	adjective
chance	3	noun
likely	3	adjective
luck	3	noun
miracle	3	noun
possible	3	adjective
absolute	4	adjective
accidental	4	adjective
bid	4	noun
casual	4	adjective
definite	4	adjective
destiny	4	noun
doom	4	noun
doubtful	4	adjective
fate	4	noun
fluke	4	noun
gamble	4	verb
hazard	4	noun
lottery	4	noun
mysterious	4	adjective
opportunity	4	noun
probable	4	adjective
stake	4	noun
uncertain	4	adjective
ambiguous	5	adjective
boon	5	noun

Word	Importance	Part of Speech
contingent	5	noun
haphazard	5	adjective
jinx	5	noun
liable	5	adjective
potential	5	adjective
random	5	adjective
venture	5	noun

262. Order and Complexity
Related Cluster: 290

Word	Importance	Part of Speech
balance	3	noun
blank	3	adjective
fancy	3	adjective
order	3	noun
plain	3	adjective
simple	3	adjective
bare	4	adjective
bleak	4	adjective
complex	4	adjective
confusion	4	noun
neutral	4	adjective
offset	4	adjective
ornate	4	adjective
pure	4	adjective
steady	4	adjective
symmetry	4	noun
tangle	4	noun
technical	4	adjective

Word	Importance	Part of Speech
uniform	4	adjective
void	4	noun
bedlam	5	noun
cosmos	5	noun
elaborate	5	adjective
equilibrium	5	noun
intricate	5	adjective
maze	5	noun
muddle	5	noun
turmoil	5	noun
wrought	5	verb

263. Clothing (General)
Related Clusters: 47, 62, 125, 129, 145, 178, 212, 224, 354, 435

Word	Importance	Part of Speech
clothes	3	noun
clothing	3	noun
costume	3	noun
suit	3	noun
uniform	3	noun
array	4	noun
attire	4	noun
design	4	noun
fad	4	noun
fashion	4	noun
outfit	4	noun
style	4	noun
wardrobe	4	noun

continued →

Word	Importance	Part of Speech
apparel	5	noun
garb	5	noun
garment	5	noun
lingerie	5	noun

264. Artists and Performers

Related Clusters: 68, 88, 146, 167, 173, 229, 236, 257, 265, 266, 297, 333, 334, 355, 356, 357, 358, 359, 360, 361, 392, 393, 394, 395, 396, 397, 436

Word	Importance	Part of Speech
artist	3	noun
choir	3	noun
drummer	3	noun
painter	3	noun
singer	3	noun
conductor	4	noun
designer	4	noun
musician	4	noun
photographer	4	noun
soprano	4	noun
violinist	4	noun

265. Public Officials

Related Clusters: 68, 88, 146, 167, 173, 229, 236, 257, 264, 266, 297, 333, 334, 355, 356, 357, 358, 359, 360, 361, 392, 393, 394, 395, 396, 397, 436

Word	Importance	Part of Speech
firefighter	3	noun
officer	3	noun
policeman	3	noun
sheriff	3	noun
soldier	3	noun
admiral	4	noun
airman	4	noun
captain	4	noun
deputy	4	noun
detective	4	noun
marshal	4	noun
policewoman	4	noun
redcoat	4	noun
trooper	4	noun
colonel	5	noun
constable	5	noun
corporal	5	noun
lieutenant	5	noun
sergeant	5	noun

266. Religious and Clergy
Related Clusters: 68, 88, 146, 167, 173, 229, 236, 257, 264, 265, 297, 333, 334, 355, 356, 357, 358, 359, 360, 361, 392, 393, 394, 395, 396, 397, 436

Word	Importance	Part of Speech
minister	3	noun
nun	3	noun
pastor	3	noun
pope	3	noun
priest	3	noun
bishop	4	noun
missionary	4	noun
monk	4	noun
prophet	4	noun
rabbi	4	noun
abbot	5	noun
apostle	5	noun
cardinal	5	noun
clergyman	5	noun
deacon	5	noun
hermit	5	noun
parson	5	noun

267. Craters and Valleys
Related Clusters: 50, 114, 139, 168, 362, 363, 398

Word	Importance	Part of Speech
hole	2	noun
canyon	3	noun
crack	3	noun
ditch	3	noun
manhole	3	noun
pit	3	noun
valley	3	noun
cavern	4	noun
cove	4	noun
crater	4	noun
gap	4	noun
groove	4	noun
gully	4	noun
notch	4	noun
ravine	4	noun
shaft	4	noun
trench	4	noun
cavity	5	noun
chasm	5	noun
cleft	5	noun
crevice	5	noun
dale	5	noun
furrow	5	noun
glen	5	noun
gulch	5	noun
rift	5	noun
rut	5	noun
silo	5	noun

268. Objects/Materials Used to Cover Things
Related Clusters: 107, 164, 181, 251, 325, 367

Word	Importance	Part of Speech
cork	3	noun
cover	3	noun
flap	3	noun
lid	3	noun
mask	3	noun
canvas	4	noun
cellophane	4	noun
foil	4	noun
plug	4	noun
thimble	4	noun
tinfoil	4	noun
wrapper	4	noun
camouflage	5	noun

269. Plants and Flowers
Related Clusters: 36, 108, 192, 421

Word	Importance	Part of Speech
berry	3	noun
blossom	3	noun
dandelion	3	noun
rose	3	noun
seed	3	noun
bouquet	4	noun
bud	4	noun
bulb	4	noun
buttercup	4	noun

Word	Importance	Part of Speech
cactus	4	noun
carnation	4	noun
daffodil	4	noun
daisy	4	noun
holly	4	noun
huckleberry	4	noun
lilac	4	noun
lily	4	noun
mistletoe	4	noun
petal	4	noun
pod	4	noun
pollen	4	noun
poppy	4	noun
sprout	4	noun
stamen	4	noun
sunflower	4	noun
thistle	4	noun
tulip	4	noun
wildflower	4	noun
anemone	5	noun
bluebell	5	noun
briar	5	noun
chrysanthemum	5	noun
cowslip	5	noun
flax	5	noun
gardenia	5	noun
geranium	5	noun
goldenrod	5	noun
hemp	5	noun
honeysuckle	5	noun

Word	Importance	Part of Speech
ivy	5	noun
jute	5	noun
larkspur	5	noun
linseed	5	noun
marigold	5	noun
petunia	5	noun
pistil	5	noun
snapdragon	5	noun
spore	5	noun

270. Curved and Circular Shapes
Related Clusters: 69, 99, 142, 193, 218, 303, 326

Word	Importance	Part of Speech
circle	2	noun
bend	3	noun
curl	3	noun
curve	3	noun
cylinder	3	noun
loop	3	noun
oval	3	noun
round	3	adjective
twist	3	noun
circuit	4	noun
circular	4	adjective
coil	4	noun
cone	4	noun
convex	4	adjective
disk	4	noun

Word	Importance	Part of Speech
flex	4	noun
halo	4	noun
sphere	4	noun
spiral	4	noun
warp	4	verb
arc	5	noun
concave	5	adjective
crescent	5	noun
kink	5	noun
parabola	5	noun

271. Light
Related Clusters: 272, 306, 372, 405

Word	Importance	Part of Speech
bright	3	adjective
clear	3	adjective
light	3	adjective
shiny	3	adjective
sunshine	3	noun
brightness	4	noun
brilliant	4	adjective
candlelight	4	noun
daylight	4	noun
gleam	4	noun
lamplight	4	noun
moonlight	4	noun
radiant	4	adjective
starlight	4	noun
sunlight	4	noun

continued ➡

Word	Importance	Part of Speech
vivid	4	adjective
glimmer	5	noun
glint	5	noun
gloss	5	verb
luminous	5	adjective
luster	5	noun
sheen	5	noun

272. Light Producers
Related Clusters: 271, 306, 372, 405

Word	Importance	Part of Speech
candle	3	noun
candlestick	3	noun
lamp	3	noun
light	3	noun
lightbulb	3	noun
beacon	4	noun
beam	4	noun
bonfire	4	noun
chandelier	4	noun
flare	4	noun
lantern	4	noun
laser	4	noun
moonbeam	4	noun
ray	4	noun
searchlight	4	noun
sunbeam	4	noun
torch	4	noun

Word	Importance	Part of Speech
filament	5	noun
fluorescent	5	noun
sunspot	5	noun

273. Cause/Effect
Related Cluster: 10

Word	Importance	Part of Speech
cause	3	noun
change	3	verb
effect	3	noun
outcome	3	noun
purpose	3	noun
reason	3	noun
result	3	noun
affect	4	verb
agent	4	noun
consequence	4	noun
impress	4	verb
incentive	4	noun
influence	4	verb
intent	4	noun
motive	4	noun
stimulate	4	verb
vary	4	verb
impact	5	noun
induce	5	verb
initiate	5	verb

274. Contractions (Would)
Related Clusters: 42, 81, 85, 150, 235

Word	Importance	Part of Speech
he'd	3	contraction
I'd	3	contraction
she'd	3	contraction
they'd	3	contraction
you'd	3	contraction

275. Engines
Related Clusters: 92, 96, 118, 119, 163, 242, 254, 276, 314, 315, 316, 419, 420

Word	Importance	Part of Speech
battery	3	noun
brake	3	noun
engine	3	noun
jet	3	noun
motor	3	noun
gear	4	noun
headset	4	noun
crankshaft	5	noun
piston	5	noun
starter	5	noun
throttle	5	noun
turbine	5	noun

276. Electronics
Related Clusters: 92, 96, 118, 119, 163, 242, 254, 275, 314, 315, 316, 419, 420

Word	Importance	Part of Speech
computer	3	noun
keyboard	3	noun
monitor	3	noun
mouse	3	noun
robot	3	noun
memory	4	noun
projector	4	noun
terminal	4	noun
transistor	4	noun
bit	5	noun
chip	5	noun
format	5	verb
network	5	noun
register	5	noun
thermostat	5	noun

277. Topics and Subjects
Related Clusters: 46, 67, 132, 137, 154, 225, 249, 347, 348, 349, 384

Word	Importance	Part of Speech
goal	3	noun
plan	3	noun
subject	3	noun
topic	3	noun
core	4	noun
essence	4	noun

continued →

Word	Importance	Part of Speech
objective	4	noun
scheme	4	noun
strategy	4	noun
theme	4	noun
viewpoint	4	noun
keynote	5	noun
scope	5	noun
thesis	5	noun

278. Pride and Confidence

Related Clusters: 211, 228, 294, 295, 332, 350, 351, 385, 386, 387, 388, 389, 429, 433, 434

Word	Importance	Part of Speech
certain	3	adjective
confident	3	adjective
hopeful	3	adjective
proud	3	adjective
sure	3	adjective
confidence	4	noun
pride	4	noun
smug	4	adjective
vain	4	adjective
conceit	5	noun
frank	5	adjective
haughty	5	adjective

279. Illustrations and Drawings

Related Clusters: 53, 71, 112, 138, 248, 256, 319, 320

Word	Importance	Part of Speech
diagram	3	noun
drawing	3	noun
graph	3	noun
map	3	noun
chart	4	noun

280. Motion (General)

Related Clusters: 38, 39, 40, 44, 66, 141, 147, 169, 170, 182, 199, 215, 216, 247, 281, 282, 283, 300, 301, 302, 322, 338, 403

Word	Importance	Part of Speech
action	3	noun
activity	3	noun
motion	3	noun
play	3	noun
movable	4	adjective
portable	4	adjective
traffic	4	noun
kinetic	5	adjective
mobile	5	adjective
osmosis	5	noun

281. Vibration

Related Clusters: 38, 39, 40, 44, 66, 141, 147, 169, 170, 182, 199, 215, 216, 247, 280, 282, 283, 300, 301, 302, 322, 338, 403

Word	Importance	Part of Speech
juggle	3	verb
shake	3	verb
shiver	3	verb
vibrate	3	verb
wiggle	3	verb
flutter	4	verb
jitter	4	verb
quake	4	verb
quiver	4	verb
scramble	4	verb
shudder	4	verb
sputter	4	verb
squirm	4	verb
throb	4	verb
tremble	4	verb
vibration	4	noun
wobble	4	verb
wriggle	4	verb
jumble	5	verb
teeter	5	verb
totter	5	verb
waver	5	noun

282. Jerking Motion

Related Clusters: 38, 39, 40, 44, 66, 141, 147, 169, 170, 182, 199, 215, 216, 247, 280, 281, 283, 300, 301, 302, 322, 338, 403

Word	Importance	Part of Speech
bounce	3	verb
fidget	3	verb
snap	3	verb
wag	3	verb
bob	4	verb
budge	4	verb
jerk	4	verb
jolt	4	verb
lurch	4	verb
twitch	4	verb
deflect	5	verb
flounce	5	verb
jounce	5	verb

283. Expanding Motion

Related Clusters: 38, 39, 40, 44, 66, 141, 147, 169, 170, 182, 199, 215, 216, 247, 280, 281, 282, 300, 301, 302, 322, 338, 403

Word	Importance	Part of Speech
blast	3	verb
expand	3	verb
explode	3	verb
magnify	3	verb
spread	3	verb
burst	4	verb

continued →

Word	Importance	Part of Speech
enlarge	4	verb
erupt	4	verb
extend	4	verb
protrude	4	verb
scatter	4	verb
swell	4	verb
discharge	5	verb
jut	5	verb

284. Furnishings and Decorations
Related Clusters: 91, 113, 123, 134, 217

Word	Importance	Part of Speech
banner	3	noun
carpet	3	noun
curtain	3	noun
rug	3	noun
vase	3	noun
accessory	4	noun
canopy	4	noun
confetti	4	noun
domestic	4	noun
furnish	4	noun
homemade	4	adjective
linoleum	4	noun
knickknack	4	noun
ornament	4	noun
pennant	4	noun
tinsel	4	noun
upholster	4	noun
varnish	4	noun

Word	Importance	Part of Speech
wallpaper	4	noun
wreath	4	noun
cornucopia	5	noun
spangle	5	noun
tapestry	5	noun
trifle	5	noun
urn	5	noun

285. Attitudinals (Truth)
Related Clusters: 30, 31, 369, 431, 439, 440

Word	Importance	Part of Speech
certainly	3	adverb
honestly	3	adverb
really	3	adverb
seriously	3	adverb
simply	3	adverb
truly	3	adverb
apparently	4	adverb
basically	4	adverb
clearly	4	adverb
definitely	4	adverb
ideally	4	adverb
indeed	4	adverb
obviously	4	adverb
plainly	4	adverb
strictly	4	adverb
surely	4	adverb
undoubtedly	5	adverb
unquestionably	5	adverb

286. Language Conventions
Related Clusters: 219, 238

Word	Importance	Part of Speech
comma	3	noun
language	3	noun
period	3	noun
vocabulary	3	noun
accent	4	noun
apostrophe	4	noun
colon	4	noun
dialect	4	noun
diction	4	noun
emphasis	4	noun
grammar	4	noun
hyphen	4	noun
parenthesis	4	noun
pronunciation	4	noun
punctuation	4	noun
slang	4	noun
syntax	4	noun
tense	4	noun
voice	4	noun
dash	5	noun
idiom	5	noun

287. Symptoms
Related Clusters: 230, 231, 305, 371, 404

Word	Importance	Part of Speech
dizzy	3	adjective
fever	3	noun
itch	3	noun
pain	3	noun
ache	4	noun
fatigue	4	noun
groggy	4	adjective
headache	4	noun
numb	4	adjective
raw	4	adjective
sore	4	noun
toothache	4	noun
coma	5	noun
delirious	5	adjective
impair	5	verb
nausea	5	noun
pang	5	noun
twinge	5	noun
vomit	5	verb
weariness	5	noun

288. Uncleanliness and Filth
Related Clusters: 185, 223

Word	Importance	Part of Speech
garbage	3	noun
junk	3	noun
litter	3	noun

continued →

Word	Importance	Part of Speech
trash	3	noun
bleak	4	adjective
clutter	4	noun
dismal	4	adjective
dreary	4	adjective
filth	4	noun
foul	4	adjective
grime	4	noun
infect	4	verb
nasty	4	adjective
pollute	4	verb
rubbish	4	noun
sewage	4	noun
slop	4	noun
smear	4	noun
smudge	4	noun
streak	4	noun
contaminate	5	verb
debris	5	noun
dingy	5	adjective
eyesore	5	noun
taint	5	verb

289. Familiarity and Popularity
Related Clusters: 261, 328

Word	Importance	Part of Speech
common	3	adjective
familiar	3	adjective
normal	3	adjective
ordinary	3	adjective
popular	3	adjective
regular	3	adjective
usual	3	adjective
appeal	4	noun
attraction	4	noun
commonplace	4	adjective
customary	4	adjective
dignity	4	noun
fame	4	noun
glory	4	noun
hip	4	adjective
honor	4	noun
legendary	4	adjective
norm	4	noun
obvious	4	adjective
patent	4	adjective
public	4	adjective
recognition	4	noun
scandal	4	noun
traditional	4	adjective
typical	4	adjective
universal	4	adjective

Word	Importance	Part of Speech
widespread	4	adjective
apparent	5	adjective
conspicuous	5	adjective
evident	5	adjective
limelight	5	noun
par	5	noun
pedestrian	5	adjective
prominent	5	adjective
repute	5	noun
standard	5	noun

290. Conformity to a Norm
Related Cluster: 262

Word	Importance	Part of Speech
odd	3	adjective
rare	3	adjective
special	3	adjective
strange	3	adjective
weird	3	adjective
distinct	4	adjective
foreign	4	adjective
original	4	adjective
peculiar	4	adjective
quaint	4	adjective
queer	4	adjective
scarce	4	adjective
uncommon	4	adjective
unfinished	4	adjective

Word	Importance	Part of Speech
unique	4	adjective
bizarre	5	adjective
defect	5	noun
eccentric	5	adjective
grotesque	5	adjective
outlandish	5	adjective
uncanny	5	adjective

291. Fear
Related Clusters: 43, 45, 55, 292, 293, 311, 312, 313, 378, 379, 380, 381, 416, 417, 422, 427, 428

Word	Importance	Part of Speech
afraid	3	adjective
alarm	3	noun
fear	3	noun
nervous	3	adjective
dread	4	noun
eerie	4	adjective
frantic	4	adjective
horror	4	noun
panic	4	noun
shock	4	noun
terror	4	noun
fright	5	noun

292. Anger
Related Clusters: 43, 45, 55, 291, 293, 311, 312, 313, 378, 379, 380, 381, 416, 417, 422, 427, 428

Word	Importance	Part of Speech
anger	3	noun
angry	3	adjective
dislike	3	verb
hate	3	noun
mad	3	adjective
fury	4	noun
hatred	4	noun
hostile	4	adjective
incense	4	verb
irritate	4	verb
offend	4	verb
rage	4	noun
resent	4	verb
tantrum	4	noun
temper	4	noun
vengeance	4	noun
contempt	5	noun
despise	5	verb
disgust	5	noun
huff	5	noun
outrage	5	noun
revenge	5	noun
scorn	5	noun
vehement	5	adjective
wrath	5	noun

293. Desire
Related Clusters: 43, 45, 55, 291, 292, 311, 312, 313, 378, 379, 380, 381, 416, 417, 422, 427, 428

Word	Importance	Part of Speech
expect	3	verb
miss	3	verb
need	3	noun
selfish	3	adjective
want	3	verb
wish	3	verb
anticipate	4	verb
crave	4	verb
desire	4	noun
lust	4	noun
seek	4	verb
greed	5	noun
hanker	5	verb
yearn	5	verb

294. Dependability and Eagerness
Related Clusters: 211, 228, 278, 295, 332, 350, 351, 385, 386, 387, 388, 389, 429, 433, 434

Word	Importance	Part of Speech
active	3	adjective
busy	3	adjective
eager	3	adjective
responsible	3	adjective
ambition	4	noun

Word	Importance	Part of Speech
ambitious	4	adjective
burden	4	noun
credible	4	adjective
depend	4	verb
dependable	4	adjective
determination	4	noun
duty	4	noun
earnest	4	adjective
efficient	4	adjective
enthusiasm	4	noun
lively	4	adjective
pep	4	noun
productive	4	adjective
reliable	4	adjective
rely	4	verb
responsibility	4	noun
service	4	noun
sincere	4	adjective
spirit	4	noun
thorough	4	adjective
trustworthy	4	adjective
diligent	5	adjective
industrious	5	adjective
vigor	5	noun
vigorous	5	adjective
zest	5	noun

295. Instability
Related Clusters: 211, 228, 278, 294, 332, 350, 351, 385, 386, 387, 388, 389, 429, 433, 434

Word	Importance	Part of Speech
crazy	3	adjective
mad	3	adjective
wild	3	adjective
frantic	4	adjective
hectic	4	adjective
uncontrolled	4	adjective
unstable	4	adjective
amuck	5	adjective
fanatic	5	noun
fickle	5	adjective
giddy	5	adjective

296. Locations For/Near Water (Manmade)
Related Clusters: 87, 101, 102, 127, 352, 353, 391, 424

Word	Importance	Part of Speech
aquarium	3	noun
canal	3	noun
dam	3	noun
dock	3	noun
pool	3	noun
aqueduct	4	noun
berth	4	noun
channel	4	noun
dike	4	noun

continued →

Word	Importance	Part of Speech
harbor	4	noun
lighthouse	4	noun
port	4	noun
reservoir	4	noun
seaport	4	noun
wharf	4	noun
breakwater	5	noun
moat	5	noun
sluice	5	noun

297. Small Businesses

Related Clusters: 68, 88, 146, 167, 173, 229, 236, 257, 264, 265, 266, 333, 334, 355, 356, 357, 358, 359, 360, 361, 392, 393, 394, 395, 396, 397, 436

Word	Importance	Part of Speech
baker	3	noun
barber	3	noun
butcher	3	noun
blacksmith	4	noun
bodyguard	4	noun
smith	4	noun
florist	5	noun
miller	5	noun
tailor	5	noun

298. Military/Police

Related Clusters: 98, 200, 258, 401

Word	Importance	Part of Speech
army	3	noun
navy	3	noun
police	3	noun
air force	4	noun
infantry	4	noun
marines	4	noun
patrol	4	noun
squadron	4	noun
troop	4	noun
brigade	5	noun
corps	5	noun
detail	5	noun
legion	5	noun
regiment	5	noun

299. Dissimilarity

Related Clusters: 5, 27, 252

Word	Importance	Part of Speech
change	3	verb
difference	3	noun
different	3	adjective
opposite	3	adjective
unequal	3	adjective
unlike	3	adjective
adapt	4	verb
contrary	4	adjective
develop	4	verb

Word	Importance	Part of Speech
development	4	noun
deviate	4	verb
differ	4	verb
diverse	4	adjective
freak	4	noun
molt	4	verb
quirk	4	noun
reform	4	verb
separate	4	verb
undergo	4	verb
variety	4	noun
various	4	adjective
vary	4	verb
discriminate	5	verb
metamorphosis	5	noun
temper	5	noun
transform	5	verb
transition	5	noun

300. Pursuit

Related Clusters: 38, 39, 40, 44, 66, 141, 147, 169, 170, 182, 199, 215, 216, 247, 280, 281, 282, 283, 301, 302, 322, 338, 403

Word	Importance	Part of Speech
chase	3	verb
follow	3	verb
track	3	verb
pursue	4	verb

301. Reducing/Diminishing

Related Clusters: 38, 39, 40, 44, 66, 141, 147, 169, 170, 182, 199, 215, 216, 247, 280, 281, 282, 283, 300, 302, 322, 338, 403

Word	Importance	Part of Speech
crumble	3	verb
crumple	3	verb
shorten	3	verb
shrink	3	verb
tighten	3	verb
diminish	4	verb
dwindle	4	verb
reduce	4	verb
shrivel	4	verb
wither	4	verb
compress	5	verb
condense	5	verb
corrugate	5	verb
cramp	5	verb
crinkle	5	verb
wilt	5	verb

302. Separating

Related Clusters: 38, 39, 40, 44, 66, 141, 147, 169, 170, 182, 199, 215, 216, 247, 280, 281, 282, 283, 300, 301, 322, 338, 403

Word	Importance	Part of Speech
divorce	3	verb
separate	3	verb
split	3	verb
disconnect	4	verb
unwind	4	verb
bisect	5	verb
detach	5	verb
divert	5	verb
ravel	5	verb

303. Shapes (General Names)

Related Clusters: 69, 99, 142, 193, 218, 270, 326

Word	Importance	Part of Speech
outline	3	noun
pattern	3	noun
shape	3	noun
figure	4	noun
form	4	noun
frame	4	noun
oblong	4	noun
profile	4	noun
skyline	4	noun
contour	5	noun
silhouette	5	noun

304. Exercise

Related Clusters: 143, 158, 183, 209, 370

Word	Importance	Part of Speech
exercise	3	noun
practice	3	noun
stretch	3	verb
cartwheel	4	noun
jog	4	verb
somersault	4	noun
sprint	4	verb
workout	4	noun
threshold	5	noun
yoga	5	noun

305. Actions Associated With Disease and Injury

Related Clusters: 230, 231, 287, 371, 404

Word	Importance	Part of Speech
blister	3	noun
burn	3	noun
scab	3	noun
sunburn	3	noun
cripple	4	verb
infect	4	verb
paralyze	4	verb
poison	4	noun
sprain	4	noun
whiplash	4	noun
wound	4	noun
abscess	5	noun

Word	Importance	Part of Speech
concussion	5	noun
fester	5	verb
gash	5	noun
venom	5	noun
welt	5	noun

306. Dark
Related Clusters: 271, 272, 372, 405

Word	Importance	Part of Speech
dark	3	adjective
shade	3	noun
shadow	3	noun
blot	4	noun
blur	4	noun
darkness	4	noun
fade	4	verb
gloom	4	noun
haze	4	noun
shady	4	adjective
splotch	5	noun

307. Natural Catastrophes
Related Clusters: 90, 226, 375, 406

Word	Importance	Part of Speech
avalanche	3	noun
earthquake	3	noun
flood	3	noun
catastrophe	4	noun
disaster	4	noun
disastrous	4	adjective
drought	4	noun
emergency	4	noun
landslide	4	noun
tragedy	4	noun
blight	5	noun
calamity	5	noun
crisis	5	noun
ordeal	5	noun

308. Jumping
Related Clusters: 63, 339, 408, 409

Word	Importance	Part of Speech
hop	3	verb
jump	3	verb
leap	3	verb
bound	4	verb
coil	4	verb
lunge	4	verb
lurch	4	verb
pounce	4	verb
spring	4	verb

309. Shellfish (and Others)
Related Clusters: 32, 35, 64, 65, 70, 82, 95, 117, 155, 188, 189, 194, 310, 341

Word	Importance	Part of Speech
lobster	3	noun
shell	3	noun
shrimp	3	noun
snail	3	noun
starfish	3	noun
clam	4	noun
coral	4	noun
crab	4	noun
crayfish	4	noun
eel	4	noun
jellyfish	4	noun
mollusk	4	noun
octopus	4	noun
oyster	4	noun
shellfish	4	noun
stingray	4	noun
plankton	5	noun
scallop	5	noun
squid	5	noun

310. Equipment Used With Animals
Related Clusters: 32, 35, 64, 65, 70, 82, 95, 117, 155, 188, 189, 194, 309, 341

Word	Importance	Part of Speech
collar	3	noun
horseshoe	3	noun
leash	3	noun
saddle	3	noun
chaps	4	noun
halter	4	noun
harness	4	noun
muzzle	4	noun
rein	4	noun
stirrup	4	noun
yoke	4	noun
bridle	5	noun

311. Cruelty and Meanness
Related Clusters: 43, 45, 55, 291, 292, 293, 312, 313, 378, 379, 380, 381, 416, 417, 422, 427, 428

Word	Importance	Part of Speech
cruel	3	adjective
mean	3	adjective
unkind	3	adjective
violent	3	adjective
cruelty	4	noun
destructive	4	adjective
fierce	4	adjective

Word	Importance	Part of Speech
merciless	4	adjective
savage	4	adjective
drastic	5	adjective
ferocious	5	adjective
vicious	5	adjective

312. General Upset
Related Clusters: 43, 45, 55, 291, 292, 293, 311, 313, 378, 379, 380, 381, 416, 417, 422, 427, 428

Word	Importance	Part of Speech
alone	3	adjective
bother	3	verb
upset	3	verb
depress	4	verb
disappoint	4	verb
discourage	4	verb
dissatisfied	4	adjective
distress	4	verb
disturb	4	verb
earnest	4	adjective
frustrate	4	verb
serious	4	adjective
solemn	4	adjective
somber	4	adjective
balk	5	verb
deject	5	verb
disrupt	5	verb
dour	5	adjective

Word	Importance	Part of Speech
impose	5	verb
infringe	5	verb
interfere	5	verb
molest	5	verb
sullen	5	adjective

313. Doubt and Hope
Related Clusters: 43, 45, 55, 291, 292, 293, 311, 312, 378, 379, 380, 381, 416, 417, 422, 427, 428

Word	Importance	Part of Speech
belief	3	noun
doubt	3	noun
hope	3	noun
trust	3	noun
desperate	4	adjective
disappointment	4	noun
faith	4	noun
hopeless	4	adjective
optimism	4	noun
despair	5	adjective

314. Lubricants and Fuels
Related Clusters: 92, 96, 118, 119, 163, 242, 254, 275, 276, 315, 316, 419, 420

Word	Importance	Part of Speech
fuel	3	noun
gas	3	noun
grease	3	noun

continued →

Word	Importance	Part of Speech
oil	3	noun
alcohol	4	noun
lubrication	4	noun
petroleum	4	noun
refuel	4	verb
diesel	5	noun
lubricate	5	verb
turpentine	5	noun

315. Handles
Related Clusters: 92, 96, 118, 119, 163, 242, 254, 275, 276, 314, 316, 419, 420

Word	Importance	Part of Speech
doorknob	3	noun
handle	3	noun
knob	3	noun
grip	4	noun
hilt	5	noun

316. Miscellaneous Devices
Related Clusters: 92, 96, 118, 119, 163, 242, 254, 275, 276, 314, 315, 419, 420

Word	Importance	Part of Speech
dial	3	noun
ladder	3	noun
pedal	3	noun
switch	3	noun
trigger	3	noun
barometer	4	noun

Word	Importance	Part of Speech
baton	4	noun
crank	4	noun
easel	4	noun
fulcrum	4	noun
platform	4	noun
pointer	4	noun
pulley	4	noun
spool	4	noun
stepladder	4	noun
wand	4	noun
reel	5	noun
sawhorse	5	noun
spindle	5	noun
toggle	5	noun

317. Lack of Permanence (People)
Related Clusters: 56, 94, 111, 203, 204, 205, 206, 227, 330, 343, 344, 382, 432, 444

Word	Importance	Part of Speech
guest	3	noun
stranger	3	noun
visitor	3	noun
gypsy	4	noun
hobo	4	noun
migrant	4	noun
passenger	4	noun
refugee	4	noun
runaway	4	noun

Word	Importance	Part of Speech
spectator	4	noun
tourist	4	noun
vacationer	4	noun
wanderer	4	noun
boarder	5	noun
fugitive	5	noun
vagabond	5	noun

318. Vehicles (Snow)

Related Clusters: 93, 97, 120, 128, 159, 234, 331

Word	Importance	Part of Speech
sled	2	noun
sleigh	2	noun
snowplow	3	noun
bobsled	4	noun
toboggan	4	noun

319. Titles and Names

Related Clusters: 53, 71, 112, 138, 248, 256, 279, 320

Word	Importance	Part of Speech
name	2	noun
title	2	noun
nickname	3	noun
autograph	4	noun
brand	4	noun
identify	4	verb

Word	Importance	Part of Speech
label	4	noun
signature	4	noun
trademark	4	noun
caption	5	noun
denomination	5	noun
dub	5	verb
monogram	5	noun
stigma	5	noun
tag	5	noun

320. Rules and Laws

Related Clusters: 53, 71, 112, 138, 248, 256, 279, 319

Word	Importance	Part of Speech
law	2	noun
rule	2	noun
regulation	3	noun
charter	4	noun
commandment	4	noun
constitution	4	noun
contract	4	noun
deed	4	noun
diploma	4	noun
policy	4	noun
treaty	4	noun
curfew	5	noun

321. Places Related to Meetings/Worship

Related Clusters: 60, 106, 121, 190, 210, 324, 335, 364, 365, 366, 399, 400

Word	Importance	Part of Speech
church	2	noun
shrine	3	noun
temple	3	noun
capitol	4	noun
cathedral	4	noun
chapel	4	noun
convent	4	noun
mission	4	noun
monastery	4	noun
synagogue	5	noun

322. Opening and Closing

Related Clusters: 38, 39, 40, 44, 66, 141, 147, 169, 170, 182, 199, 215, 216, 247, 280, 281, 282, 283, 300, 301, 302, 338, 403

Word	Importance	Part of Speech
open	2	verb
shut	2	verb
gape	4	verb
shutdown	4	noun
ajar	5	adjective
restrict	5	verb

323. Durability/Strength

Related Clusters: 202, 441

Word	Importance	Part of Speech
strong	2	adjective
weak	2	adjective
delicate	3	adjective
brittle	4	adjective
durable	4	adjective
flimsy	4	adjective
frail	4	adjective
sturdy	4	adjective
fragile	5	adjective
makeshift	5	adjective
potent	5	adjective
ramshackle	5	adjective
subtle	5	adjective

324. Storage Locations

Related Clusters: 60, 106, 121, 190, 210, 321, 335, 364, 365, 366, 399, 400

Word	Importance	Part of Speech
barn	2	noun
shed	3	noun
greenhouse	4	noun
shack	4	noun
storeroom	4	noun
warehouse	4	noun
arsenal	5	noun
hothouse	5	noun

325. Objects (General Names)
Related Clusters: 107, 164, 181, 251, 268, 367

Word	Importance	Part of Speech
thing	2	noun
object	3	noun
matter	4	noun
substance	4	noun
entity	5	noun

326. Bluntness/Sharpness
Related Clusters: 69, 99, 142, 193, 218, 270, 303

Word	Importance	Part of Speech
sharp	2	noun
dull	3	adjective
blunt	4	adjective
keen	4	adjective

327. Things That Are Commonly Measured
Related Clusters: 13, 15, 18, 19, 28, 33, 73, 130, 373, 374

Word	Importance	Part of Speech
angle	2	noun
diameter	3	noun
radius	3	noun
census	4	noun
circumference	4	noun
latitude	4	noun
longitude	4	noun
meridian	5	noun

328. Lack of Popularity/Familiarity
Related Clusters: 261, 289

Word	Importance	Part of Speech
secret	2	adjective
private	3	adjective
personal	4	adjective
privacy	4	noun
secrecy	4	noun
undiscovered	4	adjective
unknown	4	adjective
anonymous	5	adjective
solitude	5	noun

329. Growth and Survival
Related Cluster: 245

Word	Importance	Part of Speech
grow	2	verb
survive	3	verb
bloom	4	verb
cope	4	verb
mature	4	verb
stamina	4	noun
survival	4	noun
thrive	4	verb
withstand	4	verb
endure	5	verb
evolve	5	verb
flourish	5	verb
prosper	5	verb
tolerance	5	noun
tolerate	5	verb

330. Size of People
Related Clusters: 56, 94, 111, 203, 204, 205, 206, 227, 317, 343, 344, 382, 432, 444

Word	Importance	Part of Speech
giant	2	noun
dwarf	3	noun
midget	4	noun
pygmy	4	noun
runt	4	noun
troll	4	noun

331. Vehicles (Work Related)
Related Clusters: 93, 97, 120, 128, 159, 234, 318

Word	Importance	Part of Speech
tractor	3	noun
wheelbarrow	3	noun
barrow	4	noun
forklift	4	noun
harrow	4	noun
derrick	5	noun

332. Independence and Freedom
Related Clusters: 211, 228, 278, 294, 295, 350, 351, 385, 386, 387, 388, 389, 429, 433, 434

Word	Importance	Part of Speech
free	2	adjective
liberty	3	noun
obedient	3	adjective
dependent	4	adjective
independent	4	adjective
voluntary	4	adjective

333. Writers and Reporters
Related Clusters: 68, 88, 146, 167, 173, 229, 236, 257, 264, 265, 266, 297, 334, 355, 356, 357, 358, 359, 360, 361, 392, 393, 394, 395, 396, 397, 436

Word	Importance	Part of Speech
author	2	noun
speaker	3	noun
writer	3	noun
critic	4	noun
narrator	4	noun
poet	4	noun
reporter	4	noun
spokesperson	4	noun
weatherman	4	noun
publisher	5	noun
scribe	5	noun

334. People Who Clean Up

Related Clusters: 68, 88, 146, 167, 173, 229, 236, 257, 264, 265, 266, 297, 333, 355, 356, 357, 358, 359, 360, 361, 392, 393, 394, 395, 396, 397, 436

Word	Importance	Part of Speech
garbageman	2	noun
janitor	2	noun
custodian	3	noun

335. Places Related to Transportation

Related Clusters: 60, 106, 121, 190, 210, 321, 324, 364, 365, 366, 399, 400

Word	Importance	Part of Speech
station	2	noun
airport	3	noun
depot	4	noun
hangar	4	noun
terminal	4	noun

336. Organs

Related Clusters: 75, 76, 80, 115, 140, 157, 160, 191, 213, 437

Word	Importance	Part of Speech
stomach	2	noun
heart	3	noun
gland	4	noun
gut	4	noun
intestine	4	noun
kidney	4	noun
liver	4	noun
lung	4	noun
bowel	5	noun
diaphragm	5	noun
ovary	5	noun
spleen	5	noun

337. Characteristics of Rocks/Soil

Related Clusters: 133, 237, 337, 402, 438

Word	Importance	Part of Speech
sand	2	noun
pebble	3	noun
mineral	4	noun
powder	4	noun
barren	5	adjective
igneous	5	adjective

338. Halting Actions

Related Clusters: 38, 39, 40, 44, 66, 141, 147, 169, 170, 182, 199, 215, 216, 247, 280, 281, 282, 283, 300, 301, 302, 322, 403

Word	Importance	Part of Speech
quit	2	verb
stop	2	verb
avoid	4	verb
barrier	4	noun

continued →

Word	Importance	Part of Speech
blockade	4	noun
cancel	4	verb
cease	4	verb
clog	4	noun
dodge	4	verb
extinguish	4	verb
halt	4	verb
intercept	4	verb
lapse	4	verb
obstacle	4	noun
obstruct	4	verb
prevent	4	verb
resist	4	verb
smother	4	verb
abolish	5	verb
abstain	5	verb
barricade	5	noun
bondage	5	noun
boycott	5	verb
congest	5	verb
muffle	5	verb
prohibit	5	verb
refrain	5	verb
restrain	5	verb
retard	5	verb
stifle	5	verb
terminate	5	verb

339. Kicking Actions
Related Clusters: 63, 308, 408, 409

Word	Importance	Part of Speech
kick	2	verb
stamp	3	verb
stomp	4	verb
tramp	4	verb

340. Mathematical Quantities
Related Clusters: 166, 410, 423

Word	Importance	Part of Speech
sum	2	noun
average	3	noun
total	3	noun
area	4	noun
fraction	4	noun
gross	4	noun
maximum	4	noun
mean	4	noun
median	4	noun
minimum	4	noun
multiple	4	noun
percent	4	noun
percentage	4	noun
proportion	4	noun
ratio	4	noun
interest	5	noun
sine	5	noun

341. Primates

Related Clusters: 32, 35, 64, 65, 70, 82, 95, 117, 155, 188, 189, 194, 309, 310

Word	Importance	Part of Speech
monkey	2	noun
gorilla	3	noun
ape	4	noun
baboon	4	noun
chimpanzee	4	noun

342. Linking Verbs

Related Clusters: 1, 3, 4, 411

Word	Importance	Part of Speech
become	2	verb
seem	3	verb
appear	4	verb
remain	4	verb

343. Names That Indicate Permanence for People

Related Clusters: 56, 94, 111, 203, 204, 205, 206, 227, 317, 330, 344, 382, 432, 444

Word	Importance	Part of Speech
pioneer	2	noun
caveman	3	noun
citizen	3	noun
alien	4	noun
native	4	noun
newcomer	4	noun
patriot	4	noun

Word	Importance	Part of Speech
pilgrim	4	noun
puritan	4	noun
taxpayer	4	noun
tenant	4	noun
townspeople	4	noun
villager	4	noun
aborigine	5	noun
traitor	5	noun
veteran	5	noun

344. Names That Indicate Fame

Related Clusters: 56, 94, 111, 203, 204, 205, 206, 227, 317, 330, 343, 382, 432, 444

Word	Importance	Part of Speech
star	2	noun
celebrity	3	noun
savior	4	noun
idol	5	noun

345. Communication (Information Previously Withheld)

Related Clusters: 14, 61, 100, 105, 177, 198, 207, 255, 346, 383

Word	Importance	Part of Speech
tattle	3	verb
admit	4	verb
confess	4	verb
reveal	4	verb

continued →

Word	Importance	Part of Speech
confide	5	verb
divulge	5	verb
expose	5	verb

346. Recording/Translating Information

Related Clusters: 14, 61, 100, 105, 177, 198, 207, 255, 345, 383

Word	Importance	Part of Speech
record	3	noun
recording	3	noun
video	3	noun
cassette	4	noun
interpret	4	verb
score	4	verb
translate	4	verb
decode	5	verb

347. Interest

Related Clusters: 46, 67, 132, 137, 154, 225, 249, 277, 348, 349, 384

Word	Importance	Part of Speech
attention	3	noun
interest	3	noun
curiosity	4	noun
concentration	5	noun
intrigue	5	noun

348. Procedures and Processes

Related Clusters: 46, 67, 132, 137, 154, 225, 249, 277, 347, 349, 384

Word	Importance	Part of Speech
process	3	noun
recipe	3	noun
routine	3	noun
method	4	noun
procedure	4	noun
system	4	noun
convention	5	noun
function	5	noun
logic	5	noun
maneuver	5	noun
technique	5	noun

349. Beliefs

Related Clusters: 46, 67, 132, 137, 154, 225, 249, 277, 347, 348, 384

Word	Importance	Part of Speech
belief	3	noun
opinion	3	noun
custom	4	noun
habit	4	noun
ideal	4	noun
instinct	4	noun
practice	4	noun
superstition	4	noun
tradition	4	noun
creed	5	noun

Word	Importance	Part of Speech
doctrine	5	noun
mythology	5	noun
philosophy	5	noun
vice	5	noun

350. Shyness
Related Clusters: 211, 228, 278, 294, 295, 332, 351, 385, 386, 387, 388, 389, 429, 433, 434

Word	Importance	Part of Speech
bashful	3	adjective
shy	3	adjective
coy	4	adjective
helpless	4	adjective
meek	4	adjective
mild	4	adjective
skittish	4	adjective
timid	4	adjective

351. Dishonesty
Related Clusters: 211, 228, 278, 294, 295, 332, 350, 385, 386, 387, 388, 389, 429, 433, 434

Word	Importance	Part of Speech
dishonest	3	adjective
naughty	3	adjective
unfair	3	adjective
mischief	4	noun
mischievous	4	adjective
sly	4	adjective

Word	Importance	Part of Speech
unfaithful	4	adjective
cunning	5	adjective
treason	5	noun
underhanded	5	adjective

352. Equipment Used With Water/Liquid
Related Clusters: 87, 101, 102, 127, 296, 353, 391, 424

Word	Importance	Part of Speech
faucet	3	noun
hose	3	noun
sprinkler	3	noun
fountain	4	noun
funnel	4	noun
hydrant	4	noun
nozzle	4	noun
pump	4	noun
spout	4	noun
hydraulic	5	adjective
valve	5	noun

353. Moisture
Related Clusters: 87, 101, 102, 127, 296, 352, 391, 424

Word	Importance	Part of Speech
cloud	3	noun
fog	3	noun
dew	4	noun
smog	4	noun

354. Characteristics Related to Clothes/Wearing of Clothes

Related Clusters: 47, 62, 125, 129, 145, 178, 212, 224, 263, 435

Word	Importance	Part of Speech
barefoot	3	adjective
naked	3	adjective
bare	4	adjective
bareheaded	4	adjective
informal	4	adjective
nude	4	adjective
worn	4	adjective
sheer	5	adjective

355. Assistants and Supervisors

Related Clusters: 68, 88, 146, 167, 173, 229, 236, 257, 264, 265, 266, 297, 333, 334, 356, 357, 358, 359, 360, 361, 392, 393, 394, 395, 396, 397, 436

Word	Importance	Part of Speech
boss	3	noun
leader	3	noun
owner	3	noun
assistant	4	noun
chairman	4	noun
director	4	noun
foreman	4	noun
landlady	4	noun
landlord	4	noun
landowner	4	noun

Word	Importance	Part of Speech
manager	4	noun
sponsor	4	noun
superintendent	4	noun
supervisor	4	noun
apprentice	5	noun
landholder	5	noun

356. Occupations Usually Held by Youth

Related Clusters: 68, 88, 146, 167, 173, 229, 236, 257, 264, 265, 266, 297, 333, 334, 355, 357, 358, 359, 360, 361, 392, 393, 394, 395, 396, 397, 436

Word	Importance	Part of Speech
babysitter	3	noun
paperboy	3	noun

357. Discoverers and Scientists

Related Clusters: 68, 88, 146, 167, 173, 229, 236, 257, 264, 265, 266, 297, 333, 334, 355, 356, 358, 359, 360, 361, 392, 393, 394, 395, 396, 397, 436

Word	Importance	Part of Speech
astronaut	3	noun
geography	3	noun
scientist	3	noun
astronomy	4	noun
biology	4	noun
chemistry	4	noun
discoverer	4	noun

Word	Importance	Part of Speech
ecology	4	noun
economics	4	noun
geology	4	noun
inventor	4	noun
spaceman	4	noun
veterinarian	4	noun
frogman	5	noun
psychology	5	noun
researcher	5	noun
taxidermy	5	noun

358. Occupations Associated With Imprisonment/Slavery
Related Clusters: 68, 88, 146, 167, 173, 229, 236, 257, 264, 265, 266, 297, 333, 334, 355, 356, 357, 359, 360, 361, 392, 393, 394, 395, 396, 397, 436

Word	Importance	Part of Speech
guard	3	noun
prisoner	3	noun
slave	3	noun
gladiator	5	noun
warden	5	noun

359. Construction and Repairmen
Related Clusters: 68, 88, 146, 167, 173, 229, 236, 257, 264, 265, 266, 297, 333, 334, 355, 356, 357, 358, 360, 361, 392, 393, 394, 395, 396, 397, 436

Word	Importance	Part of Speech
plumber	3	noun
repairman	3	noun
carpenter	4	noun
mason	4	noun
mechanic	4	noun
draftsperson	5	noun

360. Legal Professions
Related Clusters: 68, 88, 146, 167, 173, 229, 236, 257, 264, 265, 266, 297, 333, 334, 355, 356, 357, 358, 359, 361, 392, 393, 394, 395, 396, 397, 436

Word	Importance	Part of Speech
judge	3	noun
lawyer	3	noun
attorney	4	noun
counselor	4	noun

361. Servants

Related Clusters: 68, 88, 146, 167, 173, 229, 236, 257, 264, 265, 266, 297, 333, 334, 355, 356, 357, 358, 359, 360, 392, 393, 394, 395, 396, 397, 436

Word	Importance	Part of Speech
maid	3	noun
servant	3	noun
butler	4	noun
chauffeur	4	noun
doorman	4	noun
housekeeper	4	noun
usher	4	noun
bellhop	5	noun
redcap	5	noun

362. Woodlands and Forests

Related Clusters: 50, 114, 139, 168, 267, 363, 398

Word	Importance	Part of Speech
forest	3	noun
jungle	3	noun
glade	4	noun
grove	4	noun
thicket	4	noun
woodland	4	noun

363. Pastures and Fields

Related Clusters: 50, 114, 139, 168, 267, 362, 398

Word	Importance	Part of Speech
field	3	noun
prairie	3	noun
battleground	4	noun
countryside	4	noun
meadow	4	noun
orchard	4	noun
paddy	4	noun
pasture	4	noun
vineyard	4	noun

364. Structures That Are Manmade

Related Clusters: 60, 106, 121, 190, 210, 321, 324, 335, 365, 366, 399, 400

Word	Importance	Part of Speech
building	3	noun
tower	3	noun
construction	4	noun
skyscraper	4	noun
structure	4	noun
silo	5	noun

365. Factories, Mills, and Offices
Related Clusters: 60, 106, 121, 190, 210, 321, 324, 335, 364, 366, 399, 400

Word	Importance	Part of Speech
office	3	noun
shop	3	noun
factory	4	noun
headquarters	4	noun
mill	4	noun
sawmill	4	noun
studio	4	noun
windmill	4	noun
workshop	4	noun
treadmill	5	noun

366. Ranches and Farms
Related Clusters: 60, 106, 121, 190, 210, 321, 324, 335, 364, 365, 399, 400

Word	Importance	Part of Speech
farm	3	noun
ranch	3	noun
dairy	4	noun
plantation	5	noun

367. Packing and Wrapping
Related Clusters: 107, 164, 181, 251, 268, 325

Word	Importance	Part of Speech
pack	3	verb
tape	3	verb

Word	Importance	Part of Speech
tie	3	verb
wrap	3	verb
bind	4	verb
furl	4	verb
unravel	4	verb

368. Failure and Success
Related Clusters: 58, 72, 243

Word	Importance	Part of Speech
fail	3	verb
succeed	3	verb
deserve	4	verb
merit	4	verb
qualify	4	verb
bumble	5	verb
bungle	5	verb
muff	5	verb

369. Attitudinals (Fortunate/Unfortunate)
Related Clusters: 30, 31, 285, 431, 439, 440

Word	Importance	Part of Speech
luckily	3	adverb
unfortunately	3	adverb
happily	4	adverb

370. Magic
Related Clusters: 143, 158, 183, 209, 304

Word	Importance	Part of Speech
magic	3	noun
trick	3	noun
stunt	4	noun
astrology	5	noun
gimmick	5	noun
sorcery	5	noun

371. Disabilities and Diseases
Related Clusters: 230, 231, 287, 305, 404

Word	Importance	Part of Speech
blind	3	noun
cold	3	noun
deaf	3	noun
blindness	4	noun
cancer	4	noun
chord	4	noun
croup	4	noun
lame	4	noun
mumps	4	noun
polio	4	noun
rabies	4	noun
scurvy	4	noun
stress	4	noun
diphtheria	5	noun
influenza	5	noun
malaria	5	noun
mute	5	noun
smallpox	5	noun

Word	Importance	Part of Speech
starvation	5	noun
tuberculosis	5	noun

372. Actions Related to Light
Related Clusters: 271, 272, 306, 405

Word	Importance	Part of Speech
reflect	3	verb
shine	3	verb
twinkle	3	verb
brighten	4	verb
dazzle	4	verb
flash	4	verb
glitter	4	verb
glow	4	verb
lighten	4	verb
radiate	4	verb
shimmer	4	verb
sparkle	4	verb
glisten	5	verb
illuminate	5	verb

373. Actions Related to Measurement
Related Clusters: 13, 15, 18, 19, 28, 33, 73, 130, 327, 374

Word	Importance	Part of Speech
measure	3	verb
weigh	3	verb
fathom	5	verb

374. Devices Used for Measurement

Related Clusters: 13, 15, 18, 19, 28, 33, 73, 130, 327, 373

Word	Importance	Part of Speech
thermometer	3	noun
yardstick	3	noun
compass	4	noun
measurement	4	noun
scale	4	noun
speedometer	4	noun
gauge	5	noun

375. Characteristics Associated With Weather

Related Clusters: 90, 226, 307, 406

Word	Importance	Part of Speech
dry	3	adjective
overcast	3	adjective
sunny	3	adjective
muggy	4	adjective
arid	5	adjective
sultry	5	adjective

376. Products of Fire

Related Clusters: 78, 220, 414, 442

Word	Importance	Part of Speech
ash	3	noun
smoke	3	noun
cinder	4	noun
ember	5	noun

377. Chemicals

Related Clusters: 418, 425, 443

Word	Importance	Part of Speech
caffeine	3	noun
helium	3	noun
oxygen	3	noun
ammonia	4	noun
chemical	4	noun
cholesterol	4	noun
compound	4	noun
hydrogen	4	noun
neon	4	noun
nitrogen	4	noun
sodium	4	noun
sulfur	4	noun
carbon	5	noun
chlorine	5	noun
enzyme	5	noun

378. Guilt and Worry

Related Clusters: 43, 45, 55, 291, 292, 293, 311, 312, 313, 379, 380, 381, 416, 417, 422, 427, 428

Word	Importance	Part of Speech
guilt	3	noun
shame	3	noun
worry	3	noun
anxious	4	adjective
concern	4	noun
fret	4	noun
humiliation	4	noun

continued →

Word	Importance	Part of Speech
strain	4	noun
suspense	4	noun
tense	4	verb
tension	4	noun
uncomfortable	4	adjective
uneasy	4	adjective
anxiety	5	noun

379. Irritability

Related Clusters: 43, 45, 55, 291, 292, 293, 311, 312, 313, 378, 380, 381, 416, 417, 422, 427, 428

Word	Importance	Part of Speech
grouch	3	noun
grumpy	3	adjective
rude	3	adjective
disagreeable	4	adjective
gruff	4	adjective
grumble	4	verb
impertinent	5	adjective

380. Excitement and Attention

Related Clusters: 43, 45, 55, 291, 292, 293, 311, 312, 313, 378, 379, 381, 416, 417, 422, 427, 428

Word	Importance	Part of Speech
amaze	3	verb
excite	3	verb
surprise	3	verb
amazement	4	noun
astonish	4	verb
awe	4	noun
disbelief	4	noun
rejoice	4	verb
thrill	4	verb
tingle	4	verb
appall	5	verb
astonishment	5	noun
ecstasy	5	noun
hubbub	5	noun
kindle	5	verb
marvel	5	verb
passion	5	noun
spellbound	5	adjective

381. General Human Traits
Related Clusters: 43, 45, 55, 291, 292, 293, 311, 312, 313, 378, 379, 380, 416, 417, 422, 427, 428

Word	Importance	Part of Speech
skill	3	noun
talent	3	noun
attitude	4	noun
attribute	4	noun
capacity	4	noun
discipline	4	noun
feature	4	noun
knack	4	noun
manner	4	noun
personality	4	noun
quality	4	noun
bearing	5	noun
flair	5	noun
heredity	5	noun
trait	5	noun

382. Experience/Expertise
Related Clusters: 56, 94, 111, 203, 204, 205, 206, 227, 317, 330, 343, 344, 432, 444

Word	Importance	Part of Speech
beginner	3	noun
expert	3	noun
ace	4	noun
genius	4	noun
pro	4	noun

Word	Importance	Part of Speech
scholar	4	noun
source	4	noun
specialist	4	noun
amateur	5	noun
novice	5	noun
veteran	5	noun
virgin	5	noun

383. Promises
Related Clusters: 14, 61, 100, 105, 177, 198, 207, 255, 345, 346

Word	Importance	Part of Speech
promise	3	noun
vow	4	noun
guarantee	5	noun
pact	5	noun
plea	5	noun
pledge	5	noun

384. Definition/Meaning
Related Clusters: 46, 67, 132, 137, 154, 225, 249, 277, 347, 348, 349

Word	Importance	Part of Speech
define	3	verb
definition	4	noun
interpret	4	verb
meaning	4	noun
represent	4	verb

385. Lack of Initiative

Related Clusters: 211, 228, 278, 294, 295, 332, 350, 351, 386, 387, 388, 389, 429, 433, 434

Word	Importance	Part of Speech
lazy	3	adjective
casual	4	adjective
idle	4	adjective
dormant	5	adjective
lax	5	adjective
listless	5	adjective

386. Luck and Success

Related Clusters: 211, 228, 278, 294, 295, 332, 350, 351, 385, 387, 388, 389, 429, 433, 434

Word	Importance	Part of Speech
lucky	3	adjective
successful	4	adjective
unfortunate	4	adjective

387. Stubbornness and Strictness

Related Clusters: 211, 228, 278, 294, 295, 332, 350, 351, 385, 386, 388, 389, 429, 433, 434

Word	Importance	Part of Speech
strict	3	adjective
grave	4	adjective
ornery	4	adjective

Word	Importance	Part of Speech
severe	4	adjective
sober	4	adjective
steadfast	4	adjective
stern	4	adjective
stubborn	4	adjective
obstinate	5	adjective
perverse	5	adjective
rigor	5	noun

388. Spirituality

Related Clusters: 211, 228, 278, 294, 295, 332, 350, 351, 385, 386, 387, 389, 429, 433, 434

Word	Importance	Part of Speech
holy	3	adjective
religious	4	adjective
sacred	4	adjective
spiritual	4	adjective
supernatural	4	adjective
divine	5	adjective
heathen	5	noun
pious	5	adjective
skeptic	5	noun

389. Caution
Related Clusters: 211, 228, 278, 294, 295, 332, 350, 351, 385, 386, 387, 388, 429, 433, 434

Word	Importance	Part of Speech
careful	3	adjective
careless	4	adjective
reckless	4	adjective
slack	4	adjective
stingy	4	adjective
suspicious	4	adjective
watchful	4	adjective
gingerly	5	adjective
lax	5	adjective
painstaking	5	adjective
prudent	5	adjective
wary	5	adjective

390. Geometric Planes
Related Clusters: 9, 17, 20, 21, 22, 23, 25, 26, 37, 49, 430

Word	Importance	Part of Speech
sideways	3	adjective
diagonal	4	adjective
horizontal	4	adjective
perpendicular	4	adjective
vertical	4	adjective
broadside	5	noun
lateral	5	adjective

391. Water-Related Directions
Related Clusters: 87, 101, 102, 127, 296, 352, 353, 424

Word	Importance	Part of Speech
afloat	3	adverb
ashore	4	adverb
downstream	4	noun
inland	4	noun
offshore	4	noun
midstream	5	noun

392. Food Service Occupations
Related Clusters: 68, 88, 146, 167, 173, 229, 236, 257, 264, 265, 266, 297, 333, 334, 355, 356, 357, 358, 359, 360, 361, 393, 394, 395, 396, 397, 436

Word	Importance	Part of Speech
waiter	3	noun
waitress	3	noun
chef	4	noun
dishwasher	4	noun
busboy	5	noun

393. Messengers

Related Clusters: 68, 88, 146, 167, 173, 229, 236, 257, 264, 265, 266, 297, 333, 334, 355, 356, 357, 358, 359, 360, 361, 392, 394, 395, 396, 397, 436

Word	Importance	Part of Speech
mailman	3	noun
courier	4	noun
postmaster	4	noun

394. Occupations Associated With the Outdoors

Related Clusters: 68, 88, 146, 167, 173, 229, 236, 257, 264, 265, 266, 297, 333, 334, 355, 356, 357, 358, 359, 360, 361, 392, 393, 395, 396, 397, 436

Word	Importance	Part of Speech
cowboy	3	noun
cavalry	4	noun
cowgirl	4	noun
cowhand	4	noun
deckhand	4	noun
hunter	4	noun
lumberjack	4	noun
miner	4	noun
prospector	4	noun
rancher	4	noun
shepherd	4	noun

395. People Who Buy and Sell

Related Clusters: 68, 88, 146, 167, 173, 229, 236, 257, 264, 265, 266, 297, 333, 334, 355, 356, 357, 358, 359, 360, 361, 392, 393, 394, 396, 397, 436

Word	Importance	Part of Speech
customer	3	noun
agent	4	noun
merchant	4	noun
seller	4	noun
shopper	4	noun
broker	5	noun
client	5	noun
vendor	5	noun

396. People Who Work in Offices

Related Clusters: 68, 88, 146, 167, 173, 229, 236, 257, 264, 265, 266, 297, 333, 334, 355, 356, 357, 358, 359, 360, 361, 392, 393, 394, 395, 397, 436

Word	Importance	Part of Speech
secretary	3	noun
clerk	5	noun
receptionist	5	noun
typist	5	noun

397. Occupations Associated With Transportation
Related Clusters: 68, 88, 146, 167, 173, 229, 236, 257, 264, 265, 266, 297, 333, 334, 355, 356, 357, 358, 359, 360, 361, 392, 393, 394, 395, 396, 436

Word	Importance	Part of Speech
pilot	3	noun
aviator	4	noun
driver	4	noun
skipper	4	noun
porter	5	noun
steward	5	noun
stewardess	5	noun

398. Characteristics of Places
Related Clusters: 50, 114, 139, 168, 267, 362, 363

Word	Importance	Part of Speech
desert	3	adjective
landscape	4	noun
mountainous	4	adjective
rural	4	adjective
rustic	4	adjective
tundra	4	noun
urban	4	adjective
wilderness	4	noun
heath	5	noun
moor	5	noun
municipal	5	adjective
steppe	5	noun

399. Medical Facilities
Related Clusters: 60, 106, 121, 190, 210, 321, 324, 335, 364, 365, 366, 400

Word	Importance	Part of Speech
hospital	3	noun
clinic	4	noun
morgue	5	noun
mortuary	5	noun
ward	5	noun

400. Monuments
Related Clusters: 60, 106, 121, 190, 210, 321, 324, 335, 364, 365, 366, 499

Word	Importance	Part of Speech
monument	3	noun
landmark	4	noun
memorial	4	noun
sphinx	4	noun
tomb	4	noun
tombstone	4	noun
headstone	5	noun
totem	5	noun

401. Business and Social Groups
Related Clusters: 98, 200, 258, 298

Word	Importance	Part of Speech
audience	3	noun
assembly	4	noun
association	4	noun
committee	4	noun

continued →

Word	Importance	Part of Speech
company	4	noun
conference	4	noun
convention	4	noun
council	4	noun
foundation	4	noun
league	4	noun
membership	4	noun
organization	4	noun
session	4	noun
staff	4	noun
troupe	4	noun
union	4	noun
auxiliary	5	noun
commission	5	noun
conglomerate	5	noun
institute	5	noun
partnership	5	noun

402. Actions Associated With Crops/Soil
Related Clusters: 133, 237, 259, 337, 438

Word	Importance	Part of Speech
plant	3	verb
cultivate	4	verb
fertilize	4	verb
harvest	4	verb
irrigate	4	verb
plow	4	verb
sow	4	verb

Word	Importance	Part of Speech
grub	5	verb
harrow	5	verb
tend	5	verb
thresh	5	verb
till	5	verb

403. Force
Related Clusters: 38, 39, 40, 44, 66, 141, 147, 169, 170, 182, 199, 215, 216, 247, 280, 281, 282, 283, 300, 301, 302, 322, 338

Word	Importance	Part of Speech
force	3	verb
energy	4	noun
pressure	4	noun
propulsion	5	noun

404. Germs and Genes
Related Clusters: 230, 231, 287, 305, 371

Word	Importance	Part of Speech
germ	3	noun
bacteria	4	noun
organism	4	noun
virus	4	noun
microbe	5	noun
septic	5	adjective

405. Clarity
Related Clusters: 271, 272, 306, 372

Word	Importance	Part of Speech
invisible	3	adjective
clarity	4	noun
dim	4	adjective
drab	4	adjective
dull	4	adjective
faint	4	adjective
murky	4	adjective
pale	4	adjective
transparent	4	adjective
visible	4	adjective
opaque	5	adjective
vague	5	adjective

406. Clouds
Related Clusters: 90, 226, 307, 375

Word	Importance	Part of Speech
cloud	3	noun
cirrus	4	noun
cumulus	4	noun
thunderhead	4	noun

407. Neatness/Sloppiness
Related Clusters: 186, 187, 253

Word	Importance	Part of Speech
neat	3	adjective
sloppy	4	adjective
tangle	4	noun
tidy	4	adjective
prim	5	adjective
shipshape	5	adjective

408. Creeping/Lurking Actions
Related Clusters: 63, 308, 339, 409

Word	Importance	Part of Speech
crawl	3	verb
creep	4	verb
prowl	4	verb
slink	4	verb
sneak	4	verb
lurk	5	verb
slither	5	verb

409. Standing/Stationary
Related Clusters: 63, 308, 339, 408

Word	Importance	Part of Speech
stand	3	verb
posture	4	noun
recline	4	verb
pose	5	verb
prone	5	adjective
straddle	5	verb

410. Branches of Mathematics
Related Clusters: 166, 340, 423

Word	Importance	Part of Speech
math	3	noun
algebra	4	noun
arithmetic	4	noun
geometry	4	noun
mathematics	4	noun
trigonometry	5	noun

411. Semi-Auxiliary Verbs
Related Clusters: 1, 3, 4, 342

Word	Importance	Part of Speech
have to	3	verb
had best	4	verb
had better	4	verb

412. Events and Dates (General)
Related Clusters: 179, 413

Word	Importance	Part of Speech
event	3	noun
affair	4	noun
attempt	4	noun
condition	4	noun
development	4	noun
environment	4	noun
experience	4	noun
happening	4	noun

Word	Importance	Part of Speech
occasion	4	noun
occurrence	4	noun
project	4	noun
situation	4	noun
circumstance	5	noun
context	5	noun
enterprise	5	noun
feat	5	noun
incident	5	noun
instance	5	noun

413. Political Events
Related Clusters: 179, 412

Word	Importance	Part of Speech
vote	3	verb
campaign	4	noun
crusade	4	noun
elect	4	verb
nominate	4	verb
voter	4	noun
ballot	5	noun

414. Products Associated With Fire

Related Clusters: 78, 220, 376, 442

Word	Importance	Part of Speech
pipe	3	noun
cigar	4	noun
tobacco	4	noun
wick	4	noun
cigarette	5	noun
paraffin	5	noun

415. Paint

Related Cluster: 57

Word	Importance	Part of Speech
paint	3	noun
dye	4	noun
stain	4	noun
tint	4	noun
enamel	5	noun
lacquer	5	noun

416. Actions Related to Fear

Related Clusters: 43, 45, 55, 291, 292, 293, 311, 312, 313, 378, 379, 380, 381, 417, 422, 427, 428

Word	Importance	Part of Speech
scare	3	verb
cringe	4	verb
haunt	4	verb
horrify	4	verb
startle	4	verb
terrify	4	verb
wince	4	verb
flinch	5	verb
petrify	5	verb

417. Envy and Jealousy

Related Clusters: 43, 45, 55, 291, 292, 293, 311, 312, 313, 378, 379, 380, 381, 416, 422, 427, 428

Word	Importance	Part of Speech
jealous	3	adjective
envy	4	noun
grudge	4	noun
jealousy	4	noun
possessive	4	adjective

418. Electricity and Magnetism

Related Clusters: 377, 425, 443

Word	Importance	Part of Speech
magnet	3	noun
charge	4	noun
electric	4	noun
hydroelectric	4	adjective
radiation	4	noun
microwave	5	noun
radioactive	5	adjective

419. Machines

Related Clusters: 92, 96, 118, 119, 163, 242, 254, 275, 276, 314, 315, 316, 420

Word	Importance	Part of Speech
machine	3	noun
appliance	4	noun
clockwork	4	noun
equipment	4	noun
hardware	4	noun
machinery	4	noun
mechanical	4	adjective
apparatus	5	noun
contraption	5	noun
gadget	5	noun
rig	5	noun

420. Vision-Related Equipment

Related Clusters: 92, 96, 118, 119, 163, 242, 254, 275, 276, 314, 315, 316, 419

Word	Importance	Part of Speech
camera	3	noun
binoculars	4	noun
lens	4	noun
microscope	4	noun
telescope	4	noun
eyepiece	5	noun

421. Trees/Bushes (Types)

Related Clusters: 36, 108, 192, 269

Word	Importance	Part of Speech
aspen	4	noun
balsa	4	noun
beech	4	noun
birch	4	noun
cedar	4	noun
citrus	4	noun
cottonwood	4	noun
dogwood	4	noun
elm	4	noun
fir	4	noun
hickory	4	noun
locust	4	noun
maple	4	noun
mulberry	4	noun
oak	4	noun
pine	4	noun
poplar	4	noun
redwood	4	noun
spruce	4	noun
willow	4	noun
eucalyptus	5	noun
evergreen	5	noun
hemlock	5	noun

422. Contentment and Comfort

Related Clusters: 43, 45, 55, 291, 292, 293, 311, 312, 313, 378, 379, 380, 381, 416, 417, 427, 428

Word	Importance	Part of Speech
comfort	4	noun
comfortable	4	adjective
content	4	adjective
cozy	4	adjective
mellow	4	adjective
peaceful	4	adjective
pity	4	noun
relief	4	noun
satisfy	4	verb
snug	4	adjective
soothe	4	verb
sympathize	4	verb
sympathy	4	noun
tame	4	adjective
welfare	4	noun
console	5	verb

423. Mathematical Constructs

Related Clusters: 166, 340, 410

Word	Importance	Part of Speech
denominator	4	noun
equation	4	noun
exponent	4	noun
formula	4	noun

Word	Importance	Part of Speech
identity	4	noun
product	4	noun
quotient	4	noun
rate	4	noun
evaluate	5	verb
function	5	noun
plane	5	noun
range	5	noun
slope	5	noun
term	5	noun

424. Slimy Substances

Related Clusters: 87, 101, 102, 127, 296, 352, 353, 391

Word	Importance	Part of Speech
foam	4	noun
quicksand	4	noun
scum	4	noun
sediment	4	noun
silt	4	noun
slime	4	noun
froth	5	noun
goo	5	noun
muck	5	noun

425. Atoms and Molecules
Related Clusters: 377, 418, 443

Word	Importance	Part of Speech
atom	4	noun
atomic	4	adjective
molecule	4	noun
neutron	4	noun
nuclear	4	adjective
electron	5	noun
ion	5	noun
nucleus	5	noun
proton	5	noun

426. Freedom/Lack of Freedom
Related Clusters: 41, 89, 148, 171, 184

Word	Importance	Part of Speech
escape	4	verb
flee	4	verb
parole	4	noun
release	4	verb
sacrifice	5	verb
surrender	5	verb

427. General Names for Feelings
Related Clusters: 43, 45, 55, 291, 292, 293, 311, 312, 313, 378, 379, 380, 381, 416, 417, 422, 428

Word	Importance	Part of Speech
impression	4	noun
impulse	4	noun
mood	4	noun
sensation	4	noun
sense	4	noun
emotion	5	noun

428. Actions Related to Neglect
Related Clusters: 43, 45, 55, 291, 292, 293, 311, 312, 313, 378, 379, 380, 381, 416, 417, 422, 427

Word	Importance	Part of Speech
maroon	4	verb
omit	4	verb
overlook	4	verb
exclude	5	verb
isolate	5	verb
neglect	5	verb

429. Prudence
Related Clusters: 211, 228, 278, 294, 295, 332, 350, 351, 385, 386, 387, 388, 389, 433, 434

Word	Importance	Part of Speech
modest	4	adjective
modesty	4	noun
sensible	4	adjective
chaste	5	adjective
discreet	5	adjective

430. Absence/Presence
Related Clusters: 9, 17, 20, 21, 22, 23, 25, 26, 37, 49, 390

Word	Importance	Part of Speech
absence	4	noun
absent	4	adjective
available	4	adjective
present	4	adjective
unavailable	4	adjective

431. Attitudinals (Expected/Unexpected)
Related Clusters: 30, 31, 285, 369, 439, 440

Word	Importance	Part of Speech
amazingly	4	adverb
naturally	4	adverb
typically	4	adverb
inevitably	5	adverb

432. Financial Status
Related Clusters: 56, 94, 111, 203, 204, 205, 206, 227, 317, 330, 343, 344, 382, 444

Word	Importance	Part of Speech
beggar	4	noun
bum	4	noun
millionaire	4	noun
peasant	4	noun

433. Patience
Related Clusters: 211, 228, 278, 294, 295, 332, 350, 351, 385, 386, 387, 388, 389, 429, 434

Word	Importance	Part of Speech
patience	4	noun
patient	4	adjective
restless	4	adjective

434. Humor
Related Clusters: 211, 228, 278, 294, 295, 332, 350, 351, 385, 386, 387, 388, 389, 429, 433

Word	Importance	Part of Speech
hilarious	4	adjective
humorous	4	adjective
witty	4	adjective

435. Armor
Related Clusters: 47, 62, 125, 129, 145, 178, 212, 224, 263, 354

Word	Importance	Part of Speech
armor	4	noun
sheath	4	noun
shield	4	noun

436. Occupations Associated With Transportation
Related Clusters: 68, 88, 146, 167, 173, 229, 236, 257, 264, 265, 266, 297, 333, 334, 355, 356, 357, 358, 359, 360, 361, 392, 393, 394, 395, 396, 397

Word	Importance	Part of Speech
banker	4	noun
cashier	4	noun
teller	5	noun

437. Body Systems
Related Clusters: 75, 76, 80, 115, 140, 157, 160, 191, 213, 336

Word	Importance	Part of Speech
circulation	4	noun
digest	4	noun
perspire	4	verb
digestion	5	noun

438. Actions Associated With Metals
Related Clusters: 133, 237, 259, 337, 402

Word	Importance	Part of Speech
rust	4	verb
corrode	5	verb
tarnish	5	verb

439. Attitudinals (Correctness/Incorrectness)
Related Clusters: 30, 31, 285, 369, 431, 440

Word	Importance	Part of Speech
correctly	4	adverb
incorrectly	4	adverb
wrongly	4	adverb

440. Attitudinals (Wisdom/ Lack of Wisdom)
Related Clusters: 30, 31, 285, 369, 431, 439

Word	Importance	Part of Speech
cleverly	4	adverb
reasonably	4	adverb
wisely	4	adverb

441. Consistency
Related Clusters: 202, 323

Word	Importance	Part of Speech
elastic	4	adjective
gel	4	noun
supple	4	adjective

442. Insulation

Related Clusters: 78, 220, 376, 414

Word	Importance	Part of Speech
fireproof	5	adjective
insulate	5	verb

443. Acids

Related Clusters: 377, 418, 425

Word	Importance	Part of Speech
acid	4	noun
alkaline	5	adjective

444. Names That Indicate Political Disposition

Related Clusters: 56, 94, 111, 203, 204, 205, 206, 227, 317, 330, 343, 344, 382, 432

Word	Importance	Part of Speech
confederate	5	adjective
democratic	5	adjective
independent	5	adjective
republican	5	adjective
tory	5	adjective
whig	5	adjective

APPENDIX B

Hardcopy Diagnostic Assessment

Copyright © 2009 by Robert J. Marzano

The hardcopy diagnostic assessment may be used in lieu of the online diagnostic assessment to place students in the continuum of 420 clusters. Where the online assessment involves students responding to selected response items for each cluster, the hardcopy assessment involves students responding to a pair of words for each cluster.

The first two terms are from the first cluster, the next two terms are from the second cluster, and so on. To illustrate, the first term is *can* and the second term is *will*. Both are from the first cluster titled *Modals*. Terms for cluster 50 are *moon* and *planet*. Both are from the 50th cluster titled *Bodies in Space*.

To place a student on the continuum of 420 clusters, the teacher begins with the first two test words. Again, they are *can* and *will*. The teacher asks the student to use each of the two terms in a sentence. For example, the teacher points to the word *can* and pronounces it for the student and then says, "Please use *can* in a sentence." If the answer provided by the student leaves the teacher in doubt regarding the student's understanding of the term, the teacher simply asks the student to use the term in another sentence or asks the student to explain the term.

If the student misses one or both terms for cluster 1, the teacher stops there and begins instruction on the words from cluster 1. If the student addresses both terms correctly, the teacher moves up to cluster 25. If the student addresses both of these terms correctly, the teacher jumps up to cluster 50. The teacher keeps jumping up 25 clusters until the student does not respond correctly to one or both of the test terms. In such cases, the teacher starts moving back one cluster at a time until the student reaches a cluster where he or she addresses both terms correctly.

To illustrate this progression, assume that a student addresses both terms correctly for cluster 1. The teacher moves up to cluster 25 and the student again addresses both terms correctly. The teacher moves up to cluster 50 where the student addresses only one of the terms correctly. The teacher then moves down to cluster 49 were the student does not address either of the terms correctly. The teacher moves down to cluster 48 where the student addresses one of the terms correctly. The teacher moves down to cluster 47 where the students addresses both terms correctly. At this point, the teacher stops the assessment and considers cluster 48 the starting point for the student.

Hardcopy Diagnostic Assessment

1	can will	**2**	during while	**3**	do have	**4**	am is
5	too with	**6**	they him	**7**	her its	**8**	what when
9	to at	**10**	to since	**11**	that which	**12**	how why
13	each either	**14**	good-bye maybe	**15**	more very	**16**	ready early
17	left right	**18**	almost enough	**19**	half less	**20**	far apart
21	forward backwards	**22**	indoors outside	**23**	under underneath	**24**	late afterward
25	where anywhere	**26**	top overhead	**27**	without instead	**28**	number dozen
29	Tuesday February	**30**	maybe allegedly	**31**	please hopefully	**32**	turkey ostrich
33	big tiny	**34**	any nobody	**35**	tadpole kitten	**36**	tree flower
37	corner edge	**38**	catch toss	**39**	climb lift	**40**	do use
41	own belong	**42**	we're they're	**43**	sad sorry	**44**	carry mail
45	happy celebrate	**46**	choice appoint	**47**	helmet glasses	**48**	breakfast dessert
49	point address	**50**	moon planet	**51**	drink chew	**52**	month decade
53	lullaby rhyme	**54**	ballet solo	**55**	care enjoy	**56**	person hero
57	blue green	**58**	best important	**59**	fast hurry	**60**	kindergarten classroom
61	say recite	**62**	glove sandal	**63**	run hike	**64**	dog lion
65	horse kangaroo	**66**	go travel	**67**	idea forget	**68**	student graduate
69	empty hollow	**70**	fish seal	**71**	read trace	**72**	truth mistake
73	foot spoonful	**74**	mix mustard	**75**	finger shoulders	**76**	leg ankle
77	show cartoon	**78**	cold hot	**79**	noon overnight	**80**	tooth tongue

81	he's here's	82	turtle dinosaur	83	today ancient	84	bell siren
85	I'll she'll	86	butter cheese	87	island coast	88	nurse doctor
89	win champion	90	air weather	91	kitchen hallway	92	rope glue
93	driveway drawbridge	94	aunt grandparent	95	caterpillar dragonfly	96	cup mug
97	row glide	98	pile bunch	99	deep tall	100	greet thank
101	snow rainbow	102	lake ocean	103	noise quiet	104	money dime
105	talk discuss	106	shelter jail	107	fix build	108	twig branch
109	bank purse	110	help protect	111	lady female	112	paper chalkboard
113	chair cradle	114	lot place	115	face forehead	116	free expensive
117	fly soar	118	oven furnace	119	hammer shovel	120	plane helicopter
121	home tent	122	buy earn	123	floor doorstep	124	snack spaghetti
125	jeans nightgown	126	once annual	127	sink leak	128	train motorcycle
129	fold wrinkle	130	flake slice	131	hug cuddle	132	nap dream
133	mud soil	134	blanket pillowcase	135	look focus	136	ham bacon
137	smart wise	138	story mystery	139	garden playground	140	ear nostril
141	drop tumble	142	square cube	143	doll toy	144	calendar watch
145	jacket cape	146	work hire	147	start try	148	steal attract
149	wave salute	150	they've we've	151	grin frown	152	kiss lick
153	syrup brownie	154	coach study	155	beak fin	156	laugh yawn
157	skin beard	158	ball softball	159	canoe submarine	160	body lap
161	hurt shoot	162	grill fry	163	scissors axe	164	basket tank
165	ring creak	166	add multiply	167	clown model	168	hill cliff

169	rest delay	170	sit kneel	171	keep hide	172	city downtown
173	mayor candidate	174	banana strawberry	175	meow purr	176	milk coffee
177	ask question	178	rag cotton	179	circus party	180	country continent
181	stick log	182	pull yank	183	game race	184	lose trade
185	clean sweep	186	pretty handsome	187	fat skinny	188	mouse squirrel
189	zoo birdhouse	190	theater stadium	191	blood sweat	192	lawn seaweed
193	flat steep	194	pet fossil	195	flag badge	196	blow pant
197	hit knead	198	blame scold	199	roll spin	200	family democracy
201	prize medal	202	soft hard	203	boy man	204	child teenager
205	friend neighbor	206	villain pest	207	command forbid	208	corn tomato
209	bicycle football	210	grocery restaurant	211	brave loyal	212	button sleeve
213	bone muscle	214	price rent	215	last finish	216	rock slide
217	gate fence	218	line zigzag	219	alphabet Braille	220	burn ignite
221	easy difficult	222	sweet sour	223	brush shampoo	224	comb ribbon
225	search investigate	226	wind thunder	227	cupid fairy	228	gentle grateful
229	runner batter	230	sick disease	231	pill crutch	232	hunger thirsty
233	time bedtime	234	tire cockpit	235	couldn't won't	236	job chore
237	jewel stone	238	sentence noun	239	art photograph	240	safe risk
241	sneeze snort	242	cut carve	243	evil worst	244	piano banjo
245	dead born	246	food seafood	247	meet connect	248	dictionary diary
249	solve compose	250	break crash	251	bar pipe	252	copy example
253	strong clumsy	254	gun sword	255	recommend convince	256	postcard poster

257	medicine religion	258	band team	259	steel metal	260	fight war
261	luck chance	262	plain blank	263	costume uniform	264	choir singer
265	firefighter policeman	266	pastor bishop	267	hole canyon	268	mask flap
269	rose daisy	270	circle loop	271	light bright	272	candle lamp
273	purpose cause	274	I'd you'd	275	battery engine	276	keyboard robot
277	plan goal	278	proud confident	279	map graph	280	play motion
281	shake vibrate	282	bounce fidget	283	magnify expand	284	curtain banner
285	seriously honestly	286	language vocabulary	287	itch fever	288	trash litter
289	popular common	290	rare weird	291	fear nervous	292	mad dislike
293	expect miss	294	responsible eager	295	crazy wild	296	pool dam
297	butcher baker	298	police navy	299	change opposite	300	follow chase
301	crumble shorten	302	split separate	303	shape pattern	304	practice stretch
305	blister sunburn	306	dark shadow	307	avalanche earthquake	308	hop jump
309	shrimp lobster	310	saddle leash	311	mean violent	312	upset disappoint
313	hope doubt	314	oil fuel	315	handle knob	316	ladder pedal
317	guest stranger	318	sled snowplow	319	title nickname	320	rule regulation
321	church shrine	322	open shut	323	strong delicate	324	barn storeroom
325	thing object	326	sharp dull	327	angle radius	328	secret private
329	grow survive	330	giant dwarf	331	tractor wheelbarrow	332	free obedient
333	author speaker	334	janitor garbageman	335	station airport	336	stomach heart
337	sand pebble	338	stop avoid	339	kick stamp	340	sum total
341	gorilla monkey	342	become seem	343	pioneer citizen	344	star celebrity

345	tattle admit	346	record video	347	attention interest	348	recipe routine
349	opinion belief	350	shy bashful	351	naughty dishonest	352	hose faucet
353	cloud fog	354	naked informal	355	leader owner	356	babysitter paperboy
357	astronaut scientist	358	guard slave	359	carpenter plumber	360	judge lawyer
361	maid butler	362	forest jungle	363	prairie field	364	tower building
365	shop office	366	farm ranch	367	tape pack	368	fail succeed
369	happily luckily	370	magic trick	371	blind deaf	372	shine reflect
373	measure weigh	374	thermometer yardstick	375	dry overcast	376	smoke ash
377	oxygen caffeine	378	concern guilt	379	grumpy rude	380	surprise amaze
381	skill talent	382	expert beginner	383	promise vow	384	define represent
385	lazy casual	386	lucky successful	387	strict stubborn	388	holy heathen
389	careful slack	390	sideways diagonal	391	afloat inland	392	waiter chef
393	mailman postmaster	394	cowboy lumberjack	395	customer merchant	396	secretary clerk
397	pilot skipper	398	desert rural	399	hospital clinic	400	monument landmark
401	audience council	402	plant irrigate	403	force pressure	404	germ bacteria
405	invisible dim	406	cloud thunderhead	407	neat tidy	408	crawl sneak
409	stand posture	410	math algebra	411	have to had better	412	event attempt
413	vote elect	414	pipe cigar	415	paint dye	416	scare startle
417	jealous grudge	418	magnet electric	419	machine appliance	420	camera telescope

APPENDIX C

This appendix contains the tier three subject-matter terms in grades K–5 for ELA, mathematics, science, and social studies. Terms are organized into topics referred to as *measurement topics* for each grade level and subject area.

ELA K–5 Vocabulary Terms

Table C.1: Kindergarten ELA Vocabulary Terms

Kindergarten ELA Measurement Topics	Vocabulary Terms
Decoding	consonant, letter, long vowel, short vowel, vowel, word
Phonological Awareness	rhyme, consonant, vowel, syllable
Print Concepts	back cover, front cover, left, right, space
Analyzing Text Organization and Structure	compare, different, similar
Text Features	author, illustration
Text Types	author, fiction, nonfiction, poem, rhythm, title
Analyzing Main Ideas	main topic, character, detail, event, setting
Analyzing Claims and Reasons	opinion, reason
Analyzing Narratives	beginning, end, middle, character, setting
Comparing Texts	detail, character
Analyzing Words	meaning, word, root word, opposite
Generating Sentences	action, capital letter, sentence, subject, exclamation mark, period, question mark
Generating Text Organization and Structure	information, opinion, story, topic, detail, fact
Generating Claims	opinion, statement
Sources and Research	question
Generating Narratives	character, event, narrative, setting, story, describe
Parts of Speech	noun, plural, singular, verb, preposition, how many, what, when, where, who, why
Spelling	alphabet, consonant, letter, sound, spell, vowel

Table C.2: Grade 1 ELA Vocabulary Terms

Grade 1 ELA Measurement Topics	Vocabulary Terms
Decoding	final-e, vowel team, syllable, irregular
Phonological Awareness	consonant blend, syllable
Analyzing Text Organization and Structure	order
Text Features	bold word, caption, glossary, heading, illustration
Text Types	fiction, nonfiction

Analyzing Main Ideas	important, paragraph, lesson, message, question
Analyzing Claims and Reasons	fact
Analyzing Narratives	main character, character, place, time
Analyzing Point of View	dialogue, first person, narrator, quotation marks, third person
Comparing Texts	category, compare
Analyzing Words	context, attribute, category, type
Analyzing Language	emotion, sense
Generating Sentences	capitalize, comma, declarative, end punctuation, exclamatory, imperative, interrogative, conjunction
Generating Text Organization and Structure	introduction, relevant, conclusion
Generating Claims and Reasons	opinion, support
Sources and Research	heading, source
Generating Narratives	narrative, adjective, five senses, order, sequence
Parts of Speech	possessive, proper noun, personal pronoun, possessive pronoun, article, determiner, plural, singular, future, past, present
Spelling	pronounce, spelling, consonant
Editing	comma, list

Table C.3: Grade 2 ELA Vocabulary Terms

Grade 2 ELA Measurement Topics	Vocabulary Terms
Decoding	r-controlled vowel, affix, prefix, suffix, associate
Analyzing Text Organization and Structure	climax, conflict, plot, relationship
Text Features	chapter, index, table of contents, caption
Analyzing Main Ideas	keyword, passage, time line
Analyzing Claims and Reasons	opinion
Analyzing Narratives	location, time period, challenge, trait
Analyzing Point of View	perspective, point of view, persuade
Comparing Texts	Venn diagram, purpose
Analyzing Words	definition, dictionary, compound word, prefix, suffix, synonym, thesaurus
Analyzing Language	alliteration

continued →

Grade 2 ELA Measurement Topics	Vocabulary Terms
Generating Sentences	coordinating conjunction, fragment, predicate, adverb
Generating Text Organization and Structure	response, category, conclusion
Generating Claims and Reasons	fact, reason
Sources and Research	index, sidebar, table of contents, restate
Generating Narratives	event, descriptive detail
Revision	formal, informal, slang, draft, revise
Parts of Speech	collective, reflexive pronoun, verb, adverb
Spelling	compound word, irregular, alphabetical, dictionary, guide word
Editing	apostrophe, contraction, common noun, body, closing, greeting, signature

Table C.4: Grade 3 ELA Vocabulary Terms

Grade 3 ELA Measurement Topics	Vocabulary Terms
Decoding	diphthong, root
Analyzing Text Organization and Structure	signal word, section, structure, diagram
Text Features	concept
Text Types	explanatory
Analyzing Ideas and Themes	linking word, folktale, moral
Analyzing Claims, Evidence, and Reasoning	evidence
Analyzing Narratives	impact, character trait, feeling, motivation
Analyzing Point of View	react
Comparing Texts	compare, theme, storyline
Analyzing Words	context, antonym
Analyzing Language	literal, nonliteral
Generating Sentences	complex sentence, compound sentence, simple sentence, linking word, subordinating conjunction
Generating Text Organization and Structure	prompt, body, main idea
Generating Claims, Evidence, and Reasoning	specific, vocabulary
Sources and Research	diagram, call number, database, research, summary, website
Generating Narratives	storyboard, thesaurus, dialogue tag, motivation

Revision	slang, thesis
Parts of Speech	future tense, past tense, present tense, abstract, comparative, modifier, superlative, antecedent, feminine, masculine, pronoun
Editing	historical period, direct address, homophone

Table C.5: Grade 4 ELA Vocabulary Terms

Grade 4 ELA Measurement Topics	Vocabulary Terms
Decoding	affix, sight word
Analyzing Text Organization and Structure	causation, problem/solution, graph, multimedia
Text Features	text feature
Text Types	act, character list, line, meter, scene, stanza, verse, third person
Analyzing Ideas and Themes	outline, paraphrase, topic sentence, theme
Analyzing Claims, Evidence, and Reasoning	personal experience, quote
Analyzing Narratives	trait
Analyzing Point of View	narration, persona
Comparing Texts	firsthand, secondhand, oral, representation, visual, culture, myth
Analyzing Words	text feature, homophone
Analyzing Language	metaphor, simile
Generating Text Organization and Structure	introduce, section, link, transition, main idea
Generating Claims, Evidence, and Reasoning	convince, inference, paraphrase
Sources and Research	encyclopedia, research question, cause, effect, procedure
Generating Narratives	chronological, describe, dialogue tag
Revision	dependent clause, independent clause, topic sentence
Parts of Speech	modal auxiliary verb, future progressive, past progressive, present progressive, relative adverb, relative pronoun, adjective
Editing	double negative, proper adjective, compound sentence, spellcheck

Table C.6: Grade 5 ELA Vocabulary Terms

Grade 5 ELA Measurement Topics	Vocabulary Terms
Analyzing Text Organization and Structure	comparison, description, epilogue, prologue, line break, stanza break
Analyzing Ideas and Themes	summarize, conflict
Analyzing Claims, Evidence, and Reasoning	claim, direct, indirect, objective, subjective, anecdote
Analyzing Narratives	setting, circumstance
Analyzing Point of View	limited, omniscient, second person
Comparing Texts	second person, genre, dialect, register
Analyzing Language	context, adage, idiom, proverb, imagery, sensory language, symbol
Generating Text Organization and Structure	focus, heading, example, summarize
Generating Claims, Evidence, and Reasoning	claim, anecdote
Sources and Research	search engine, paraphrase
Generating Narratives	resolve, action verb, linking verb, show, tell, dialogue
Audience, Purpose, and Task	entertain, inform, audience, style
Revision	anecdote, style, tangent, clause, complex, compound, compound-complex, run-on, simple
Parts of Speech	past participle, perfect tense, simple tense, correlative conjunction, interjection
Editing	shift, tense, proper adjectives, proper nouns, italics, underline, interrupters, nonessential, series, root

Mathematics K–5 Vocabulary Terms

Table C.7: Kindergarten Mathematics Vocabulary Terms

Kindergarten Mathematics Measurement Topics	Vocabulary Terms
Number Sequence	count, number, digit
Counting Objects	number, total, group, order, count
Comparing Quantities	equal to, fewer than, match, more than, greater than, less than
Decomposing Numbers	equation, part, whole, compose, decompose

Addition	add, addition, equal, equation, plus, addend, sum, break apart, decompose
Subtraction	difference, minus, subtract, subtraction, break apart, decompose
Measurement	area, attribute, heavy, height, length, light, long, measurable, attribute, measure, narrow, short, tall, temperature, volume, wide, width, balance scale, compare, thermometer, weight
Geometric Figures	closed, corner, curved, open, side, straight, edge, equal faces, face, flat, point, solid, vertex, circle, cone, cube, cylinder, hexagon, rectangle, sphere, square, trapezoid, triangle
Constructing Geometric Figures	above, below, beside, equal corners, equal sides, flat, solid, three-dimensional, two-dimensional
Categorical Data	attribute, category, different, similar, sort

Table C.8: Grade 1 Mathematics Vocabulary Terms

Grade 1 Mathematics Measurement Topics	Vocabulary Terms
Place Value	ones, ones place, tens, tens place, place value, greater than, less than
Addition	tens, ones, tens place, ones place, place value
Subtraction	ones, tens, ones place, tens place
Addition and Subtraction Concepts	equals, difference, sum
Length	longer, shorter, centimeter, endpoint, inch
Time	analog clock, clockwise, half hour, hour, hour hand, minute, minute hand, digital clock, hour display, minute display, o'clock
Geometric Figures	rhombus, angle, right angle, three-dimensional
Partitions and Compositions of Geometric Figures	equal portions, fourth, half, quarter, rhombus, three-dimensional
Representing Categorical Data	category label, graph, graph title, picture graph, tally

Table C.9: Grade 2 Mathematics Vocabulary Terms

Grade 2 Mathematics Measurement Topics	Vocabulary Terms
Counting	ones place, skip count, tens place, hundred, hundreds place
Even and Odd Numbers	equal groups, even, odd
Number Lines and Line Plots	hash mark, number line, range, unit, line plot, unit type
Place Value	expanded form, hundred, hundreds place, standard form, inequality, greater than, less than
Addition	hundreds, hash mark, number line, range, unit
Subtraction	hundreds, minuend, subtrahend, hash mark, number line, range, unit
Word Problems	difference, sum, measurement, unit
Rectangular Arrays	cell, column, rectangular array, row
Fractions	third, whole
Length	hash mark, length unit, measuring tape, meter stick, ruler, yardstick, zero mark, foot, key, unit
Time	a.m., minute mark, p.m.
Money	bill, cent, coin, dime, dollar, nickel, penny, quarter, change, dollars, cents
Geometric Figures	pentagon, quadrilateral, right angle
Representing Categorical Data	key, title, axis, bar graph, count scale, range, unit

Table C.10: Grade 3 Mathematics Vocabulary Terms

Grade 3 Mathematics Measurement Topics	Vocabulary Terms
Estimation	estimate, round
Multiplication	array, factor, multiplication, multiply, product, associative property of multiplication, commutative property of multiplication, distributive property of multiplication, parentheses, numerical expression, times
Division	divide, dividend, divisor, quotient, associative property, commutative property, distributive property, factor, product, division
Word Problems	numerical expression, operation, order of operations, parentheses, variable, diagram

Fractions	denominator, fraction, numerator, whole number, improper fraction, proper fraction, unit fraction
Equivalent Fractions	fraction, whole number, equivalent fractions, denominator, numerator
Fraction Measurements	fraction, mixed number, unit fraction, whole unit, equivalent fractions, scale, whole number
Patterns	associative property of addition, commutative property of addition, associative property, commutative property, distributive property, multiplication table
Time	a.m., p.m., midnight, noon
Mass and Liquid Volume	gram, kilogram, mass, metric system, ounce, pound, scale, U.S. customary system, cup, fluid ounce, gallon, liquid volume, liter, milliliter
Area	area, square units, unit square, array, distributive property
Perimeter	perimeter, side length, area
Two-Dimensional Figures	category
Representing Categorical Data	scale, key

Table C.11: Grade 4 Mathematics Vocabulary Terms

Grade 4 Mathematics Measurement Topics	Vocabulary Terms
Place Value	hundred thousands, millions, ten thousands, place value
Addition and Subtraction	carry, standard algorithm for addition, borrow, regroup, standard algorithm for subtraction
Multiplication	area model, times
Division	quotient, multiple, remainder
Factors and Multiples	composite number, multiple, prime number
Equivalent Fractions	equivalent fractions, reduced form, benchmark fraction, least common multiple
Fraction Addition and Subtraction	common denominator, like denominators, regroup
Fraction Multiplication	multiple
Decimal Fractions	power of ten, decimal point, decimal value, hundredths, tenths, thousandths, decimal place value
Patterns	rule, term, pattern
Measurement Conversions	kiloliter, kilometer, mile, millimeter, pint, quart, ton, yard, liquid volume, mass

continued →

Grade 4 Mathematics Measurement Topics	Vocabulary Terms
Area and Perimeter	area, perimeter, square units
Two-Dimensional Figures	acute, acute triangle, angle, equilateral triangle, isosceles triangle, obtuse, obtuse triangle, opposite angles, parallel, parallelogram, perpendicular, right angle, right triangle, scalene triangle, line of symmetry, rotational symmetry, flip, image, line of reflection, point of rotation, reflection, rotation, slide, translation, turn
Angles	acute, angle, degree, obtuse, protractor, ray, right angle, straight angle, vertex, angle measure, adjacent angles, congruent
Lines	dimension, end point, line, line segment, point, ray, degree, intersect, oblique, parallel, perpendicular, plane, right angle

Table C.12: Grade 5 Mathematics Vocabulary Terms

Grade 5 Mathematics Measurement Topics	Vocabulary Terms
Multiplication and Division	standard algorithm for multiplication, quotient, remainder, power of ten
Fraction Addition and Subtraction	unlike denominators, least common multiple
Fraction Multiplication	fraction, denominator, numerator, equivalent fractions, whole number
Fraction Division	quotient, unit fraction, whole number
Decimal Place Values	thousandths, decimal place value
Decimal Addition and Subtraction	thousandths
Decimal Multiplication and Division	decimal place value, whole number
Exponents	base, cube, exponent, power, raise, square, exponential notation, power of ten
Numerical Expressions	brackets, numerical expression
Numerical Patterns	table of values, sequence, coordinate plane, ordered pair
Measurement Conversions	tablespoon, teaspoon, centi, deci, decimeter, kilo, metric ton, milli, milligram
Volume	base, unit cube, volume, cubic units, right rectangular prism
Two-Dimensional Figures	decagon, heptagon, irregular, nonagon, octagon, polygon, regular, concave, convex
Coordinate Planes	Cartesian coordinate plane, coordinates, ordered pair, origin, point, x-axis, x-coordinate, y-axis, y-coordinate, horizontal, vertical

Science K–5 Vocabulary Terms

Grade-band scales should be applied at every grade level within the specified band.

Table C.13: Grades K–5 Science Vocabulary Terms

Grades K–5 Science Measurement Topics	Vocabulary Terms
Scientific Method	analysis, conclusion, data, experiment, hypothesis, observation, scientific method

Table C.14: Grades K–2 Science Vocabulary Terms

Grades K–2 Science Measurement Topics	Vocabulary Terms
Defining Engineering Design Problems	engineering, need, observation, problem, situation, tool
Solutions for Engineering Design Problems	models, problem, solution, predict, solve, test

Table C.15: Grades 3–5 Science Vocabulary Terms

Grades 3–5 Science Measurement Topics	Vocabulary Terms
Defining Engineering Design Problems	criteria, design problem, feature, constraint, limitation
Solutions for Engineering Design Problems	design problem, research, source, topic, collaborate, constraint, criteria, condition, difficulty, element, failure point, investigate

Table C.16: Kindergarten Science Vocabulary Terms

Kindergarten Science Measurement Topics	Vocabulary Terms
Solar Energy	cooler, soil, sun, sunlight, warmer, heat, material, shade, structure, surface, temperature
Force and Motion	force, push, pull, strength, direction, motion
Weather	cloudy, foggy, rainy, season, snowy, sunny, weather, windy, blizzard, drought, flood, hail, high wind, hurricane, ice storm, lightning, predict, prepare, severe weather, tornado
Human Impact	environment, organism, resource, solution
Organism Needs	animal, carbon dioxide, energy, food, need, oxygen, plant, shelter, desert, mountain, ocean, polar, region, savannah, tropical, adapt, environment, organism
Comparing Organisms	category, crawl, fly, jump, organism, swim, walk, air, habitat, land, manmade, shelter, water, fin, fur, gill, horn, lung, scales, tail, wing

Table C.17: Grade 1 Science Vocabulary Terms

Grade 1 Science Measurement Topics	Vocabulary Terms
Electricity	convert, electricity, light
Light	beam, light, opaque, reflective, shadow, translucent, transparent, eye, luminous, nonluminous, reflect, visibility
Sound and Vibration	brain, ear, high, low, sound, vibration, wave
Celestial Motion	observation, sunrise, sunset, planet, satellite, star, crescent, full moon, gibbous, new moon, phase, quarter, waning, waxing
Seasons	autumn, day, night, spring, summer, winter
Organism Needs	external, needle, pouch, root, scale, seed, shell, stem, thorn
Comparing Organisms	difference, mature, similarity, young, adult, offspring
Organism Behavior	behavior, comforting, feeding, offspring, parent, protecting, copy, survive

Table C.18: Grade 2 Science Vocabulary Terms

Grade 2 Science Measurement Topics	Vocabulary Terms
Object Composition	compose, disassemble, assemble, form, function, structure
Properties of Materials	classify, flexibility, gas, hardness, liquid, property, solid, ceramic, metal, plastic, purpose, wood
Changes to Materials	condensation, evaporation, freeze, gas, liquid, melt, solid, state, cool, dissolve, irreversible, mix, reversible, solution
Geographic Features	body of water, flow, fresh water, glacier, ice cap, lake, river, salt water, sea, bay, beach, compass rose, continent, island, landform, legend, plain, plateau, scale, tributary, valley, wetland
Weathering and Erosion	erosion, sand dunes, sediment, weathering, windbreak, canyon, flow, riverbed, thaw, vegetation
Earth's History	earthquake, erosion, flooding, landslide, timescale, volcano, weathering
Organism Needs	leaf, photosynthesis, anther, flower, fruit, nectar, ovary, ovule, petal, pollen, reproduce, sepal, stamen, stigma, style
Biodiversity	amphibian, carnivore, diversity of life, forest, herbivore, mammal, omnivore, plain, rainforest, tundra

Table C.19: Grade 3 Science Vocabulary Terms

Grade 3 Science Measurement Topics	Vocabulary Terms
Force	balanced force, force, friction, net force, resultant force, unbalanced force
Motion	force, pattern, position, unbalanced force, variable
Electricity	electrical charge, friction, negative charge, neutral charge, positive charge, static electricity
Magnets	magnet, magnetic field, magnetic force, magnetic, nonmagnetic, north pole, south pole
Climate and Weather	atmosphere, atmospheric pressure, Celsius, Fahrenheit, humidity, precipitation, climate, climate zone, continental climate, dry climate, equator, mild climate, polar climate, polar zone, pole, temperate zone, torrid zone, Tropic of Cancer, Tropic of Capricorn, tropical climate
Natural Hazards	evacuation, extreme weather, mitigation, natural disaster, natural hazard, preparedness, prevention, recovery, risk
Comparing Organisms	adulthood, birth, death, egg, germination, growth, larva, life cycle, metamorphosis, reproduction
Organism Behavior	community, competition, group behavior, member, pack, solitary
Organism Traits	inherited, physical, trait, acquired
Organism Habitats	arctic, characteristic, savanna, inherited, trait, variation, migrate

Table C.20: Grade 4 Science Vocabulary Terms

Grade 4 Science Measurement Topics	Vocabulary Terms
Energy	energy, kinetic energy, law of conservation of energy, potential energy, system, chemical energy, circuit, electrical energy, heat, sound energy, thermal energy
Motion	frame of reference, kinetic energy, mass, potential energy, speed, velocity, work, energy, heat, law of conservation of energy, sound energy, system, transfer
Light and Vision	angle of incidence, angle of reflection, cone, cornea, iris, lens, optic nerve, pupil, reflection, retina, rod
Waves	amplitude, frequency, mass, midline, period, wave, wave cycle, wavelength, crest, energy, longitudinal wave, matter, medium, oscillate, transverse wave, trough
Information Transfer	code, decode, key, Morse code, receiver, sender, symbol

continued →

Grade 4 Science Measurement Topics	Vocabulary Terms
Geographic Features	contour interval, contour line, contour map, topographic map
Earth Changes	acid rain, chemical weathering, deposition, mechanical weathering, cave, relative dating, rock layer, sedimentary rock, soil
Earth's History	fossil, fossil record, relative dating, rock layer
Natural Hazards	response, sinkhole, tsunami
Natural Resources	biomass, coal, fossil fuel, geothermal power, hydroelectric power, natural gas, natural resource, nonrenewable, nuclear power, oil, renewable, solar power, wind power, consumption, production, waste
Plant Needs	adaptation, external structure, internal structure, phloem, seed coat, stoma, xylem
Animal Needs	adaptation, external structure, function, internal structure, structure, terrain, response, sense, sense organ, stimulus

Table C.21: Grade 5 Science Vocabulary Terms

Grade 5 Science Measurement Topics	Vocabulary Terms
Gravity	gravity, orbit
Matter	atom, matter, volume, weight, conservation of mass, deposition, physical change, sublimation, vaporization, chemical change, chemical reaction, closed system, mixture, open system, product, reactant, solute, solvent
Properties of Matter	boiling point, density, electrical conductivity, elasticity, melting point, plasticity, thermal conductivity, unit, viscosity
Celestial Motion	axis, rotation, angle, east, west, circumpolar constellation, constellation, northern hemisphere, orbit, revolution, seasonal constellation, southern hemisphere, year
Celestial Objects	apparent brightness, luminosity, star
Earth Systems	atmosphere, biosphere, geosphere, hydrosphere, sphere, groundwater, polar icecap, water vapor
Ecosystem Interactions	chlorophyll, nutrient, photosynthesis, stomata, ecosystem, food chain, transfer, cycle, decomposer, food web, inorganic, organic, waste

Social Studies K–5 Vocabulary Terms

Table C.22: Kindergarten Social Studies Vocabulary Terms

Kindergarten Social Studies Measurement Topics	Vocabulary Terms
The Globe	boundary, Earth, globe, land, map, model, water
Cooperation	agree, benefit, compromise, cooperate, share
Time	category, future, order, past, present, time, today, tomorrow, yesterday, April, August, calendar, day, December, February, Friday, January, July, June, March, May, Monday, month, November, October, Saturday, September, Sunday, Thursday, Tuesday, Wednesday, week, year
Exchange	barter system, buy, goods, money, sell, trade, buyer, exchange, market, pay, price, seller, services
Authority	authority, fair, power, rule, responsibility, confidence, determination, leader, leadership

Table C.23: Grade 1 Social Studies Vocabulary Terms

Grade 1 Social Studies Measurement Topics	Vocabulary Terms
Position and Arrangement of Physical and Human Features	area, arrangement, distance, line, location, point, size, volume
Human Dependence on the Environment	air, environment, natural resource, need
Places and Regions	community, human characteristic, physical characteristic, place, population, rural, suburban, urban, city, harbor, settlement, town, village
Personal History	aunt, brother, culture, family, father, generation, grandfather, grandmother, heritage, mother, cousin, parents, sister, tradition, uncle, chronology, event, history, time line
Production and Consumption	consumer, consumption, distribution, producer, production, resource
Cultures	belief, ceremony, cultural marker, culture, custom, language, practice, symbol, tradition, value, fable, folktale, legend, myth
Change and Continuity	cause, change, continuity, different, result, similar

continued →

Grade 1 Social Studies Measurement Topics	Vocabulary Terms
Rights and Justice	crime, enforce, government, justice, law, right, society, Abraham Lincoln, Cesar Chavez, civil rights, Clara Barton, Eleanor Roosevelt, Elizabeth Blackwell, Frederick Douglass, human rights, Jackie Robinson, Martin Luther King, Jr., Mary McLeod Bethune, Rosa Parks, Sojourner Truth, Susan B. Anthony
Historical Family Life	communication, community, cultural tradition, religious observance, role, technology, transportation
American Independence	Benjamin Franklin, George Washington, Second Continental Congress, Thomas Jefferson, Yorktown
Symbols and Holidays	Angel Island, eagle, Ellis Island, flag, Fourth of July, Liberty Bell, Lincoln Memorial, Martin Luther King Jr. Day, Memorial Day, Mt. Rushmore, Statue of Liberty, White House, history, monument, motto, statue, symbol
The Local Community	communication, community, ecosystem, transportation
Finding Food	domesticate, farmer, gatherer, hunter, surplus
Exploration and Discovery	Christopher Columbus, native, Marco Polo, journey, people group, route

Table C.24: Grade 2 Social Studies Vocabulary Terms

Grade 2 Social Studies Measurement Topics	Vocabulary Terms
Geographic Representations	cardinal direction, compass rose, coordinate, east, geospatial information, grid, intermediate direction, latitude, legend, longitude, north, orientation, position, scale, south, west, chart, climate map, economic map, geographic representation, physical map, political map, resource map, road map, topographic map
Locations and Geographic Characteristics	absolute location, boundary, human feature, intersection, landmark, physical feature, relative location
Technology	airplane, automobile, canal, gesture, hieroglyphics, internet, pictograph, printing, railroad, satellite, ship, signal, telegraph, telephone, wagon, writing
Conflict and Cooperation	commercial, disagreement, industrial, land use, negotiation, residential, zoning, conflict, cooperation, goal, motivation, party, perspective
The Environment	arctic, biome, climate, desert, ecosystem, forest, freshwater, grassland, marine, rainforest, savannah, temperate, tropical, tundra, wetland, avalanche, blizzard, earthquake, environmental hazard, flood, hurricane, landslide, severe weather, tornado, volcano, wildfire

Migration	cultural diffusion, emigrant, immigrant, media, migration, origin
Pioneer and Colonial Communities	colonist, colony, covered wagon, frontier, lean-to, log house, Native American, pioneer, sod house
Scientists and Inventors	Alexander Graham Bell, crop rotation, Galileo, George Washington Carver, Jonas Salk, Louis Pasteur, Marie Curie, Nobel Prize, pasteurization, polio, radioactivity, telescope, vaccine, X-ray
Incentive and Choice	cost, need, satisfaction, value, choice, consume, scarcity, want
Types of Rights	conflict, cost, limit, object of privacy, personal space, privacy, private, public, right to privacy, U.S. Constitution
Types of Justice	corrective justice, deserve, distribute, distributive justice, just, procedural justice, right, wrong
Native Peoples, Explorers, and Settlers	adapt, explorer, goal, region, settler, state

Table C.25: Grade 3 Social Studies Vocabulary Terms

Grade 3 Social Studies Measurement Topics	Vocabulary Terms
Components of Ecosystems	biomass, coastal, continental, organism, soil, vegetation
The Environment	response, constraint, fertile, human activity, landform, opportunity, recreation, terrain, weather, biodiversity, deforestation, endangered species, erosion, extinct, invasive species, nonrenewable resource, pollution, renewable resource, stress
Earth's Physical Processes	atmosphere, biosphere, canyon, deposition, drainage basin, hill, hydrosphere, lake, leeward, lithosphere, mountain range, ocean, physical process, plain, plateau, river, tectonic plate, water cycle, windward, valley
Locations and Geographic Characteristics	Africa, Antarctica, Asia, Australia, continent, developed, developing, Europe, North America, region, scale, South America
Geographic Representations	cartogram, choropleth map, equator, geographic information system [GIS], global positioning system [GPS], isopleth map, kilometer, meridian, mile, parallel, prime, meridian, projection, thematic map, topography, Tropic of Cancer, Tropic of Capricorn
Modeling Physical and Human Systems	cycle, human system, model, network, physical system, system

continued →

Grade 3 Social Studies Measurement Topics	Vocabulary Terms
Flow of Economic Resources	bank, borrow, check, currency, deposit, interest, lend, market value, savings, store of value, taxes, unit of account, withdraw, business, capital good, capital resource, household, human resource, income, labor, productive resource
Incentive and Choice	activity, alternative, opportunity cost, scarce, trade-off, incentive, individual, influence, penalty, reward
Authority	dispute, source
Conflict and Cooperation	alliance, ambassador, cultural contact, diplomacy, international, military force, trade agreement
American Society	citizen, civic responsibility, common good, community, individual, personal responsibility, equal protection, equal opportunity, fundamental, universal public education, voluntarism
Change and Continuity	cyclical
Exploration and Discovery	Columbian exchange, Eastern Hemisphere, Indian, Indies, Old World, smallpox, Western Hemisphere, Age of Exploration, Cape of Good Hope, Ferdinand Magellan, Gulf of Saint Lawrence, Jacques Cartier, New World, Prince Henry the Navigator, Strait of Magellan, Vasco da Gama, Zheng He
Time Lines	century, decade
Methods of Historical Study	anthropology, archaeology, artifact, folklore, oral tradition, prehistory, record
Changes in Native American and Hawaiian Life	Apache, Battle of Little Bighorn, Black Hawk War, Cherokee, Geronimo, Hopi, Indian, Inuit, Iroquois, Kamehameha I, Kingdom of Hawaii, Nez Perce, Polynesia, reservation, Sioux, Sitting Bull, smallpox, Tecumseh, Trail of Tears, treaty
Symbols and Holidays	Columbus Day, e pluribus unum, Great Seal, Labor Day, Pledge of Allegiance, Presidents' Day, statue of justice, Thanksgiving, Uncle Sam, Veterans Day
Personal and Civic Responsibility	civic responsibility, education, election, ethical standards, financial choices, personal responsibility
Historical Family Life	dream, ideal, structure
Pioneer and Colonial Communities	agriculture, Far West, old northwest, Plymouth, Post Vincennes, prairie, San Antonio, Southwest, St. Augustine, Williamsburg
Earth-Sun Relationship	agriculture, axis, revolution, rotation, tilt

Table C.26: Grade 4 Social Studies Vocabulary Terms

Grade 4 Social Studies Measurement Topics	Vocabulary Terms
Distributions of People, Places, and Environments	density, dispersed, distribution, irregularity, linear, nucleated, sequence, spatial pattern
Settlement Development Patterns	boomtown, company town, decline, function, ghost town, growth, settlement pattern
History of Cities	industrial revolution, public transportation, sanitation, urbanization
Places and Regions	distinguishing characteristic, human criteria, identity, physical criteria, human process
Location and Economic Activity	economic activity, manufacture, valuation, variation
Economic Specialization	economic specialization, interdependent, self-sufficient
The Characteristics of Government	anarchy, govern, institution, mandate, order, consent, constitution, dictatorship, economic right, liberty, limited government, personal right, political right, unlimited government, court, democracy, president, representative, self-government, senator, United States of America, U.S. Congress, U.S. House of Representatives, U.S. Senate
Participating in Government	campaign, candidate, demonstration, elected official, interest group, monitor, petition, political party, public official, vote
Historic American Documents	Bill of Rights, Declaration of Independence, Emancipation Proclamation, James Madison, Mayflower Compact
Demographic Characteristics	birth rate, census, death rate, demographic, ethnicity, infant mortality, life expectancy, marital status, occupation, religion, statistic, survey
Natural Resources	extract, flow resource, replenish, conserve, deplete, manage, recycle, reuse, waste
The Local Community	founding, infrastructure, local, activist, charity, community service, philanthropy, public service, volunteer
The State or Region	inhabitant, settle, statehood
Technology	breakthrough, efficiency, invention, tool, trial and error, alphabet, Braille, computer, cuneiform, Johannes Gutenberg, printing press, radio, sign language, telecommunication, aircraft, Amelia Earhart, caravan, cargo, freeway, Henry Ford, highway, John Glenn, marine, rocket, Sally Ride, spaceship, submarine, vessel, wheel, Wright brothers

continued →

Grade 4 Social Studies Measurement Topics	Vocabulary Terms
American Independence	American Revolutionary War, Betty Zane, Boston Tea Party, Common Sense, Declaration of Independence, Great Britain, James Armistead, John Adams, King George III, Lydia Darragh, Nathan Beman, Parliament, Samuel Adams, Stamp Act, Sybil Ludington, "taxation without representation," Thomas Paine
American Democracy	diversity, equal protection of the law, equality of opportunity, freedom of religion, freedom of speech, majority rule, minority rights, civic-mindedness, civility, compassion, critical-mindedness, democracy, individual responsibility, open-mindedness, patriotism, respect for the law, respect for the rights of others, self-discipline, self-governance, class, ethnicity, religion
American Citizenship	allegiance, citizenship, naturalization, public office

Table C.27: Grade 5 Social Studies Vocabulary Terms

Grade 5 Social Studies Measurement Topics	Vocabulary Terms
Cultures	gradual, achievement, social organization, way of life
Geographic Context	context, geography, spatial distribution
Differences in Perceptions	mental map, perception
Political and Economic Units	country, economic unit, metropolitan area, political unit
Migration	destination, emigration, immigration, migrant, refugee, enclave, experience, living conditions, port of entry, screening
Diversity	gender, kaleidoscope, linguistic, melting pot, national origin, racial, religious, salad bowl, background, empathy, synthesis, bias, discrimination, ignorance, impartial, integration, prevent, resolve, segregation, tension, tolerance
Culture Hearths	civilization, culture hearth, Fertile Crescent, Ganges River Valley, Indus River Valley, Mesoamerica, Mesopotamia, Nile River Valley, Wei-Huang Valley, West Africa
Supply and Demand	competition, demand, demand curve, equilibrium price, firm, law of demand, law of supply, market clearing price, product, profit, supply, supply curve
Government Revenues and Services	budget, health services, income tax, Medicaid, Medicare, national defense, payroll tax, property tax, public project, public safety, public utilities, revenue, sales tax, social security
Entrepreneurship and Innovation	capital, entrepreneur, innovation, investor, marketing, risk, venture
Labor Productivity	cottage industry, division of labor, labor productivity, mass production, specialization

Economic Systems	command economy, economic system, market economy, mixed economy, traditional economy
Historical Interpretation	anachronism, evidence, historical fiction, historical interpretation, norm
Historical Impact	chance, consequence
American Cultural History	Billy the Kid, Daniel Boone, Davy Crockett, folk hero, Jedediah Smith, Jesse James, John Henry, Johnny Appleseed, mountain man, Paul Bunyan, Pecos Bill, Stormalong, Wild West
The Functions of Government	appoint, governor, jurisdiction, lieutenant governor, local government, mayor, state government, state house of representatives, state representative, state senate, state senator, Cabinet, congressman, congresswoman, executive branch, federal court, federal government, judge, judicial branch, legislative branch, legislator, Supreme Court, vice president
Evaluating Candidates for Leadership	evaluate, qualification
Types of Rights	infringe
Rights and Justice	Anne Frank, Booker T. Washington, Dalai Lama, Harriet Tubman, Mahatma Gandhi, Malala Yousafzai, Nelson Mandela, principle, W.E.B. DuBois, William Wilberforce

REFERENCES AND RESOURCES

Adams, M. J. (1990). *Beginning to read: Thinking and learning about print.* Cambridge, MA: MIT Press.

Anderson, R. C., & Freebody, P. (1979, August). *Vocabulary knowledge* (Tech. Rep. No. 136). Urbana-Champaign: University of Illinois, Center for the Study of Reading.

Anderson, R. C., & Freebody, P. (1985). Vocabulary knowledge. In H. Singer & R. B. Ruddell (Eds.), *Theoretical models and processes of reading* (3rd ed., pp. 343–371). Newark, DE: International Reading Association.

Beck, I. L., & McKeown, M. G. (1985). Teaching vocabulary: Making the instruction fit the goal. *Educational Perspectives, 23*(1), 11–15.

Beck, I. L., & McKeown, M. G. (1991). Conditions of vocabulary acquisition. In R. Barr, M. L. Kamil, P. Mosenthal, & P. D. Pearson (Eds.), Handbook of reading research (Vol. 2, pp. 789–814). New York: Longman.

Beck, I. L., & McKeown, M. G. (2007). Increasing young low-income children's oral vocabulary repertoires through rich and focused instruction. *Elementary School Journal, 107*(3), 251–271.

Beck, I. L., McKeown, M. G., & Kucan, L. (2002). *Bringing words to life: Robust vocabulary instruction.* New York: Guilford Press.

Beck, I. L., Perfetti, C. A., & McKeown, M. G. (1982). Effects of long-term vocabulary instruction on lexical access and reading comprehension. *Journal of Educational Psychology, 74*(4), 506–521.

Berne, J. I., & Blachowicz, C. L. Z. (2008). What reading teachers say about vocabulary instruction: Voices from the classroom. *Reading Teacher, 62*(4), 314–323.

Biemiller, A. (2005). Size and sequence in vocabulary development: Implications for choosing words for primary grade vocabulary instruction. In E. H. Hiebert & M. L. Kamil (Eds.), *Teaching and learning vocabulary: Bringing research to practice* (pp. 223–242). Mahwah, NJ: Erlbaum.

Biemiller, A., & Slonim, N. (2001). Estimating root word vocabulary growth in normative and advantaged populations: Evidence for a common sequence of vocabulary acquisition. *Journal of Educational Psychology, 93*(3), 498–520.

Blachowicz, C. L. Z., & Fisher, P. (2008). Attentional vocabulary instruction: Read-alouds, word play, and other motivating strategies for fostering informal word learning. In A. E. Farstrup & S. J. Samuels (Eds.), *What research has to say about vocabulary instruction* (pp. 32–55). Newark, DE: International Reading Association.

Blachowicz, C. L. Z., & Fisher, P. (2012). Keep the "fun" in fundamental: Encouraging word consciousness and incidental word learning in the classroom through word play. In E. J. Kame'enui & J. F. Baumann (Eds.), *Vocabulary instruction: Research to practice* (2nd ed., pp. 189–209). New York: Guilford Press.

Cain, K., Oakhill, J. V., Barnes, M. A., & Bryant, P. E. (2001). Comprehension skill, inference-making ability, and their relation to knowledge. *Memory and Cognition, 29*(6), 850–859.

Carey, S. (1978). The child as word learner: Linguistic theory and psychological reality. In M. Halle, J. Bresnan, & G. A. Miller (Eds.), *Linguistic theory and psychological reality* (pp. 264–293). Cambridge, MA: MIT Press.

Carleton, L., & Marzano, R. J. (2010). *Vocabulary games for the classroom.* Bloomington, IN: Marzano Resources.

Casale, U. P. (1985). Motor imaging: A reading-vocabulary strategy. *Journal of Reading, 28*(7), 619–621.

Cunningham, A. E., & Stanovich, K. E. (1997). Early reading acquisition and its relation to reading experience and ability 10 years later. *Developmental Psychology, 33*(6), 934–945.

Dalton, B., & Grisham, D. L. (2011). eVoc strategies: 10 ways to use technology to build vocabulary. *Reading Teacher, 64*(5), 306–317.

Davis, F. B. (1942). Two new measures of reading ability. *Journal of Educational Psychology, 33*(5), 365–372.

Davis, F. B. (1944). Fundamental factors of comprehension in reading. *Psychometrika, 9*(3), 185–197.

Davis, F. B. (1968). Research in comprehension in reading. *Reading Research Quarterly, 3*(4), 499–545.

Dodson, C. (2019) *The critical concepts in social studies.* Bloomington, IN: Marzano Resources. Accessed at www.marzanoresources.com/critical-components-social-studies on December 18, 2019.

Elleman, A. M., Lindo, E. J., Morphy, P., & Compton, D. L. (2009). The impact of vocabulary instruction on passage-level comprehension of school-age children: A meta-analysis. *Journal of Research on Educational Effectiveness, 2*(1), 1–44.

Farkas, G., & Beron, K. (2004). The detailed age trajectory of oral vocabulary knowledge: Differences by class and race. *Social Science Research, 33*(3), 464–497.

Freeman, Y. S., & Freeman, D. E. (2009). *Academic language for English language learners and struggling readers: How to help students succeed across content areas.* Portsmouth, NH: Heinemann.

Fry, E. B., Kress, J. E., & Fountoukidis, D. L. (2000). *The reading teacher's book of lists* (4th ed.). San Francisco: Jossey-Bass.

Graves, M. F. (2006). *The vocabulary book: Learning and instruction.* New York: Teachers College Press.

Graves, M. F., & Slater, W. H. (1987, April 20–24). *The development of reading vocabularies in rural disadvantaged students, inner-city disadvantaged students, and middle-class suburban students.* Paper presented at the meeting of the American Educational Research Association, Washington, DC.

Hart, B., & Risley, T. R. (1995). *Meaningful differences in the everyday experience of young American children.* Baltimore: Brookes.

Hart, B., & Risley, T. R. (2003). The early catastrophe: The 30 million word gap by age 3. *American Educator, 27*(1), 4–9.

Hattie, J. A. C. (2009). *Visible learning: A synthesis of over 800 meta-analyses relating to achievement.* New York: Routledge.

Haystead, M. W., & Marzano, R. J. (2009, August). *Meta-analytic synthesis of studies conducted at Marzano Research on instructional strategies.* Englewood, CO: Marzano Resources. Accessed at www.marzanoresources.com/meta-analytic-synthesis-of-studies on January 15, 2020.

Hiebert, E. H., & Cervetti, G. N. (2012). What differences in narrative and informational texts mean for the learning and instruction of vocabulary. In E. J. Kame'enui & J. F. Baumann (Eds.), *Vocabulary instruction: Research to practice* (2nd ed., pp. 322–344). New York: Guilford Press.

Jenkins, J. R., & Dixon, R. (1983). Vocabulary learning. *Contemporary Educational Psychology, 8*(3), 237–260.

Jenkins, J. R., Stein, M. L., & Wysocki, K. (1984). Learning vocabulary through reading. *American Educational Research Journal, 21*(4), 767–787.

Just, M. A., & Carpenter, P. A. (1987). *The psychology of reading and language comprehension.* Boston: Allyn & Bacon.

Kamil, M. L., & Hiebert, E. H. (2005). Teaching and learning vocabulary: Perspectives and persistent issues. In E. H. Hiebert & M. L. Kamil (Eds.), *Teaching and learning vocabulary: Bringing research to practice* (pp. 1–23). Mahwah, NJ: Erlbaum.

Klesius, J. P., & Searls, E. F. (1990). A meta-analysis of recent research in meaning vocabulary instruction. *Journal of Research and Development in Education, 23*(4), 226–235.

Levelt, W. J. M., Roelofs, A., & Meyer, A. S. (1999). A theory of lexical access in speech production. *Behavioral and Brain Sciences, 22*(1), 1–38.

Manzo, U. C., & Manzo, A. V. (2008). Teaching vocabulary-learning strategies: Word consciousness, word connection, and word prediction. In A. E. Farstrup & S. J. Samuels (Eds.), *What research has to say about vocabulary instruction* (pp. 80–105). Newark, DE: International Reading Association.

Marmolejo, A. (1990). *The effects of vocabulary instruction with poor readers: A meta-analysis.* Unpublished master's thesis, Columbia University Teachers College, New York.

Marulis, L. M., & Neuman, S. B. (2010). The effects of vocabulary intervention on young children's word learning: A meta-analysis. *Review of Educational Research, 80*(3), 300–335.

Marzano, R. J. (2004). *Building background knowledge for academic achievement: Research on what works in schools.* Alexandria, VA: Association for Supervision and Curriculum Development.

Marzano, R. J. (2006). *Classroom assessment and grading that work.* Alexandria, VA: Association for Supervision and Curriculum Development.

Marzano, R. J. (2010a). *Formative assessment and standards-based grading.* Bloomington, IN: Marzano Resources.

Marzano, R. J. (2010b). *Teaching basic and advanced vocabulary: A framework for direct instruction.* Boston: Cengage ELT.

Marzano, R. J. (2018a). *Building basic vocabulary: Tracking my progress.* Bloomington, IN: Marzano Resources.

Marzano, R. J. (2018b). *Making classroom assessments reliable and valid.* Bloomington, IN: Solution Tree Press.

Marzano, R. J., & Marzano, J. S. (1988). *A cluster approach to elementary vocabulary instruction.* Newark, DE: International Reading Association.

Marzano, R. J., Paynter, D. E., Kendall, J. S., Pickering, D., & Marzano, L. (1991). *Literacy plus: Teacher reference book to words in semantic clusters.* Columbus, OH: Zaner-Bloser.

Marzano, R. J., & Pickering, D. J. (2005). *Building academic vocabulary: Teacher's manual.* Alexandria, VA: Association for Supervision and Curriculum Development.

Marzano, R. J., Rogers, K., & Simms, J. A. (2015). *Vocabulary for the new science standards.* Bloomington, IN: Marzano Resources.

Marzano, R. J., & Simms, J. A. (2013). *Vocabulary for the Common Core.* Bloomington, IN: Marzano Resources.

McKeown, M. G. (1991). Learning word meanings from definitions: Problems and potential. In P. J. Schwanenflugel (Ed.), *The psychology of word meanings* (pp. 137–156). Hillsdale, NJ: Erlbaum.

McKeown, M. G. (1993). Creating effective definitions for young word learners. *Reading Research Quarterly, 28*(1), 16–31.

McKeown, M. G., Beck, I. L., Omanson, R. C., & Perfetti, C. A. (1983). The effects of long-term vocabulary instruction on reading comprehension: A replication. *Journal of Reading Behavior, 15*(1), 3–18.

McKeown, M. G., Beck, I. L., Omanson, R. C., & Pople, M. T. (1985). Some effects of the nature and frequency of vocabulary instruction on the knowledge and use of words. *Reading Research Quarterly, 20*(4), 522–535.

McLaughlin, B., August, D., Snow, C., Carlo, M., Dressler, C., White, C., et al. (2000, April 19–20). *Vocabulary improvement and reading in English language learners: An intervention study.* Paper presented at the Research Symposium on High Standards in Reading for Students from Diverse Language Groups: Research, Practice & Policy, Washington, DC: U.S. Department of Education, Office of Bilingual Education and Minority Languages Affairs.

Mezynski, K. (1983). Issues concerning the acquisition of knowledge: Effects of vocabulary training on reading comprehension. *Review of Educational Research, 53*(2), 253–279.

Miller, G. A., & Gildea, P. M. (1987). How children learn words. *Scientific American, 257*(3), 94–99.

Mol, S. E., Bus, A. G., & de Jong, M. T. (2009). Interactive book reading in early education: A tool to stimulate print knowledge as well as oral language. *Review of Educational Research, 79*(2), 979–1007.

Mol, S. E., Bus, A. G., de Jong, M. T., & Smeets, D. J. H. (2008). Added value of dialogic parent-child book readings: A meta-analysis. *Early Education and Development, 19*(1), 7–26.

Nagy, W., Berninger, V., Abbott, R., Vaughan, K., & Vermeulen, K. (2003). Relationship of morphology and other language skills to literacy skills in at-risk second-grade readers and at-risk fourth-grade writers. *Journal of Educational Psychology, 95*(4), 730–742.

Nagy, W. E., & Anderson, R. C. (1984). How many words are there in printed school English? *Reading Research Quarterly, 19*(3), 304–330.

Nagy, W. E., & Herman, P. A. (1984, October). *Limitations of vocabulary instruction* (Tech. Rep. No. 326). Urbana, IL: University of Illinois, Center for the Study of Reading. (ERIC Document Reproduction Service No. ED248498)

Nagy, W. E., & Herman, P. A. (1987). Breadth and depth of vocabulary knowledge: Implications for acquisition and instruction. In M. G. McKeown & M. E. Curtis (Eds.), *The nature of vocabulary acquisition* (pp. 19–35). Hillsdale, NJ: Erlbaum.

National Early Literacy Panel. (2008). *Developing early literacy: Report of the National Early Literacy Panel.* Washington, DC: National Institute for Literacy.

National Reading Panel. (2000). *Teaching children to read: An evidence-based assessment of the scientific research literature on reading and its implications for reading instruction—Reports of the subgroups.* Bethesda, MA: National Institute of Child Health and Human Development.

Neuman, S. B., & Dwyer, J. (2011). Developing vocabulary and conceptual knowledge for low-income preschoolers: A design experiment. *Journal of Literacy Research, 43*(2), 103–129.

Nye, C., Foster, S. H., & Seaman, D. (1987). Effectiveness of language intervention with the language/learning disabled. *Journal of Speech and Hearing Disorders, 52*(4), 348–357.

Padak, N., Newton, E., Rasinski, T., & Newton, R. M. (2008). Getting to the root of word study: Teaching Latin and Greek word roots in elementary and middle grades. In A. E. Farstrup & S. J. Samuels (Eds.), *What research has to say about vocabulary instruction* (pp. 6–31). Newark, DE: International Reading Association.

Poirier, B. M. (1989). *The effectiveness of language intervention with preschool handicapped children: An integrative review.* Unpublished doctoral dissertation, Utah State University, Logan.

Rasinski, T., Padak, N., Newton, R. M., & Newton, E. (2007). *Building vocabulary from word roots.* Huntington Beach, CA: Teacher Created Materials.

Roehr, S., & Carroll, K. (Eds.). (2010). *Collins COBUILD illustrated basic dictionary of American English.* Boston: Heinle Cengage Learning.

Scarborough, H. S. (2001). Connecting early language and literacy to later reading (dis)abilities: Evidence, theory, and practice. In S. B. Neuman & D. K. Dickinson (Eds.), *Handbook of literacy research* (Vol. 1, pp. 97–110). New York: Guilford Press.

Scott, J. A., Miller, T. F., & Flinspach, S. L. (2012). Developing word consciousness: Lessons from highly diverse fourth-grade classrooms. In E. J. Kame'enui & J. F. Baumann (Eds.), *Vocabulary instruction: Research to practice* (2nd ed., pp. 169–188). New York: Guilford Press.

Scott, J. A., & Nagy, W. E. (1997). Understanding the definitions of unfamiliar verbs. *Reading Research Quarterly, 32*(2), 184–200.

Simms, J. A. (2017). *The critical concepts: Alignment to source standards.* Bloomington, IN: Marzano Resources. Accessed at www.marzanoresources.com/technology/critical-concepts-atss on December 18, 2019.

Singer, H. (1965). A developmental model of speed of reading in grades 3 through 6. *Reading Research Quarterly, 1*(1), 29–49.

Stahl, K. A. D., & Stahl, S. A. (2012). Young word wizards! Fostering vocabulary development in preschool and primary education. In E. J. Kame'enui & J. F. Baumann (Eds.), *Vocabulary instruction: Research to practice* (2nd ed., pp. 72–92). New York: Guilford Press.

Stahl, S. (1983). Differential word knowledge and reading comprehension. *Journal of Reading Behavior, 15*(4), 33–50.

Stahl, S. A. (1999). *Vocabulary development.* Cambridge, MA: Brookline Books.

Stahl, S. A. (2005). Four problems with teaching word meanings (and what to do to make vocabulary an integral part of instruction). In E. H. Hiebert & M. L. Kamil (Eds.), *Teaching and learning vocabulary: Bringing research to practice* (pp. 95–114). Mahwah, NJ: Erlbaum.

Stahl, S. A., & Fairbanks, M. M. (1986). The effects of vocabulary instruction: A model-based meta-analysis. *Review of Educational Research, 56*(1), 72–110.

Stahl, S. A., & Nagy, W. E. (2006). *Teaching word meanings.* Mahwah, NJ: Erlbaum

Stanovich, K. E. (1986). Matthew effects in reading: Some consequences of individual differences in the acquisition of literacy. *Reading Research Quarterly, 21*(4), 360–407.

Stanovich, K. E., Cunningham, A. E., & Feeman, D. J. (1984). Intelligence, cognitive skills, and early reading progress. *Reading Research Quarterly, 19*(3), 278–303.

Storch, S. A., & Whitehurst, G. J. (2002). Oral language and code-related precursors to reading: Evidence from a longitudinal structural model. *Developmental Psychology, 38*(6), 934–947.

Swanborn, M. S. L., & de Glopper, K. (1999). Incidental word learning while reading: A meta-analysis. *Review of Educational Research, 69*(3), 261–285.

Thurstone, L. L. (1946). Note on a reanalysis of Davis' reading tests. *Psychometrika, 11*(3), 185–188.

Umbel, V. M., Pearson, B. Z., Fernández, M. C., & Oller, D. K. (1992). Measuring bilingual children's receptive vocabularies. *Child Development, 63*(4), 1012–1020.

Whipple, G. (Ed.). (1925). *The 24th yearbook of the National Society for the Study of Education: Report of the National Committee on Reading.* Bloomington, IL: Public School.

White, T. G., Sowell, J., & Yanagihara, A. (1989). Teaching elementary students to use word-part clues. *Reading Teacher, 42*(4), 302–308.

INDEX

Formative Assessment & Standards-Based Grading
Robert J. Marzano
Learn everything you need to know to implement an integrated system of assessment and grading. The author details the specific benefits of formative assessment and explains how to design and interpret three different types of formative assessments, how to track student progress, and how to assign meaningful grades. Detailed examples bring each concept to life, and chapter exercises reinforce the content.
BKL003

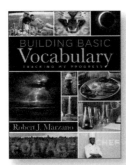

Building Basic Vocabulary
Robert J. Marzano
A companion to *Teaching Basic, Advanced, and Academic Vocabulary* by Robert J. Marzano, this notebook is carefully designed to help students learn and practice more than 2,500 basic vocabulary terms and 2,889 challenge vocabulary terms. Students use space provided beside each term to take notes, rate their level of understanding, or draw pictures to help them retain specific word meanings.
BKL039

Vocabulary for the New Science Standards
Robert J. Marzano, Katie Rogers, and Julia A. Simms
Discover how to use the power of assessment to instill hope, efficacy, and achievement in your students. With this research-based resource, you'll explore six essential tenets of assessment—assessment purpose, communication of assessment results, accurate interpretation, assessment architecture, instructional agility, and student investment—that will help deepen your understanding of assessment to not only meet standards but also enhance students' academic success and self-fulfillment.
BKL026

Vocabulary Games for the Classroom
Lindsay Carleton and Robert J. Marzano
Make direct vocabulary instruction fun and successful with this simple, straightforward, and easy-to-use book. Hundreds of critical vocabulary terms handpicked by Dr. Marzano cover four content areas and all grade levels. Each game identifies the appropriate grade level and subject area, as well as whether or not the students should already be familiar with the vocabulary.
BKL007

Vocabulary for the Common Core
Robert J. Marzano and Julia A. Simms
The Common Core State Standards present unique demands on students' ability to learn vocabulary and teachers' ability to teach it. The authors address these challenges in this resource. Work toward the creation of a successful vocabulary program, guided by both academic and content-area terms taken directly from the mathematics and English language arts standards.
BKL014

MARZANO Resources

Visit MarzanoResources.com or call 800.733.6786 to order.

Professional Development
Designed for Success

Empower your staff to tap into their full potential as educators. As an all-inclusive research-into-practice resource center, we are committed to helping your school or district become highly effective at preparing every student for his or her future.

Choose from our wide range of customized professional development opportunities for teachers, administrators, and district leaders. Each session offers hands-on support, personalized answers, and accessible strategies that can be put into practice immediately.

Bring Marzano Resources experts to your school for results-oriented training on:

▶ Assessment & Grading
▶ Curriculum
▶ Instruction
▶ School Leadership

▶ Teacher Effectiveness
▶ Student Engagement
▶ Vocabulary
▶ Competency-Based Education

LEARN MORE at MarzanoResources.com/PD